SCIENCE
HORIZONS

Silver Burdett Ginn

MORRISTOWN, NJ ▪ NEEDHAM, MA

Atlanta, GA ▪ Dallas, TX ▪ Deerfield, IL ▪ Menlo Park, CA

SCIENCE HORIZONS

Sterling Edition

George G. Mallinson
Distinguished Professor
of Science Education
Western Michigan University

Jacqueline B. Mallinson
Associate Professor of Science
Western Michigan University

Linda Froschauer
Science Senior Teacher
Central Middle School
Greenwich, CT

James A. Harris
Principal, D.C. Everest
Area School District
Schofield, Wisconsin

Melanie C. Lewis
Professor, Department of Biology
Southwest Texas State University
San Marcos, Texas

Catherine Valentino
Former Director of Instruction
North Kingstown School Department
North Kingstown, Rhode Island

Acknowledgments appear on pages 462–464, which constitute an extension of this copyright page.

4 5 6 7 8 9 VH 99 98 97 96 95 94 93   ISBN 0-382-31836-6

Dear Boys and Girls,

Welcome to SCIENCE HORIZONS! Is science one of your favorite subjects? We hope so. Science can be as exciting as an adventure movie. For example, did you know that one kind of beetle fires a boiling liquid at its enemies? You will discover how the beetle does this. Then you will mix things together to make a surprising change.

Science can be more puzzling than any detective story. Did you know that explosions on our sun might be causing static on your radio? These explosions are called solar flares. This year you will make a model to show how big a solar flare can be.

What else will you do in science? You will take part in many problem-solving adventures. Do you like whales? Most people do. Some people would even go a long way to rescue a whale in danger. You will help to solve the problem of how to rescue some whales surrounded by ice. On this adventure you will learn some amazing facts about whales.

Enjoy the adventure of exploring your world of science.

Best wishes,
The Authors

Contents

UNIT TWO
PHYSICAL SCIENCE

3 UNIT THREE
EARTH SCIENCE

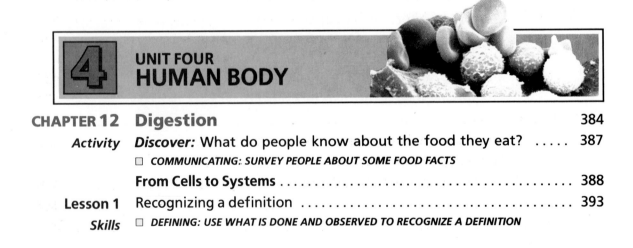

4 UNIT FOUR
HUMAN BODY

A Whale of a Story

The temperature was well below freezing. Fierce winds were blowing across the Arctic Ocean. Although it was early October, the water near Point Barrow, Alaska, was already covered with ice.

Most of the gray whales had begun the long journey south to the warm waters of Mexico. But three whales had stayed behind. Now they were trapped in a small hole in the ice, more than 6 km (4 miles) from the open ocean.

Because whales breathe air, the three whales could not swim under the ice to freedom. They needed to come to the surface every few minutes to breathe.

Day after day the frigid weather continued. Soon the breathing hole began to freeze over. Again and again the whales poked their noses through the closing hole to breathe. Their skin became bruised and bloody as it scraped against the sharp edges of the ice.

Finally, help arrived. A group of Eskimos traveled on snowmobiles to reach the whales. They used ice picks and chain saws to cut the ice and keep the breathing hole open.

News of the trapped whales spread quickly. Newspaper and television reporters arrived. Scientists joined the rescue team. People all over the world offered money and equipment.

But days passed, and the whales still were not free. A jumbo helicopter tried dropping a concrete-and-steel weight onto the ice to punch open more breathing holes. The Soviet Union sent a huge icebreaker ship to cut a path through the ice for the whales.

Although the rescuers were cold and tired, they kept working around the clock. Nobody gave up trying to save the whales they had nicknamed Snowflake, Ice, and Ice Hole. "It's kind of personal now," one worker said. "We can identify them, and we've become attached."

At last the scientists had an idea. They decided to cut a path of breathing holes all the way to the open ocean. But how would the scientists get the whales to follow the holes?

ACTIVITY

Problem Solving

Sink or Swim

Finding a way to get the whales to move is an example of problem solving. This science book has activities in which you can practice solving problems. There are four steps to follow.

First, **think** about the problem. List facts about the problem that you know. Gather other facts that you need. Second, use the facts to **plan** a way to solve the problem. Make a list of the things you will need. Third, gather the things you need and **do** what you planned. Record your results and conclusions. Fourth, **share** your results and conclusions with your classmates.

Working day and night, a team of Eskimos cut 24 holes in the ice. The holes would help move the whales closer to the open ocean. At first the whales did not leave their main

How would you get whales to follow a path of breathing holes?

Think Think of ways that might make whales move from one hole to another. What do you know about whales that might help you? What reference books might help you collect the facts you need to know?

Plan Using what you learned, plan a way to get the whales to move from one hole to another.

Do Collect the things you need. Then make a drawing or build a model of your plan.

Share Show the drawing or model to the class. Explain why you think your plan might work.

breathing hole. But teamwork and patience soon paid off. The whales sank below the water and came up through another hole in the line. Then two of the whales appeared in the last hole. Everyone began to celebrate while they waited for Snowflake, the smallest whale, to appear. Sadly, Snowflake had drowned under the ice.

But the scientists were not discouraged. Their plan had worked. So the Eskimos kept on cutting the path of holes. Weeks later the whales swam out into the open ocean.

Why would so many people try to rescue three whales? Once, people hunted whales. Thousands of whales were killed each year.

Today, most countries protect the small numbers of whales that are left. People are studying whales instead of killing them.

Many people learn about whales by getting a close look at them from whale-watching boats. Whales delight people by swimming and playing near the boats. They leap into the air and belly-flop onto the water. They smack the water loudly with their tails or flippers. Some whales surprise people by spraying them with water from their blowholes, or nostrils.

Scientists are also learning about whales. Scuba diving gear, special cameras, computers, and other equipment help them in their work. With these new tools, scientists are making exciting discoveries about the behavior, or actions, of whales.

Whale biologist Charles Jurasz discovered that humpback whales feed in a special way. These whales spin a net much as a spider spins a web. But the net is made of bubbles. First, the whale dives deep. Next, it swims upward in a circle while blowing air bubbles through its blowhole. The bubbles form a net that traps shrimplike animals called krill. Finally, the whale comes to the surface inside the net with its mouth wide open.

The whale gulps large amounts of water and krill. Instead of teeth, humpback whales have long, stiff plates, called baleen (buh LEEN). The whale strains the water through its baleen. Then it swallows the krill trapped within its mouth.

▼ Baleen of humpback whale

▼ Humpback whale bubble-net feeding

THINKING

Skills

Measuring the amount of space objects take up

A skill is something you do well. In science, you will learn many thinking skills. Whenever you do a **Skills** lesson, you will follow three steps. First, you will **practice** so that you can learn how to do the skill. Second, you will **think** about how you used the skill. Third, you will **apply,** or use, the new skill on your own.

A humpback whale can eat about a ton of krill each day. You can measure the amount of space that uneven objects, such as krill, take up. Measuring is an example of a skill.

Practicing the skill

1. Put some water and some pebbles into a small paper cup. The pebbles are like krill.

2. Pour the pebbles and water into a graduate. Record the water level.

3. Pour the mixture through a strainer into a beaker. The strainer is like the whale's baleen.

4. Pour the strained water back into the graduate.

5. Use a calculator to find the difference between the two water levels. That difference is the amount of space the pebbles take up.

Thinking about the skill

Suppose you put 50 mL of water into the graduate. Predict how much the water level will go up if you add the pebbles.

Applying the skill

Shape a piece of clay into a model whale.
Measure the amount of space the whale takes up.

▼ Singing humpback whale

▲ Dr. Roger Payne recording whale noises

Scientists are also learning that whales "talk" to each other. Each kind of whale has a special language of sounds. The sounds are like whistles, hums, groans, and clicks.

But humpback whales actually sing "songs" to each other! Whale biologist Roger Payne makes recordings of these songs. He found that the whales are always composing new melodies. The songs, he says, can be "as different as Beethoven from the Beatles."

How do whales behave while they sing? Underwater photographer Flip Nicklin took this picture. A singing whale hangs head down without moving. One scientist says the song booms out like "a stereo with the volume cranked up."

Another exciting discovery is that whales, like people, do not look alike. Scientists have found ways to identify thousands of individual whales by their markings. They have even nicknamed many whales.

Dr. Roger Payne has found a way to identify individual right whales. These whales have white patches of rough, thick skin on their heads. The size, shape, number, and pattern of the patches are different for each whale. This makes it easy to tell the whales apart by sight.

Steve Katona and a team of scientists have found a way to identify individual humpback whales. These whales have black and white markings on the undersides of their flukes, or tails. The markings are like a person's fingerprint. They are different for each whale. Thousands of individual whales have been identified and nicknamed by their fluke prints.

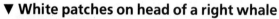
▼ White patches on head of a right whale

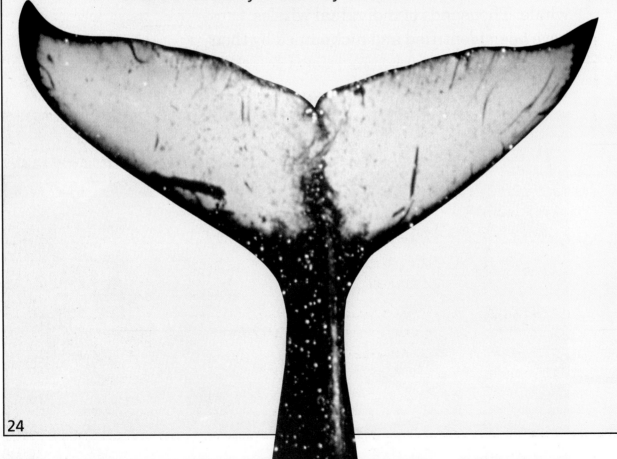

Explore Together

How can you identify a whale by its flukes?

When scientists study whales, they often work together as a team. In **Explore Together** activities, you will be part of a group, or team. Every member of the group has a special job to do.

The **Organizer** gets the materials for the activity and leads the cleanup when the activity is done. The **Investigator** carries out the activity. The **Manager** helps the Investigator. The Manager also keeps time, makes sure safety rules are followed, and does calculations. The **Recorder** writes down the ideas and observations of the group. The **Reporter** shares these observations with the rest of the class. When the **Group** is named, everyone helps.

Now it is your turn to work on a team. See how a team can identify a whale by its flukes.

Materials

Organizer   8 plain file cards · marking pen

Procedure

Recorder   **A.** Use a marking pen to copy an outline of a whale's flukes on each of 8 file cards. Give four cards to the Investigator and four cards to the Manager.

"Silver"

Investigator   **B.** Look at the four pictures of the whale flukes.
On a file card, draw each pattern of black and white markings. On the opposite side of the card, write the name of each whale.

Manager   **C.** Repeat step **B** with your four file cards. Give the cards to the Investigator.

"Matthew"

Investigator   **D.** Place the cards, fluke print side up, on a table and mix them up.

Group   **E.** Compare the fluke prints and try to find matching sets of flukes.

Recorder   **F.** Check the names on the back of the cards. Record the number of correct matches.

"Cassie"

Writing and Sharing Results and Conclusions

Group, Recorder   **1.** How successful were you in matching fluke prints?

   2. Which pattern was most difficult to match?

Reporter   **3.** How do your results and conclusions compare with those of your classmates?

"Pepper"

25

While you are reading this story, a scientist somewhere in the world may be discovering something new about whales. The scientists you have read about spend their lives finding answers to questions about whales. What things do you wonder about? You may find answers to your questions as you study science.

Science is a way to ask and answer questions about the world. It is a way of learning about the world around you. Plants, animals, matter, energy, the earth, and space are part of the world around you.

When Dr. Roger Payne went to South America to study right whales, his children went, too. They were able to learn about whales and explore the beaches of South America. Dr. Payne thought his children were "the luckiest children on earth."

This science book can help you explore the world around you. With it you can come face to face with whales, study ice, explore the moon, and look inside the human body.

SCIENCE HORIZONS

LIFE SCIENCE

Seed Plants

Come and Get It

What words would you use to describe flowering plants? Would you say they are beautiful and fragrant? If an insect could describe some plants, what would it say? The insect might say that plants are dangerous. The insect might want plants to wear a warning label. Caution! Attack plant on duty. Approach at your own risk!

Can plants attack insects? Plants seem so harmless! Or do they? Look at the trap of the Venus' flytrap. Scientists once thought the trap was for protection. But this is not true.

When an insect lands on the trap, the trap closes. The insect is caught inside. Slowly, chemicals in the plant digest the insect into a liquid. The plant then absorbs this liquid. An insect is not the only animal killed by this plant. Even frogs can be caught in a Venus' flytrap.

There are other "killers" in the plant world. The sundew also catches insects. Each leaf of a sundew is covered with tiny threads, called filaments (FIHL uh munts). At the end of each filament is a drop of sticky liquid. The sweet smell of the liquid attracts insects. When an insect lands, it gets caught in the filaments. The leaf curls around the insect and begins to digest it.

The bladderwort is a water plant that catches insects. It can catch a mosquito larva that gets too close. The plant's balloonlike bladders expand and draw in water. The larva is swept into the trap. Then the bladder snaps shut, sealing the larva inside.

Plants can make their own food. So why do they catch insects? These plants live in places where the soil is poor. There may not be enough minerals in the soil. So the plants digest insects to get minerals. The next time you see a fly, think of it as a "vitamin" pill for plants!

Discover

How does a pitcher plant trap insects?

ACTIVITY

Materials   piece of waxed paper · tape · water · tiny bead or stone

Procedure

The funnel-shaped pitcher plant is another plant that catches insects. The trap is a large leaf that rolls into a tube. The top of the trap is covered with a sweet liquid. At the bottom of the tube is a pool of liquid. Near the liquid the leaf's surface is slippery.

Make a model of a pitcher plant by folding a square of waxed paper into a cone. Seal the edges and the bottom with tape. Curl the top of the cone to make a lip. Fill the bottom of the cone with water. Study your model carefully. Place a tiny bead or stone near the lip of the cone. What happens when you release the bead? How do you think a pitcher plant traps insects? Describe your idea.

In this chapter you will learn more about the way plants get their food. You will learn how plants are grouped. What you learn will help you understand more about the different parts of a plant.

1. Classifying Plants

Words to Know
flowering plant
conifer

Getting Started Have you ever walked in a forest? Observe this drawing of a forest floor. Notice the many different kinds of plants. Which of these plants have you seen growing? Which of the plants that you have seen have seeds?

What are two main groups of plants?

Scientists classify plants into two main groups. Plants that produce new plants of the same kind from seeds are called seed plants. Those plants that produce new plants without seeds are called nonseed plants. A seed contains a tiny young plant and a supply of food.

A seed plant can have one seed or many seeds. The tiny young plant in a seed will grow under the right conditions. These conditions include the proper amounts of light, water, warmth, and space. As the young plant grows, it uses the food stored in the seed and develops stems, roots, and leaves.

Mosses and ferns are all alike in one way. They produce new plants without seeds. Some of these nonseed plants form spores. Look at the spore cases in the drawing. Spores form new living things.

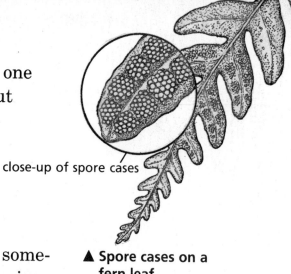

close-up of spore cases

▲ Spore cases on a fern leaf

How are seed plants grouped?

Have you ever picked flowers for someone? If so, you picked a bunch of flowering plants. A **flowering plant** is a plant that produces seeds in a flower.

▲ Magnolia tree

▲ Garden flowers

Many plants that you have seen are flowering plants. You probably have seen some of those shown here. You can see that some flowering plants have flowers with bright, colorful petals. Grasses and trees are also flowering plants. If you look at the pictures, you can see that these flowers are not as colorful.

▼ Bushy beardgrass

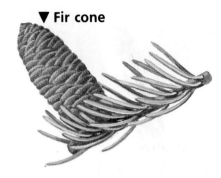
▼ Fir cone

▼ Pine cone

▼ Cypress cone

▼ Spruce cone

Not all seed plants have flowers. Instead, some produce seeds in cones. Hard woody cones protect the seeds. Such cones are found on many trees called conifers (KAHN uh furz). A **conifer** is a plant that produces seeds within cones. Pine, fir, and spruce trees are some examples of conifers. Some types of shrubs are also conifers. Conifers are often called evergreens. Why, do you think, are they called evergreens?

▼ Conifers

Lesson Review

1. What are the two main groups of plants?
2. Compare and contrast seed plants with nonseed plants.
3. How are seed plants grouped?
4. How are flowering plants and conifers the same? How are they different?

Think! Observe a variety of plants from your neighborhood. Classify each plant as a flowering plant, a conifer, or a nonseed plant.

Skills

THINKING

Classifying the same objects in different ways

You can classify some things in more than one way. For example, you can classify plants into groups that have seeds and those that do not. You can also classify plants into groups that have green stems and those that have woody stems. Classification is a way of grouping objects based on their traits.

Practicing the skill

1. Observe the seeds in the picture. Some seeds are flat, and others are not. Classify them into flat and not flat groups. Write the names of the seeds in each group.

2. Use a different trait to put the same seeds into two new groups. Record your new groups.

Apple seed

Watermelon seed

Corn seed

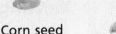
Orange seed

Pumpkin seed

Thinking about the skill

Why might people classify the same objects in different ways?

Applying the skill

What are two ways that the flowers in the pictures can be classified?

▲ Lily of the Valley

▲ Aster

▲ Bluebell

▲ Daisy

2. Roots

Getting Started Think about the last time you ate part of a plant. Did you eat a stem, a root, a leaf, a seed, or a flower? People eat all these plant parts. Examine a carrot, beet, or radish. What part of a plant is each of these?

Words to Know
root
root hair
fibrous root
 system
taproot system

*What would happen if plants stopped making food? Find out when you read **Photosynthesis Calls It Quits!** in Horizons Plus.*

What do roots do for plants?

Seed plants have roots, stems, and leaves. The part that anchors a plant in the ground is the **root.** Actually, plants are anchored by a system, or group, of roots. Roots help to keep a plant from blowing away or washing away.

Roots take in water and minerals from the soil. Plants need water and minerals to grow and to make food. Some plants have roots that store food. A beet is a root in which food is stored.

Roots also carry water and minerals upward to the other parts of a plant. There is a system of tubes within the roots. Locate the tubes in the drawing and trace the flow of materials. Some tubes carry water and minerals absorbed from the soil to the stems and leaves. Different tubes carry food made in the leaves to the roots and other parts of the plant.

▼ Bald cypress roots

How does a root absorb water and minerals? Notice the tiny threadlike objects in the picture. These are root hairs. A **root hair** grows from a root into the soil. Root hairs absorb water and minerals from the soil. The more root hairs there are, the more water and minerals the root can absorb. Most roots have millions of root hairs.

▼ Root hairs

What are two types of root systems?

There are two main types of root systems. If you pull up some grass, you will see a fibrous (FYE brus) root system. A **fibrous root system** has several main roots with many smaller branching roots. These smaller roots grow in many directions.

Look at the pictures of the fibrous root system. You can see that the roots grow near the surface of the soil. You can also see how tiny pieces of soil stick to the smaller roots. Thus the fibrous root system helps to hold the soil in place. Most grasses have fibrous root systems. Why do people often plant grasses on steep hills?

▼ Fibrous root system

▼ Fibrous roots of an African violet

The other main type of root system has one large root. It is called the taproot system. In a **taproot system** the large root grows straight down. Small roots grow outward from the taproot. Look at the pictures. You can see that a taproot system grows much deeper than a fibrous root system. Why might a taproot system anchor a plant better than a fibrous root system? Why is the taproot system able to get water from far below the surface of the soil?

▼ Taproot system

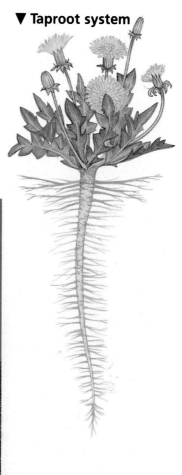

▼ Taproot of a dandelion

Lesson Review

1. Identify four things roots do for plants.
2. What are the main differences between a fibrous root system and a taproot system?

Think! Suppose a plant is dug up and its root hairs are destroyed. Describe what might happen if you replanted the plant.

Should factory farms be used to feed people?

Each day about 259,000 people are born. Will there be enough food to feed them all? With more people on the earth, there will be less farmland on which to grow food. One answer may be factory farms. These farms are indoor farms, where machines do the work. Factory farms grow more food in less space than outdoor farms.

One factory farm is called PhytoFarm. The farm building is as long as a football field. It holds rows and rows of crops. But the plants do not grow in soil. Instead, their roots hang down into boxes filled with the water and minerals that the plants need.

STS

The plant boxes sit on moving surfaces that stretch across the farm building. Workers place tiny young plants in the boxes on the surfaces at one end of the building. The young plants grow as they move slowly across the building. By the time the plants reach the other side, they are fully grown. Then workers harvest them.

Factory farms have some benefits and some problems. These farms take up much less space than outdoor farms. Crops also grow faster in them. But factory farming costs a lot. It is expensive to run the thousands of bright light bulbs needed. An indoor farm has no windows, and the lights are on 17 hours a day. This gives crops more growing time than they would get outdoors.

Factory farms do not grow much of our food now. But they might in the future. NASA is looking into the use of factory farms in space. One day your lettuce might even come from a factory farm on the moon!

Critical thinking

1. Why might factory farming be necessary on Earth someday? Why might people want to build factory farms in space?

2. How does factory farming conserve resources? How does it waste them?

Using what you learned

How well can plants grow without soil? Fill each part of half an egg carton with a different material like soil, cat litter, torn paper, or sand. Plant radish seeds in each part and water daily. Compare seeds grown in soil with those grown in other materials. Graph your results.

3. Stems

Words to Know
stem

Getting Started Hold a flower with a stem in your hand. Carefully observe the end of the stem that is opposite the flower. Touch this end of the stem. What do you feel? Now gently pull the stem apart and describe what you see inside the stem.

▲ Tulips

What does a stem do?

Have you ever seen a vase filled with cut flowers? You probably know that the part of a flower that is cut is the stem. But did you know that the trunk of a tree is also a stem? A **stem** is the part of a plant that supports the leaves, flowers, or cones. The stem also contains tubes that carry food, water, and minerals to all parts of the plant. Some stems can even store food for the plant.

42

How are materials carried from the roots to all parts of a plant? Remember that roots have a system of tubes. This system of tubes continues in the stems. Water and minerals travel from the roots to other parts of the plant through the tubes. Water moves through the tubes like liquid moving through a straw. Recall that other tubes carry food from the leaves to the rest of the plant.

What are the different kinds of stems?

There are two main kinds of stems. Some stems are thin, green, and bend easily. Tulips, lilies, and petunias have this type of stem. These stems produce their own food.

Other stems are brown and woody, like a tree trunk. A woody stem does not bend easily and grows taller and thicker every year. Trees and shrubs have woody stems.

▼ Daffodils

▼ Roses

Explore

How does water travel in a plant?

"**I**'m thirsty!" is something you might say when you need a drink. But plants do not talk. How do you know when a plant needs water? Plants wilt if they need water.

Materials

celery stalk with leaves · table knife · jar · water · red or blue food coloring · paper · pencil

Procedure

A. Slice off the bottom of the stalk of celery.

B. Observe the bottom of the stalk.
  1. Draw a picture of the bottom of the stalk.

C. Fill the jar with water to a height of 3 cm. Add five drops of food coloring. Put the stalk into the colored water and let the stalk soak overnight.
  2. What do you think will happen to the stalk after it soaks?

D. Take out the stalk and observe the end that soaked in the water. Cut off a slice of this end.
  3. Draw the end of the stalk after it has soaked overnight.

Writing and Sharing Results and Conclusions

1. Compare the way the bottom of the stalk looked before and after it has soaked.

2. How did the leaves look after the stalk soaked overnight?

3. From your observations, explain how water travels in plants.

As you know, stems have tubes like straws that carry water and food. The tubes in stems are arranged in bundles. In woody stems the bundles of tubes are arranged in a ring. Look at the section of a woody stem. Next to the bark are the tubes that carry food. In the center of the stem, you can see the tubes that carry water.

▼ Fir tree

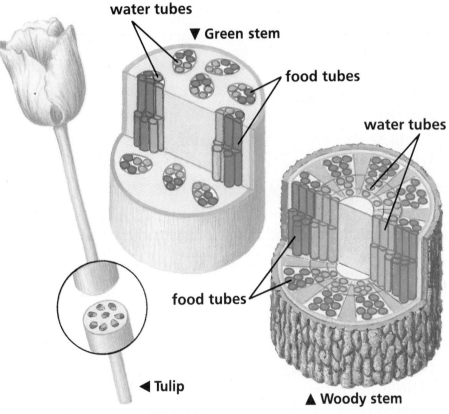

water tubes

▼ Green stem

food tubes

water tubes

food tubes

◄ Tulip

▲ Woody stem

Lesson Review

1. Name the two main jobs of a stem.

2. Compare and contrast the two types of stems.

Think! Two seeds are planted at the same time. The seeds sprout. After 2 years the stem on one plant is slender and the stem on the other plant is three times as thick. Which stem might be a tree? Explain how you decided.

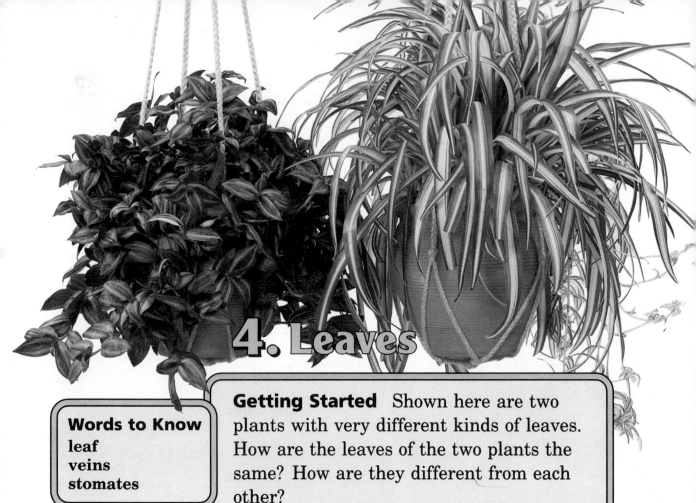

4. Leaves

Getting Started Shown here are two plants with very different kinds of leaves. How are the leaves of the two plants the same? How are they different from each other?

What is the structure of a leaf?

A **leaf** is the part of the plant where most of its food is made. You will learn more about how a plant makes food later in the chapter. Most leaves have two parts, the blade and the stalk. Look at the drawing and locate the blade. Then find the stalk, which connects the blade to the stem.

The lines or ridges on the leaf are **veins** (vayns). Veins hold tubes like those in stems. And in the same manner, some tubes in the veins transport food from the leaves to the stems. Other tubes in the veins carry water and minerals from the stems to the leaves.

▲ Leaf veins

Almost all living things need air. You get air with your lungs. But how does a plant get air? Look at the drawing. It shows tiny openings on the underside of a leaf. These tiny openings are **stomates** (STOH mayts). Air, along with water vapor, moves into and out of a leaf through the stomates. The stomates can be opened and closed. Air also moves in and out through tiny slits in stems.

stomates

What are the different types of leaves?

When you think of a leaf, you probably think of something flat, soft, and green. Many flowering plants have leaves like this. Flowering plants with wide, flat leaves are called broad-leaved plants.

◄ Aspen leaf

▼ Goldenrain tree leaf

▼ Sweet gum leaf

Problem Solving

"Where Is the Water?"

ACTIVITY

If you breathe on a mirror you can see moisture on the mirror from your breath. In much the same manner, leaves give off water. But how can you see the water given off by a plant? Try this experiment. First seal a plant in a plastic bag. Then place the plant in the sun for a few hours. Observe the plastic bag.

Do broad-leaved and needle-leaved plants lose water at the same rate?

Design an experiment that will show how fast or slow different plants lose water. Plan on using a broad-leaved and a needle-leaved plant. Then try your experiment.

▼ **Oak leaf**

▼ **Horse chestnut leaf**

There are two types of broad-leaved plants: those with simple leaves and those with compound leaves. A simple leaf has a single blade attached to a stalk. A compound leaf has one stalk with several blades attached to it. Look at the goldenrain tree leaf on page 47. On this kind of compound leaf, the blades are opposite one another along the stalk. Other compound leaves have many blades attached to the stalk at the same point. Which of these drawings shows a compound leaf?

48

The leaves on a pine tree are very different from broad leaves. Conifers have leaves that look like needles. So conifers are called needle-leaved plants. Needle-leaved plants have leaves that are small, thin, and pointed. These leaves also have a tough outer covering. The shape and covering of the leaves keep a plant from losing a lot of water into the air.

Yellow cedar leaves ▶

▲ White spruce leaves

▲ Ponderosa pine leaves

Lesson Review

1. What are the main parts of a leaf?
2. What are three ways a leaf helps a plant?
3. What are two differences between a broad-leaved plant and a needle-leaved plant?

Think! Which would survive better under hot, dry conditions: a broad-leaved plant or a needle-leaved plant? Why?

Physical Science
CONNECTION

Find out what the word evaporation *means. From which leaves does more evaporation occur — broad leaves or needle leaves?*

5. Food Making

Getting Started The picture below shows a plant only a few days old. Shown above is this plant months later. To grow, you must have food. Plants also need food to grow. You get your food by eating. But plants do not eat. How did the little plant get the food it needed to grow to be the big plant?

▼ Young sunflower plant

How do plants make food?

Your body needs food. But it cannot make its own. You must use a source outside your body. This source can be a plant or an animal that you eat. Unlike you, a plant makes its own food. **Photosynthesis** (foht oh SIHN thuh sihs) is the process by which plants produce food. This process can occur in any green part of a plant. But most photosynthesis occurs in the leaves.

A plant needs carbon dioxide (KAHR bun dye AHK syd), water, and light to make food. How does the plant get these things?

Plant leaves have a substance that traps light. **Chlorophyll** (KLOR uh fihl) is the green matter in plants that traps light used to produce food.

Carbon dioxide that is in the air enters through the stomates. Oxygen that is produced during photosynthesis exits through them. Water travels through tubes from the roots to the leaves.

Now you know how the food-making part of a leaf gets the light, carbon dioxide, and water it needs to make food. But just how is the food made?

▲ Microscope view of chlorophyll

What would happen if plants stopped making food? Find out when you read **Photosynthesis Calls It Quits!** *in Horizons Plus.*

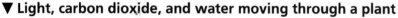

▼ Light, carbon dioxide, and water moving through a plant

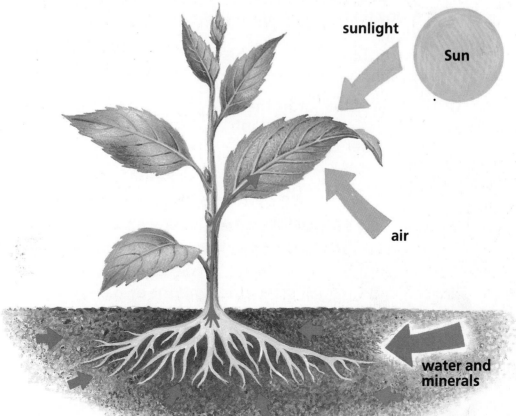

sunlight

Sun

air

water and minerals

Explore Together

How does sunlight affect photosynthesis?

Materials

Organizer

baking soda · water · wide-mouthed jar · narrow jar · small water plant · funnel · watch or clock with second hand, or seconds display

Procedure

Investigator

A. Dissolve about 2 g of baking soda in 200 mL of water. Fill the wide-mouthed jar half full with this baking soda solution. Fill the narrow jar with the baking soda solution.

Investigator

B. Set up the activity as shown in the picture. Then place the jars in darkened room.

Recorder

1. Every 30 seconds, count the number of gas bubbles.

2. Copy the graph that is shown on this page. Record the results on the graph.

Investigator

C. Now place the jar in the sunlight. Count and graph the number of gas bubbles every 30 seconds.

Recorder

3. Graph the new results.

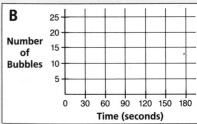

Writing and Sharing Results and Conclusions

Group and Recorder

1. What gas is released from the plant during photosynthesis?

2. How did sunlight affect the amount of gas released from the leaves?

Reporter

3. Compare your results with those of your classmates.

Look at the drawings to learn how plants make their own food. (1) Light strikes the leaf and is trapped by the chlorophyll. Water is carried to the leaf by the tubes. (2) Inside the leaf, light changes part of the water to hydrogen (HYE druh jun) and oxygen. Carbon dioxide from the air enters the leaf through the stomates. (3) The hydrogen joins with the carbon dioxide to make food for the plant. This food is carried by tubes to the rest of the plant. Oxygen gas is released through the stomates.

▼ **Photosynthesis in a leaf**

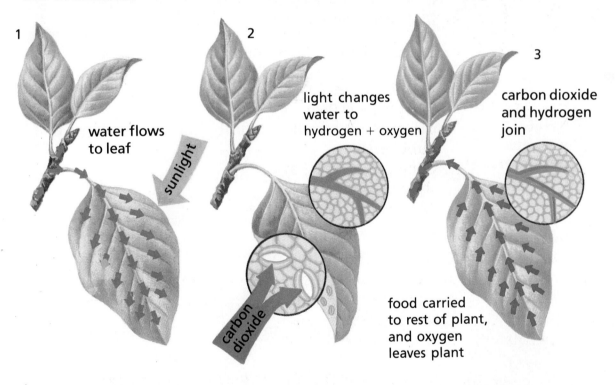

water flows to leaf

sunlight

carbon dioxide

light changes water to hydrogen + oxygen

carbon dioxide and hydrogen join

food carried to rest of plant, and oxygen leaves plant

Lesson Review

1. Where does a plant make its food?
2. Name the things a plant uses to make food.
3. Describe how a plant makes food.

Think! In what way do all living things depend on photosynthesis?

Physical Science
CONNECTION

What form of energy is used by plants during photosynthesis?

6. Producing New Plants

Words to Know
petals
stamens
pollen grain
pistil
ovary
pollination

Getting Started Tear open an orange, grapefruit, or lemon. The fleshy part you see is what you usually eat. Somewhere in the fleshy part, you will find seeds. Identify any parts of the fruit that might have been a part of a flower.

What are the parts of a flower?

All living things produce new living things of the same kind. New flowering plants grow from seeds. But where do the seeds come from? A flower is the part of flowering plants where seeds are produced.

A flower has many parts. These parts are the petals, the sepals (SEE pulz), the stamens (STAY munz), and the pistil (PIHS tihl). Look at the drawing of the flower on the next page. Locate each part of the flower as you read about it.

The **petals** surround and protect the other parts of the flower. Petals are usually brightly colored. Around the bottom of the flower are green leaflike parts called sepals.

The **stamens** are the male parts of the flower. How many stamens are in the drawing? A stamen is a small stalk with a sac on its tip. The sac forms millions of pollen (PAHL un) grains. A **pollen grain** is a small object that holds the male cells of the plant. A male cell joins with a female cell to make a seed. What material will you have on your finger if you touch the tip of a stamen?

The **pistil** is the female part of the flower. This part is found in the center of the flower. The bottom part of the pistil contains the **ovary** (OH vuh ree). The ovary contains the ovules (AHV yoolz). Ovules hold the female cells of the plant.

▼ **Parts of a flower**

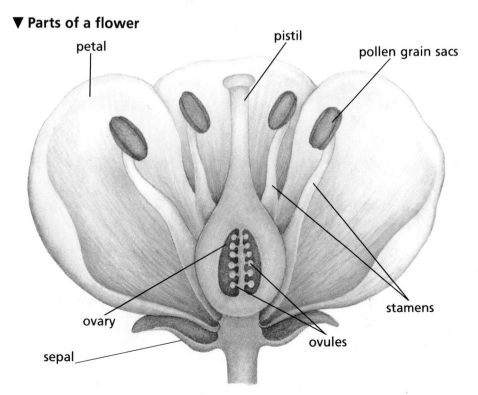

▲ Pollen grains on a bee

How does pollen move?

For a flower to make a seed, pollen grains must move from a stamen to a pistil. The process by which pollen grains move from a stamen to a pistil is called **pollination** (pahl uh NAY shun).

How does pollination occur? The colorful petals of flowers attract insects. Some of these flowers have a sweet liquid which the insect drinks. As the insect drinks, it brushes against the pollen grains on the stamen.

Some pollen grains stay on the insect. As the insect moves from flower to flower, these grains stick to the flowers' pistils. Other animals or the wind also carry pollen grains from flower to flower. For pollination to occur, the pollen grain must stick to the same kind of flower from which it came.

▼ Hummingbird drinking from a flower

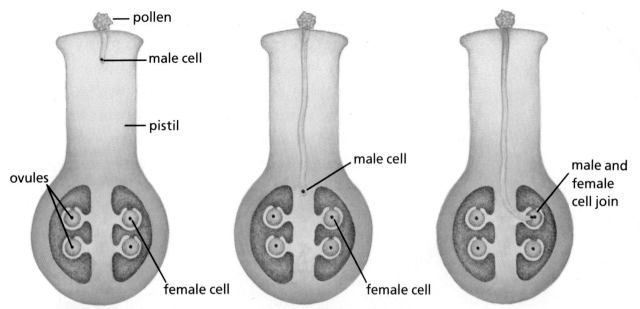

▲ Fertilization of a flower

How does a seed form?

Once a flower is pollinated, seeds may form. Look at the picture of the pistil as you read. First, the pollen grain on top of the pistil begins to form a tube. This tube grows down through the pistil to the ovary. A male cell from the pollen grain travels down the tube into the ovary.

Recall that inside the ovary are the ovules. Here the male cell enters an ovule. The male cell then joins with a female cell inside the ovule. Fertilization (fur tul ih ZAY-shun) is the joining of the male cell and the female cell.

After fertilization, the joined cells form a seed. One seed or many seeds may be formed in an ovary. As a seed develops, the ovary grows thick. An ovary is a fruit. The fruit surrounds the seeds and protects them.

*For a funny story about plants that grow from seeds, read **McBroom Tells the Truth,** page 150.*

If you have ever split open an apple or orange, you can see how the fruit protects the seeds. You can probably name many fruits. But look at the picture of foods you call vegetables. They are really fruits. A fruit is an ovary which surrounds and protects seeds. The "vegetables" in the picture are fruits because they are ovaries surrounding seeds.

▲ **Vegetables with seeds**

Lesson Review

1. What part of a flowering plant makes seeds?
2. What are the four main parts of a flower?
3. What is one way that pollen grains move from a stamen to a pistil?
4. How does a seed form?

Think! Suppose a flower did not have a stamen. Could the flower be pollinated? Explain your answer.

Chapter Connections

Write a summary of the main ideas in this chapter.
Use the graphic organizer to help you.

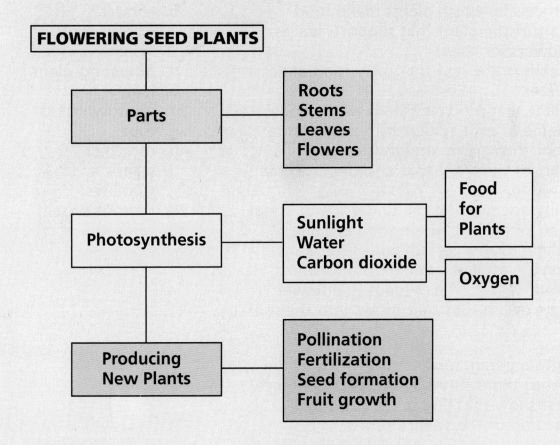

FLOWERING SEED PLANTS

Parts — Roots, Stems, Leaves, Flowers

Photosynthesis — Sunlight, Water, Carbon dioxide → Food for Plants, Oxygen

Producing New Plants — Pollination, Fertilization, Seed formation, Fruit growth

Writing About Science • Persuade

Suppose homeowners in your town have sprayed their yards to get rid of insects that bother them. The spray may affect bees. What effect will the killing of bees and other insects have on the pollination of plants? Describe what might happen if people continued to spray. Give your opinion and try to persuade others to agree with you.

Chapter 1 Review

Science Terms

A. Write the letter of the term that best matches the definition.

1. Green matter in plants that produces food
2. Process by which plants make food
3. Part of the plant that supports leaves, flowers, or cones
4. Tubes in the leaf that carry food and water
5. Plant that produces seeds within cones
6. Name of root system with single large root that grows straight down
7. Part of the plant that anchors it to the ground
8. Tiny openings on the underside of a leaf
9. Part of a plant where food is made
10. Name of root system with several main roots with many smaller branch roots
11. Plant that produces seeds in a flower
12. Part of the root that grows into the soil

a. chlorophyll
b. conifer
c. fibrous root system
d. flowering plant
e. leaf
f. photosynthesis
g. root
h. root hair
i. stem
j. stomates
k. taproot system
l. veins

B. Write a paragraph that uses each of the science terms listed below. Each sentence must show that you understand the meaning of the science terms.

ovary

petals

pistil

pollen grain

pollination

stamen

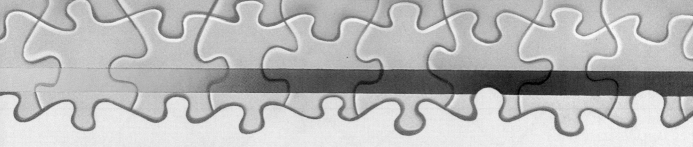

Science Ideas

Use complete sentences to answer the following.

1. Name some ways that flowering plants are like conifers. Name some ways that they are different.
2. What are the three main functions of a root?
3. List the main things a stem does.
4. Draw a leaf and label its parts.
5. What are the things a plant needs to make food?
6. Briefly describe the process by which a plant makes food.
7. Describe how seeds form and grow into plants.
8. Draw a flower and label its parts.
9. Describe the main functions of a leaf.
10. Contrast broad leaves and needlelike leaves.

Applying Science Ideas

Use complete sentences to answer the following.

1. Heavy rains in your area have caused a loss of good topsoil. Research to find what kinds of plants would help to stop this loss.
2. Imagine you are a corn farmer in the Midwest. Give your reasons for or against changing your outdoor farm into a factory farm.

Using Science Skills

Look at the leaves in the drawings. What are two ways that the leaves can be grouped?

Animals With Backbones

To the Rescue

THE RAPTOR TRUST

Len Soucy's back yard is full of huge bird cages. Sometimes he has as many as 250 birds there. But these birds are not pets. They are patients. Many of the birds are sick or injured. Others are orphans, birds who fell out of a nest and could not get back. When the birds are well enough to take care of themselves, Len lets them go.

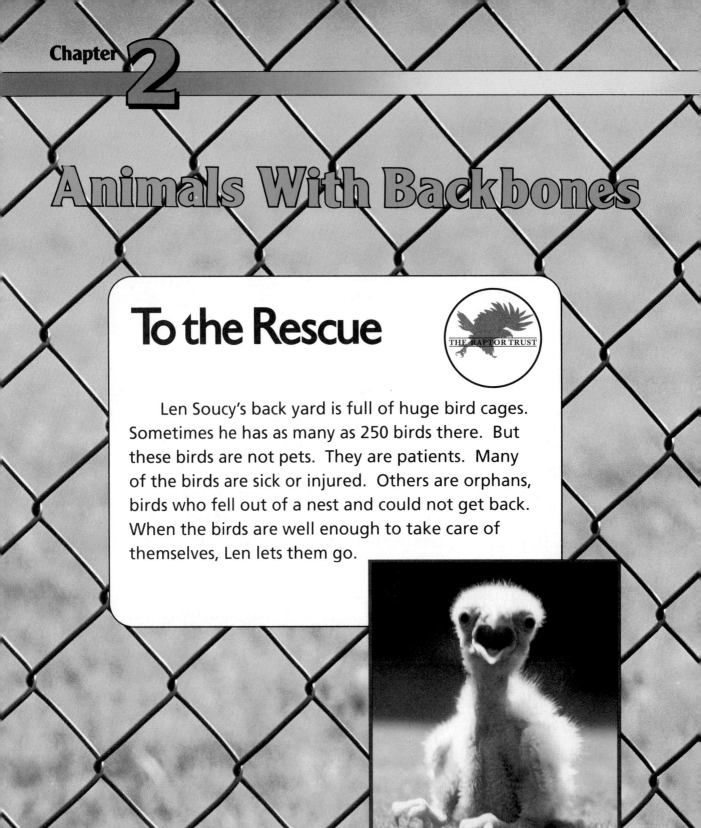

Len and his wife, Diane, started taking care of birds 20 years ago. Someone left an injured red-tailed hawk in a cardboard box on their porch. Len and Diane did not know how to help the bird, but they knew they had to find a way.

The Soucys began by calling a doctor who told them how to set broken bones. For the next 6 weeks, the hawk lived in a cardboard box, eating mice and raw hamburger. When Len removed the bandages, the hawk's wing had healed. But before the hawk could fly again, it had to exercise. Finally, the hawk was ready to be free. When Len released the bird, he knew that he wanted to go on caring for wild birds.

The Soucys have cared for over 100 kinds, from tiny songbirds to large owls. Len and Diane are well trained to care for wild animals, but they must still have a license to do so.

The Soucys have another special helper. She is Hootie, a great horned owl. When the Soucys found Hootie, she was so badly hurt that she could not fly. Len knew that she could not live on her own, so he kept her. Now, Hootie cares for orphaned great horned owlets. Living with Hootie, the owlets have almost no contact with people. So it is easy for the owlets to go back into the wild when they are grown.

Len travels around the country and gives talks about birds. He explains to students that it is against the law to keep wild animals without a permit. If you see a wild animal that is hurt, do not touch it. Instead, call a wildlife center for help.

Discover

What kinds of birds live in your area?

ACTIVITY

Materials   birdseed · empty milk carton · scissors · string · reference book

Procedure

Build a bird feeder like the one shown. Fill the bird feeder with birdseed. Hang the bird feeder in a special place in your schoolyard or back yard.

Observe the birds that visit your bird feeder. Make a chart showing the types of birds and the time that they come to the bird feeder. Draw pictures of the birds. Use a reference book from the library and identify the birds.

In this chapter you will learn more about birds and how they are alike and different from other animals. You will discover that birds, along with mammals, reptiles, amphibians, and fish, belong to an important group—animals with backbones.

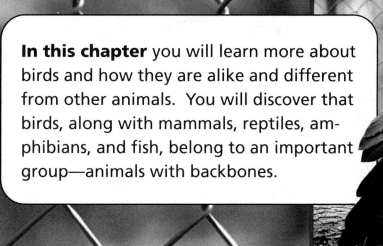

1. Grouping Living Things

Getting Started Do you like to collect things? Some people collect stamps or coins. Some people collect baseball cards. Suppose you take a trip to the beach and collect these shells. When you get home you spread out the shells on a table. What are some ways you might group these shells?

Words to Know
invertebrate
vertebrate
cold-blooded
  animal
warm-blooded
  animal

How can living things be grouped?

Suppose you could collect one of each kind of living thing on the earth. You would have a huge collection. Studying it would be difficult. How could you study living things more easily? You could classify (KLAS uh fy), or group them, as you did with the shells. The living things in each group would have traits that are alike. Traits describe a thing, or tell what it is like.

Scientists classify living things into large groups called kingdoms. All plants, for example, are placed in the plant kingdom. Every living thing in the plant kingdom makes its own food. All animals are placed in the large group called the animal kingdom. Living things in the animal kingdom use other living things as food.

How do scientists classify animals?

There are millions of animals in the animal kingdom. To make animals easier to study, scientists divide the animal kingdom into smaller groups. They do this by looking at the traits of animals. One important trait they use is whether the animal has a backbone. A backbone is a long row of connected bones in the back. Find the backbone in each of the animals shown here.

▲ Tree frog

▼ Sand boa

67

ACTIVITY

Explore Together

How can you classify the names of your classmates?

Organizer

Materials

5 file cards • paper punch • scissors • toothpick

Procedure

Investigator A. Get five file cards. Use a paper punch to punch three holes along the side of each file card as shown. Give a card to each member of your group.

Group B. Write the questions next to the holes on your file card as shown.

B

First Name _____

○ 1. Is your name a girl's name?

○ 2. Does your name have 6 or more letters?

○ 3. Does your name have 3 or more vowels?

Investigator C. Ask your group each question.

Group D. If you answer a question "yes," you should use the scissors to cut a slit next to the hole for that question as shown.

D

Manager E. Collect the cards from your group.

Investigator F. One of the Investigators should complete the rest of the procedure. Collect the cards from the Managers. Sort the cards by putting a toothpick through the first hole of the pack. All the cards with a slit will fall out of the pack.

Investigator G. Keep sorting the cards by repeating Step F for the remaining questions.

Writing and Sharing Results and Conclusions

Group, Recorder 1. What happens to the number of cards in the pack as you proceed to sort through the cards?

2. In what three ways are the names in the third group (those left on the toothpick) alike?

Reporter 3. Summarize for your class the process by which the names were classified.

68

An animal without a backbone is called an **invertebrate** (ihn VER tuh briht). Invertebrates make up one group in the animal kingdom. Animals such as worms, spiders, and insects are found in this group. Fish, amphibians (am FIHB ee unz), reptiles (REHP tuhlz), birds, and mammals (MAM uhlz) are all animals that have a backbone. An animal with a backbone is called a **vertebrate** (VER tuh briht). Vertebrates make up the other group in the animal kingdom. Which of the animals shown here is an invertebrate? Which is a vertebrate?

▲ Garden spider

All vertebrates can be placed into one of two groups. Some of these animals are cold-blooded. A **cold-blooded animal** is one whose body temperature changes as the outside temperature changes. Fish, amphibians, and reptiles are cold-blooded. All birds and mammals are warm-blooded. A **warm-blooded animal** is one whose body temperature stays about the same, even when the outside temperature changes.

▲ Koala

Lesson Review

1. How can living things be classified?
2. What are the two main groups in the animal kingdom?
3. List the five groups of vertebrates.
4. How is a cold-blooded animal different from a warm-blooded animal?

Think! Imagine you must classify items in your bedroom closet. How many groups would you have? What would you put into each group?

2. Fish

Getting Started Have you ever bought a goldfish? If so, you had to have a container of clean water in which to carry the goldfish home. How are fish different from other animals?

Words to Know
fish   gills
fin   life cycle
scale

What are the traits of fish?

Fish are cold-blooded vertebrates that live in water. Like all cold-blooded animals, fish have a body temperature that changes with the outside temperature. When the water around a fish becomes cold, the fish becomes cold. When the water becomes warm, the fish becomes warm also.

All fish have fins. A **fin** is a fanlike part on an animal's body. Fins help a fish move, steer, and balance in the water. How many fins do you count on this fish?

fins

Body of a Fish

scales

fins

70

Most fish are covered with scales. A **scale** is a hard flat plate that protects an animal's body. Look at the drawing of fish scales. As a fish grows larger, its scales grow also. As scales grow, ring-shaped lines usually form. By counting the lines on their scales, you can tell the age of some fish.

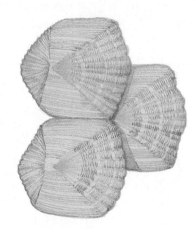

▲ Scales

Like other animals, fish need oxygen. Animals that live on land get oxygen from the air they breathe. Fish get oxygen from the water around them. Fish take in the oxygen found in water through their gills. **Gills** are thin, feathery body parts filled with blood. Most fish use gills for breathing.

How Fish Breathe

Look at the drawing to learn how gills work. (1) First, the fish takes water into its mouth. (2) Next, the water flows over the gills. The blood inside the gills contains carbon dioxide. (3) Oxygen from the water goes into the blood inside the gills. At the same time, carbon dioxide passes from the blood into the water. (4) The water then flows out of the fish's body.

Problem Solving

Something Fishy

Imagine that you have just purchased ten goldfish. You place them in a fishbowl filled with water. The next day you go to check on them. The fish appear to be acting strangely. All the fish are swimming near the surface of the water. Their mouths are partly above the water, and they appear to be gulping for air.

What could be the problem the fish are having, and how can it be solved?

What might cause the fish to act this way? Write down as many things as you can think of. How can you solve these problems?

How do fish produce young?

Like all living things, fish have a life cycle. A **life cycle** is all of the stages in the life of a living thing. During their life cycle, living things grow and change. They become adults and reproduce, or form more living things like themselves.

In their life cycle, most fish produce young fish by laying eggs. The female fish lays eggs in the water. The male fish swims over the eggs and fertilizes (FER tuh ly zehz) them. When an egg is fertilized, it can grow into a new living thing. In a few weeks a young fish hatches from the fertilized egg.

Fish lay thousands or even millions of eggs at once. But many eggs are not fertilized. Many others die or are eaten. So these eggs never hatch. But since a large number of eggs are laid, some eggs will live. Why is it important that some eggs hatch?

Life Cycle of a Fish

Newly hatched salmon ▼

▲ Adult salmon

▲ Salmon eggs

Lesson Review

1. Name three traits of fish.

2. How do fish use gills to breathe?

3. How do most fish produce young?

Think! Which fish has the higher body temperature—one that lives in the tropics or one that lives in the Arctic? Explain your answer.

Should animals be used for research?

Science has made great progress in the past 50 years. Many diseases can now be cured by using new drugs that are made in labs. People who are injured can also be helped in new ways. Today, doctors can perform lifesaving surgery that was not possible in the past.

How do scientists find out about new drugs? How do they learn if a drug will be helpful and not harmful? How can they test the new treatments for the sick and injured? Much of what they learn comes from research done on animals.

When a new drug or treatment is found, it is tested on animals. If the animal test is a success, people may then be tested.

Many of the animals that are used for research are vertebrates. Mice and rats are most often used for testing. They are small animals and do not take up a lot of lab space. Also, they do not cost a lot of money to buy.

But there is a major problem in using mice and rats. There are a great many ways in which they are not like people. So they are not useful for all types of tests. For example, doctors wanted to test a heart that they had made for people. They needed to see how well the heart would work in a large animal. So they used a cow for their test.

Some people do not want animals to be used for any research. These people want to stop research projects in which animals are killed. They are also against research that may cause pain to animals.

Other people think that research done on animals must be allowed. These people say that many human lives have been saved by such research. They also say that sometimes there is no other way to test new drugs or treatments for people.

Critical thinking

1. Would you object to new drugs or treatments being tested on mice or rats? Should cats or dogs be used for such testing? Give reasons for your answers.

2. Cosmetics such as hair dye and makeup are tested to find out if they cause rashes on the skin or make the eyes burn or itch. Do you think animals should be used for testing cosmetics? Defend your answer.

Using what you learned

Ask people you know to answer the questions in the **Critical thinking** section. Record all the answers. Compare your findings with those of your classmates.

3. Amphibians

Getting Started You have learned about one group of animals with a backbone—fish. Frogs are other animals with a backbone. Imagine a fish and a frog living in the same pond. Picture in your mind how each animal moves. How are the two animals different?

What are the traits of amphibians?

A frog belongs to a group of animals called amphibians. An **amphibian** is a cold-blooded vertebrate that lives part of its life in water and part on land.

Amphibians have some traits in common with fish. Like fish, they are cold-blooded. They lay eggs in water, where the eggs hatch. Like fish, young amphibians live in water and breathe with gills.

▼ Frog eggs

▲ Wood frog

Amphibians are different from fish in many ways. Most amphibians have thin, moist skin. They do not have scales. Most amphibians also have two pairs of legs. Unlike fish, most adult amphibians have lungs. **Lungs** are organs through which animals get oxygen from air. How does this affect where amphibians live? Animals with lungs cannot live under water. So, unlike fish, adult amphibians live on land. They must breathe air as you do.

▼ Mud puppy

One type of amphibian, called the mud puppy, lives almost its entire life under water. As you can see, a mud puppy has bushy gills outside its body. What do gills do?

▲ Red-backed salamander

Scientists classify amphibians into two main groups. One group is made up of amphibians with tails. Newts and salamanders are in this group. The second group is made up of amphibians without tails. Frogs and toads are tailless amphibians.

▲ Marine toad

▲ Green frog

What is the life cycle of an amphibian?

Most amphibians go through many changes during their life cycle. In fact, most young amphibians do not look at all like their parents. The changes in form that occur from egg to adult are called **metamorphosis** (meht uh MOR fuh sihs).

The metamorphosis of a frog is shown on the next page. As you can see, (1) a female frog lays many jelly-covered eggs in the water. The eggs are fertilized by the male frog. (2) Fishlike animals called **tadpoles** hatch from frog eggs.

▼ Newly hatched tadpole

2

3

▲ Growing tadpole

Life Cycle
of
a Frog

4

1 **▲ Frog eggs**

▲ Adult frog

A tadpole has gills, a tail, and no legs. (3) Tadpoles live in the water and eat plants. The tadpoles grow and change quickly. Back legs form and the tail disappears. Lungs and front legs form. (4) Then the full-grown frog moves onto land. Adult frogs eat insects and live near the water. They return to the water when it is time to lay eggs. Then the life cycle begins again.

Lesson Review

1. What is an amphibian?

2. How is an amphibian different from a fish?

3. Name two groups of amphibians.

4. Make a drawing of the life cycle of the frog.

Think! The jelly covering of frog eggs has a bad taste. How might this jelly protect the eggs?

Earth Science
CONNECTION

Use what you know about metamorphosis to guess what a metamorphic rock is. Then use a reference book to find out if you were right.

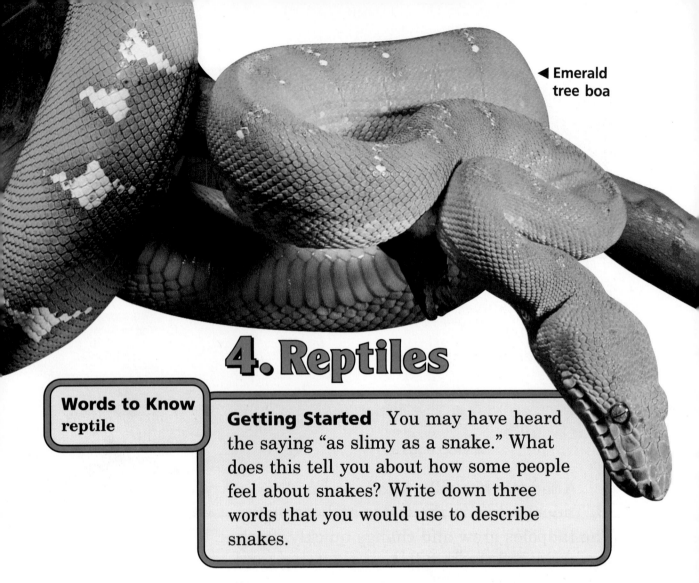

◀ Emerald
tree boa

4. Reptiles

Words to Know
reptile

Getting Started You may have heard the saying "as slimy as a snake." What does this tell you about how some people feel about snakes? Write down three words that you would use to describe snakes.

What are the traits of reptiles?

A **reptile** is a cold-blooded vertebrate that has lungs and dry skin. Almost all reptiles are covered with scales. Most have four legs with claws on the toes. Some reptiles give birth to live young. But most lay eggs that have a thick covering.

Reptiles are not like other cold-blooded vertebrates. Reptiles control their body temperature by their actions. Some reptiles lie in the sun. So even when the air is cold, they become warmer than the air around them.

Most reptiles spend their whole life on land. They do not have gills at any part of their life cycle. Reptiles get oxygen from air they breathe into their lungs.

How do reptiles produce young?

Reptiles are different from amphibians in the way they produce their young. Unlike frogs, reptiles lay eggs on land. Count the number of eggs in the picture. Most reptiles lay only a dozen eggs at a time. A frog may lay thousands.

Reptile eggs are protected from drying out by a leathery shell. They are fertilized before they are laid. As you can see in the picture below, a newly hatched reptile looks very much like its parents. How is this different from a newly hatched frog?

▼ **Bull snake hatching from egg**

▼ **Baby land turtles hatching**

What are some groups of reptiles?

There are three main groups of reptiles. These are the crocodiles and alligators, the turtles, and the lizards and snakes.

Crocodiles and alligators live in warm, shallow rivers and swamps. These reptiles can grow to be longer than a big car. They have large jaws with sharp teeth, and a long tail for swimming. One way to tell crocodiles from alligators is by the shape of their head. A crocodile's head is long and thin and comes to a point. An alligator's head is wider and more rounded. Which of these pictures, *A* or *B*, shows a crocodile?

Turtles make up a second group of reptiles. A turtle's body is protected by two hard shells. A curved shell covers the top of the body; a flat shell covers the bottom.

Like all reptiles, turtles have lungs and lay their eggs on land. Many turtles, such as the sea turtle, live in water. These turtles must breathe air at the water's surface. They must also find land on which to lay eggs.

Green sea turtle ▶

▲ Garter snake shedding skin

Snakes and lizards make up the third group of reptiles. Both snakes and lizards have skin covered by scales. The skin does not grow as the animals grow. From time to time old skin is shed. The shedding of a body covering is called molting. During molting a new and larger body covering forms.

Most lizards are found in hot, dry places. They usually do not grow very large. But snakes are found all over the world. They can be very large or very small. An anaconda (an uh KAHN duh) would stretch from one end of your classroom to the other. But a thread snake would fit on your hand.

Lesson Review

1. What are three traits of reptiles?
2. How do reptiles and amphibians differ in the way they lay eggs?
3. List three main groups of reptiles.

Think! Many turtles pull their heads and legs inside their shell. How does this help a turtle?

**Earth Science
CONNECTION**

Use reference books to find out about the Mesozoic Era.

5. Birds

Words to Know
bird
feather

Getting Started You learned that a reptile is covered with scales. A bird has a body covering that is different from scales. What is this body covering? Look at the bird shown here. How is a bird different from a reptile? How are they alike?

Blue jay ▶

down feather

contour feather

What are the traits of birds?

A **bird** is a warm-blooded vertebrate that has a body covering of feathers. Feathers are the one trait that makes birds different from all other animals. A **feather** is a light body part that is found on a bird's skin.

A bird has two types of feathers. Contour (KAHN toor) feathers are large, strong, and smooth. They give a bird a sleek shape for flight. Down feathers are small and fluffy. They are found under the contour feathers. Down feathers help keep birds warm.

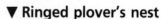

All birds have a pair of legs and a pair of wings. Birds use their wings and feathers for flying. A bird's bones are very light and filled with air. The bones make a bird's body light enough to fly.

How do birds produce their young?

Birds are a lot like reptiles in the way they produce young. All birds lay eggs. Bird eggs are many sizes and colors. The eggs are fertilized before they are laid. Like reptile eggs, bird eggs are covered by a shell. But a bird eggshell is hard and breakable. How is this shell different from that of a reptile egg?

Most birds build nests for their eggs. Nests can be made of twigs, leaves, feathers, mud, or anything else a bird can find. Nests can hang from trees, rest on the ground, or float on water. Some birds lay eggs on bare ground, without a nest. As you can see, different birds build different kinds of nests. Where might you find the nests shown?

▼ **Robin's nest**

▼ **Ringed plover's nest**

▲ Penguin with baby

▲ Male flamingo feeding its baby

Many birds sit on their eggs to keep them warm until they hatch. After hatching, many kinds of baby birds are weak and helpless. They have very few feathers and cannot see. Both parents feed the baby birds and protect them. In a few weeks the young birds learn to fly and get food on their own.

Some kinds of young birds, like chicks and ducklings, need less care. Soon after they hatch, these baby birds can feed themselves, walk, and swim. How are the young birds shown here being cared for?

Lesson Review

1. Identify two traits of birds.
2. How do contour and down feathers help a bird?
3. How do most birds care for their young?

Think! Most eggs laid on bare ground are speckled or brown. How is this coloring helpful?

86

THINKING

Skills

Making an inference

Asking questions is something you do every day. An inference is a possible answer to a question about how or why something happens. It is a guess based on what you can observe and what you already know.

Practicing the skill

1. Look at the drawing carefully. Suppose you wonder, How did the broken eggshell get there? Make a list of all the things you can observe that might help answer the question: The eggshell is near the tree, feathers are on the ground, and so on.

2. Now make a list of what you already know that might help to explain what happened: Wind can blow things out of trees, some animals eat bird eggs, and so on.

3. Think of some possible answers to the question.
   a. The wind blew the eggshell out of the nest.
   b. An animal ate the egg.
   Add your own to this list.

4. Pick the best inference. A good inference fits well with the facts that you have collected. Explain why you have chosen this inference.

Thinking about the skill

Why did you try to think of several possible answers?

Applying the skill

Suppose you see some jelly-covered eggs along the edge of a pond. Later you notice that the eggs are gone. Make an inference to answer this question: What happened to the eggs?

6. Mammals

Getting Started Touch the top of your head. What do you feel? Hair is a trait that people have. What are some animals that also have hair or fur? In what other ways are these animals alike?

Words to Know
mammal

What are the traits of mammals?

A **mammal** is a warm-blooded vertebrate that has hair and feeds milk to its young. Mammals are the only animals with hair or fur. Like feathers on birds, hair helps to keep a mammal warm. Not all mammals have the same amount of hair. Can you think of a mammal that has a lot of hair?

▼ Blue whale

Mammals are also the only animals that feed milk to their young. Female mammals have body parts, called milk glands, that produce milk. The milk is food for the young.

Mammals live in many different places. Most mammals live on land. But some, like whales, live in water. One group, the bats, can fly. Mammals are many different sizes. Look at the picture of the shrew, the smallest mammal. It is not even as long as your finger. Have you ever been close to an elephant? As big as this mammal is, it is not the largest mammal. The largest mammal is the blue whale. A blue whale weighs more than the total weight of 20 elephants.

▼ Shrew

▼ African elephants

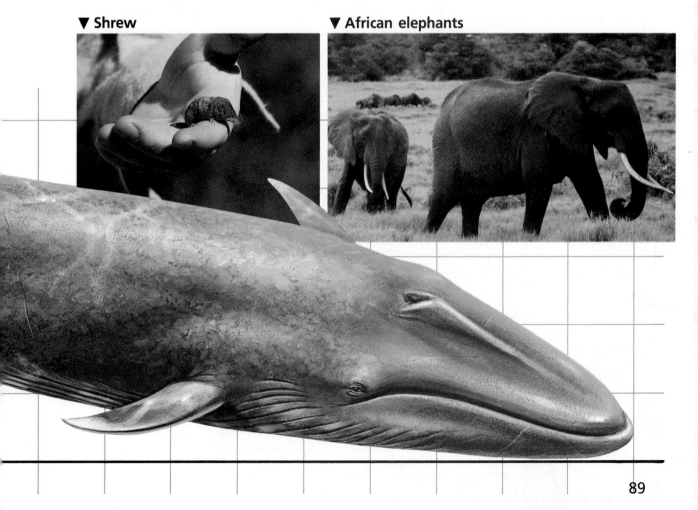

Explore

Does hair help keep an animal warm?

Mush! With this simple command the Iditarod Dog Sled Race begins. By the time the sled teams finish the race, they will have run over 1,840 km (1,150 mi) through Alaska. Along the way the dogs will have faced temperatures that can fall to −35°C (−31°F).

Materials
hot water · 2 thermometers · 2 tin cans · glue · cotton · aluminum foil · timer

Procedure

A. Remove the labels from two tin cans. Coat the outside of one can with glue.

B. Put a layer of cotton over the glued surface. Wait a few minutes for the glue to dry. Fluff the cotton outward.

C. Fill both cans with the same amount of hot water from the same container.

D. Place a thermometer in each can. Cover the tops of the cans with aluminum foil as shown.

E. Measure and record the temperature of the water in each can every 5 minutes for the next half hour.

F. Make a bar graph of the temperature data to show how the temperatures compare.

Writing and Sharing Results and Conclusions

1. From which can was heat lost more quickly?
2. In what way is fluffed cotton like the hair of an animal's coat?
3. How do your results and conclusions compare with those of your classmates?

What are three groups of mammals?

Scientists divide mammals into three groups. The first group contains egg-laying mammals. One kind of egg-laying mammal is the duckbilled platypus (PLAT ih puhs).

As you can see here, the platypus has some traits in common with birds. Like a duck, it has webbed feet, a bill, and no teeth. It lays eggs in a nest near a lake or river. But when the young hatch, the furry babies are fed milk by their mother.

The second group of mammals is called the marsupials (mahr SOO pee uhlz). A kangaroo and an opossum (uh PAHS uhm) are marsupials. A young marsupial begins to form inside its mother's body. When it is born, it is very small and not fully formed. The young marsupial crawls into a pouch, or pocket, on its mother's body. There it feeds on milk and continues to grow and change.

▲ **Duckbilled platypus**

▼ **Newborn kangaroo**   **Kangaroo in mother's pouch** ▶

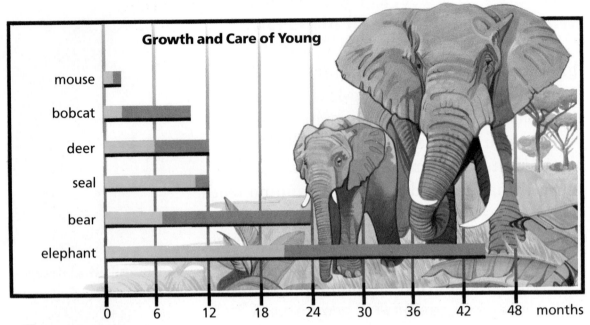

Growth and Care of Young

mouse
bobcat
deer
seal
bear
elephant

0   6   12   18   24   30   36   42   48   months

■ Length of time inside mother

■ Length of time parents care for young

Most of the mammals you know belong to a third group. These mammals have young that grow and change inside the mother's body. The young are fully formed when they are born. But the young still need to be cared for by their parents.

Usually, the smaller the mammal, the shorter the time it grows inside the mother. This graph shows how long some mammal babies grow inside the mother. It also shows how long the parents care for the young after birth. Which mammal takes the shortest time to grow inside its mother? Which mammal takes the longest? Which mammal cares for its young the longest?

Lesson Review

1. List three traits of mammals.

2. How do scientists group mammals?

Think! Which baby would probably grow faster inside the mother — a kitten or a bear cub?

Chapter 2 Putting It All Together

Chapter Connections

List as many different animals as you can that belong to each vertebrate group. Use the graphic organizer to help you.

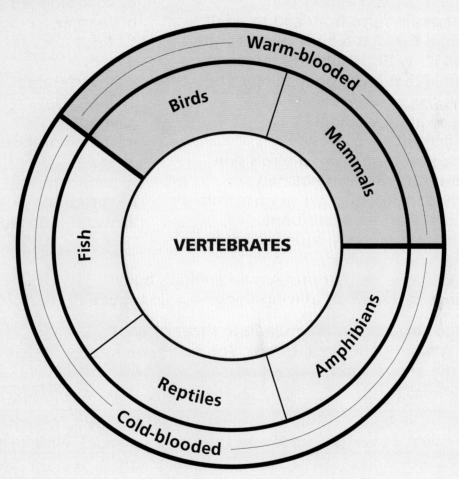

Writing About Science • Classify

Make a vertebrate scrapbook with a section for each of the five vertebrate groups. Paste or draw pictures of animals in each group and label each picture with the animal's name. Write a paragraph telling why a section of your scrapbook is your favorite.

Chapter 2 Review

Science Terms

A. Write the letter of the term that best matches the definition.

1. Fanlike part on a fish's body
2. Changes in form from egg to adult
3. Animal that has a body temperature that changes with the outside temperature
4. Animal that has a body temperature that stays the same, even when the outside temperature changes
5. Animal with a backbone
6. Body part that covers a bird's skin
7. Frogs that have just hatched
8. Body parts used to get oxygen from air
9. Animal without a backbone
10. Thin feathery body parts used for breathing in water
11. Hard, flat plate that protects an animal's body
12. Stages in the life of a living thing

a. cold-blooded animal
b. feather
c. fin
d. gills
e. invertebrate
f. life cycle
g. lungs
h. metamorphosis
i. scale
j. tadpoles
k. vertebrate
l. warm-blooded animal

B. Copy the chart below on a separate sheet of paper. Leave room to write in each box. For each term listed, fill in the answers to the questions.

	Cold- or warm-blooded?	How do they produce young?	How do they breathe?	What is their body covering?
fish				
amphibian				
reptile				
bird				
mammal				

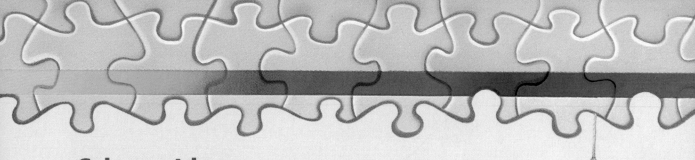

Science Ideas

Use complete sentences to answer the following.

1. Why are fish, amphibians, reptiles, birds, and mammals placed in one animal group?
2. Which groups of vertebrates are cold-blooded? Which groups are warm-blooded?
3. How does a fish get oxygen from water?
4. Why do fish lay large numbers of eggs?
5. Name two kinds of amphibians with tails. Name two kinds without tails.
6. How is a tadpole different from an adult frog?
7. How does the leathery shell help protect reptile eggs?
8. Describe one trait of (a) crocodiles and alligators, (b) turtles, (c) snakes and lizards.
9. How do birds care for their young before the eggs hatch?
10. How does a young marsupial form?

Purple Finch

Applying Science Ideas

Use complete sentences to answer the following.

1. All mammals have lungs. Some mammals live in the ocean. How do ocean mammals breathe?
2. Why do some people think that animals should be used to test new drugs? Why are some people against using animals for scientific research?

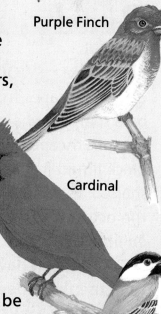

Cardinal

Chickadee

Using Science Skills

Suppose you want to feed the birds shown on this page. You put sunflower seeds in this feeder and hang it on a tree. The cardinals eat seeds that fall on the ground. But they do not eat the seeds in the feeder. Make an inference about why the cardinals do not feed at the feeder.

Tufted titmouse

95

Animal Adaptations

Ready, Aim, Fire

SQUIRT! SWOOSH! In a matter of seconds an octopus escapes from an enemy. The enemy might be a shark, a whale, or even a person. How did the octopus escape so quickly? An octopus can squirt a black liquid from its siphon (SYE fun), a funnel-shaped opening under its head. The liquid hides the octopus so that it can move away from the enemy.

All animals have ways to protect themselves. Deer use their speed to run from enemies. Birds and insects fly away from danger. Other animals fight back if attacked. Dogs and wolves have strong teeth. Cats scratch with sharp claws. And kangaroos kick with powerful legs.

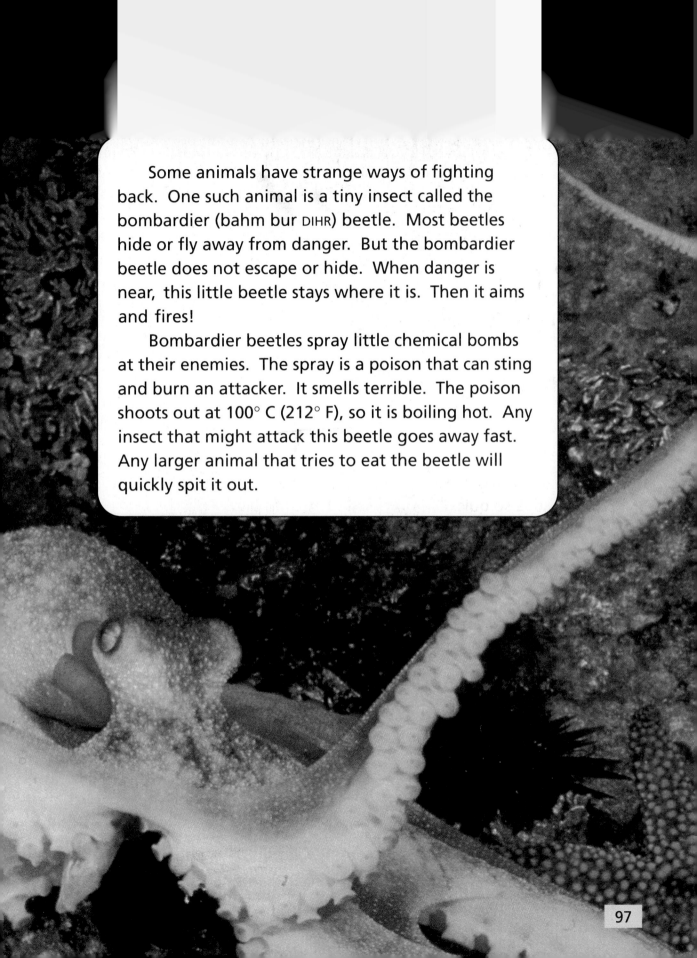

Some animals have strange ways of fighting back. One such animal is a tiny insect called the bombardier (bahm bur DIHR) beetle. Most beetles hide or fly away from danger. But the bombardier beetle does not escape or hide. When danger is near, this little beetle stays where it is. Then it aims and fires!

Bombardier beetles spray little chemical bombs at their enemies. The spray is a poison that can sting and burn an attacker. It smells terrible. The poison shoots out at 100° C (212° F), so it is boiling hot. Any insect that might attack this beetle goes away fast. Any larger animal that tries to eat the beetle will quickly spit it out.

How is the poison made? The beetle has two sacs inside the back of its body. Each sac has two sections. And each section makes a different chemical. The chemicals are stored in the sacs.

There is a tube that connects the two sections of each sac. When the beetle is attacked by an enemy, the chemicals in each section mix. This mixing causes a chemical reaction, which gives off a gas. The gas helps to shoot the chemicals out of the beetle's body.

The sacs have openings on the surface of the beetle's body. When the openings are pointed at an attacker, the attacker gets squirted. And the bombardier   does not often miss its target!

Discover

How can you mix chemicals to produce a gas?

ACTIVITY

Materials vinegar · graduate · small plastic soda bottle · spoon · baking soda · balloon · funnel

Procedure

Caution: *Wear safety glasses for this activity.* Inside the bombardier beetle's body, chemicals mix to produce a gas. You can mix chemicals to produce a different gas.

Pour about 100 mL (3 oz) of vinegar into a small plastic bottle. Spoon about 2 tablespoons of baking soda into a balloon. You may need a funnel to get the baking soda into the balloon.

Stretch the opening of the balloon across the opening of the bottle. Be careful not to let the baking soda fall into the bottle. When the balloon is attached to the bottle, lift the end of the balloon and let the baking soda fall into the bottle. Describe what happens.

In this chapter you will learn more about how an animal's body helps it stay alive. You will also find out what body parts and actions help animals stay alive.

1. How Animals Stay Alive

Words to Know
environment
adaptation

Getting Started Do you have a pet? If so, you know how to take care of it. Make a list of things your pet needs to keep it healthy. Now think about the things you need to stay healthy. How are your needs the same as those of your pet?

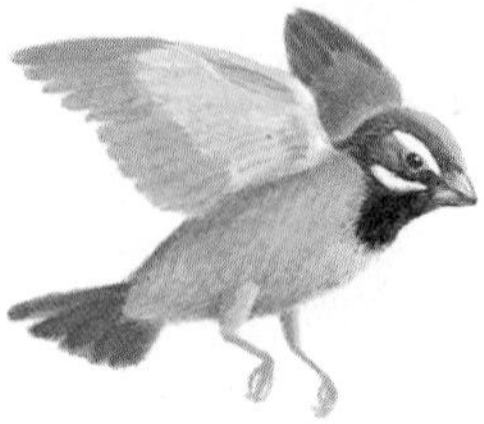

What do animals need to stay alive?

To survive (sur VYV), or stay alive, animals need certain things. They need food, water, and oxygen. They also need a place to live. These things are found where an animal lives and are part of its environment (en VYE-run munt). The **environment** is everything that surrounds and affects an animal. The environment includes both living and nonliving things. What living and nonliving things are parts of this jack rabbit's environment?

▼ Sonoran Desert of Arizona

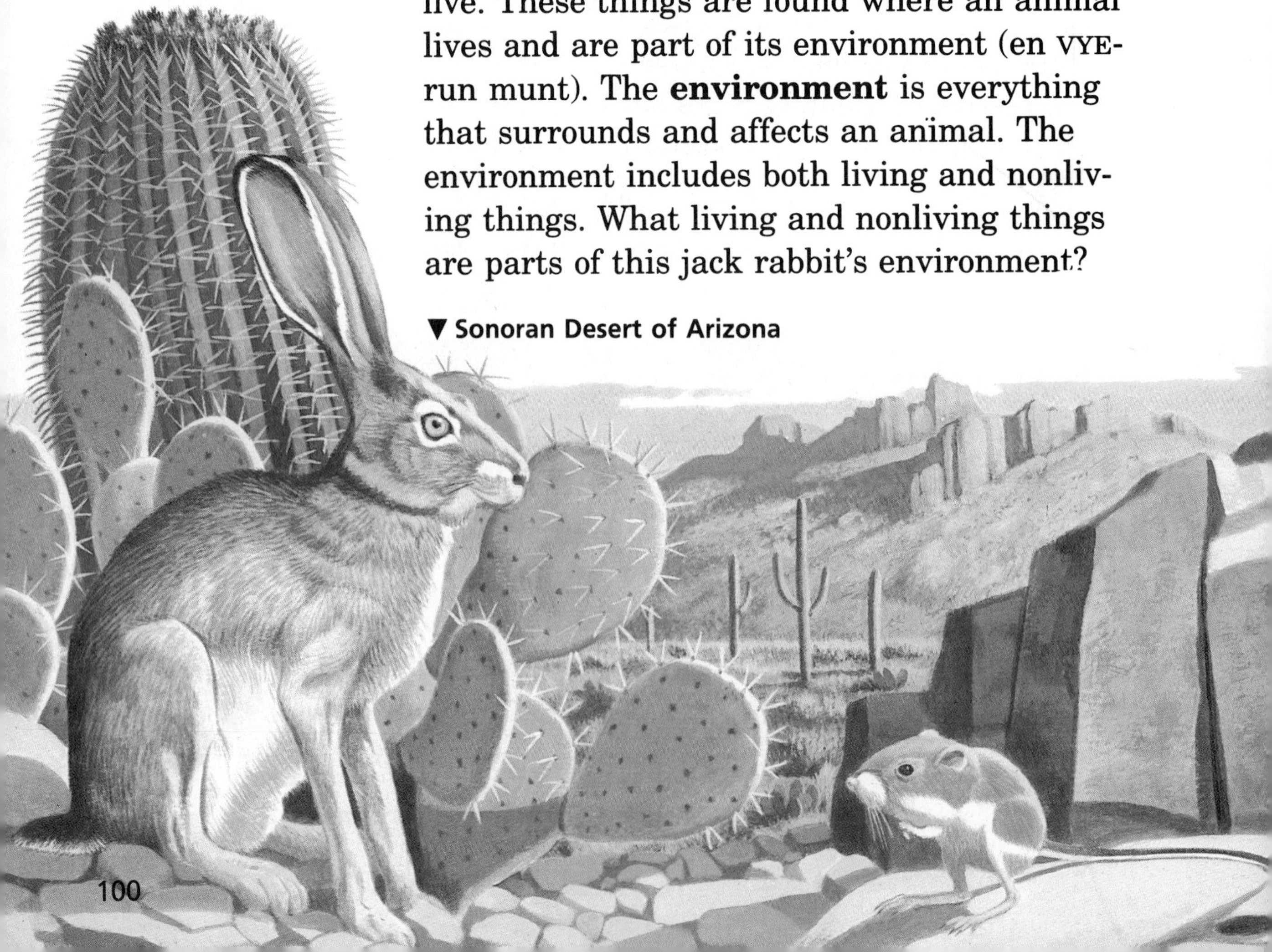

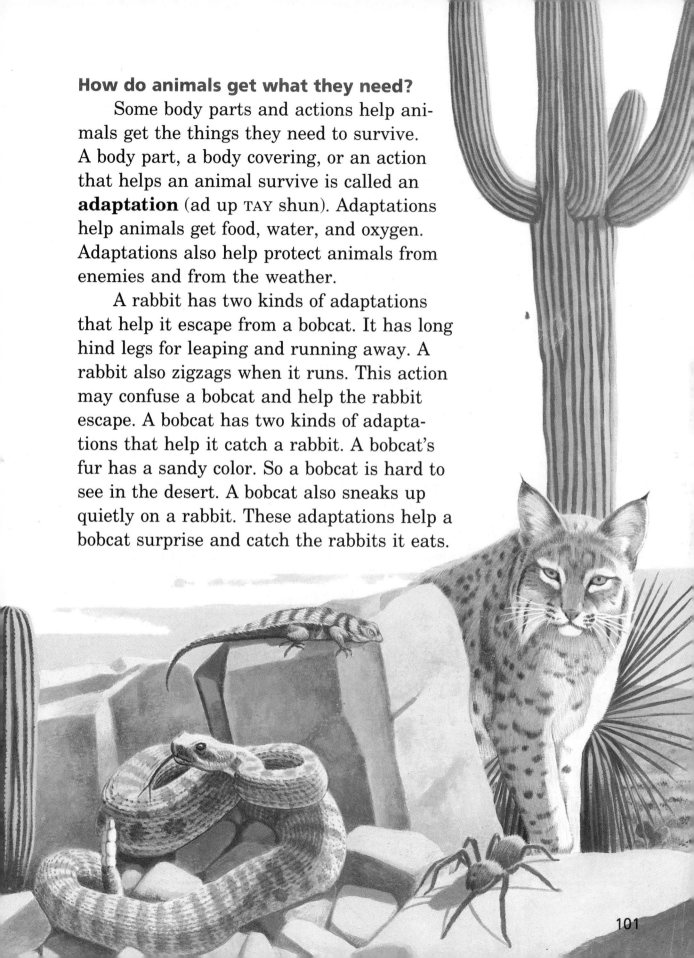

How do animals get what they need?

Some body parts and actions help animals get the things they need to survive. A body part, a body covering, or an action that helps an animal survive is called an **adaptation** (ad up TAY shun). Adaptations help animals get food, water, and oxygen. Adaptations also help protect animals from enemies and from the weather.

A rabbit has two kinds of adaptations that help it escape from a bobcat. It has long hind legs for leaping and running away. A rabbit also zigzags when it runs. This action may confuse a bobcat and help the rabbit escape. A bobcat has two kinds of adaptations that help it catch a rabbit. A bobcat's fur has a sandy color. So a bobcat is hard to see in the desert. A bobcat also sneaks up quietly on a rabbit. These adaptations help a bobcat surprise and catch the rabbits it eats.

▼ **Three kinds of teeth**

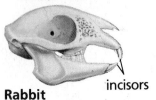

Rabbit

incisors

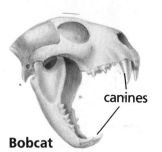

Bobcat

canines

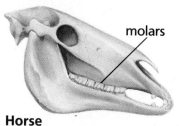

molars

Horse

What body parts help animals get food?

Many body parts help animals get food. As the drawings show, animals have three different kinds of teeth. Teeth help animals eat different kinds of food. Rats, mice, and squirrels have long, sharp front teeth called incisors. Beavers and rabbits do, too. These teeth help animals cut and gnaw hard plant parts, such as seeds, nuts, and wood. Meat-eating animals have long pointed teeth called canines near the front of the mouth. Canines help cats, dogs, and bears bite and tear the meat they eat. Plant-eating animals have large flat teeth called molars along the sides of the mouth. Molars help cows, horses, and deer crush and grind the grass they eat. You have these three kinds of teeth. How do your teeth help you eat different foods?

10   20   30   40   50   60   70

The way animals move also helps them get food. Body parts, such as arms, legs, and wings, help animals find or catch their food. This monkey lives in trees. Its long, strong arms help it swing through branches to look for fruits to eat.

Now look at the long legs of this cheetah. A cheetah's powerful legs help it run about 113 kilometers per hour (70 miles per hour). This is about as fast as a fast car moves. At this speed a cheetah can outrun and catch the animals it eats. How fast can you run?

As fast as a cheetah can run, it is not the fastest animal. This falcon can outfly and catch other birds. Its long pointed wings help it dive swiftly and steeply to snatch up a bird in the air. Look at the drawing. What other body parts might help the falcon catch food?

▲ Spider monkey

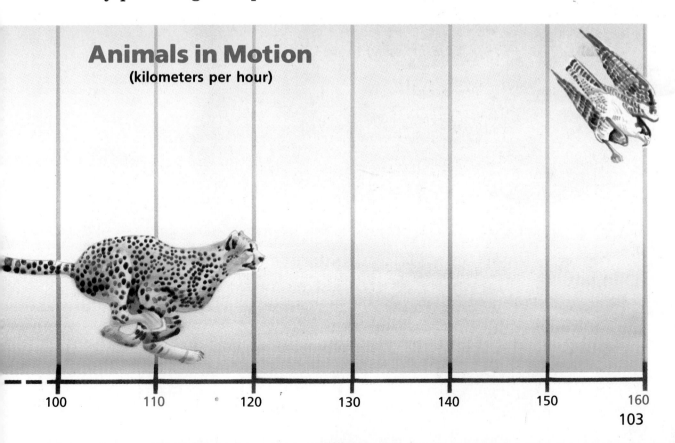

Animals in Motion
(kilometers per hour)

100   110   120   130   140   150   160

How do body coverings help animals survive?

Body coverings help animals in different ways. Coverings help animals get oxygen and other things they need. Coverings also help protect animals in their environment.

Skin, for example, helps some animals get oxygen from the air. Frogs and worms have thin, moist skin that allows oxygen to pass through it. Have you ever seen worms on a sidewalk after it rains? Once their skin dries, they cannot get oxygen. What happens to the worms then?

Many body coverings protect animals from the weather. Thick scales cover a lizard's body. Water cannot pass through the scales. The water stays inside the lizard's body. So scales protect lizards from losing water in hot, dry places like a desert.

▲ Brown and gold tree frog

▼ Desert spiny lizard

Feathers and fur protect some animals from the cold. The thick fur that covers this polar bear helps keep the bear warm. So the bear can survive the very cold temperatures and fierce winds of its arctic environment.

▲ Polar bear

Sometimes a body covering helps protect an animal from enemies. A porcupine is covered with sharp quills. The quills are like needles that are about as long as a piece of chalk. They can come loose and get stuck in an enemy's body. So not many animals will try to eat a porcupine.

▼ Porcupine

Lesson Review

1. List three things animals need to stay alive.
2. What three kinds of teeth help animals eat different foods?
3. Name two body coverings that protect animals from the weather.

Think! What body part helps a giraffe eat the leaves of tall trees?

2. Colors and Shapes

Getting Started Do you like to wear costumes? A costume makes you look like someone or something else. Think about the last time you wore a costume. Your friends may have guessed what you were pretending to be. How could they tell?

▲ Pink praying mantis from Malaysia

How do looks help animals survive?

Sometimes the way an animal looks helps it survive. Find the caterpillar in the picture. It looks like a twig on a tree. Its color and shape are adaptations that help it hide in its environment.

A color or shape that helps an animal blend in with its environment is called **camouflage** (KAM uh flahzh). Camouflage can hide animals from enemies. It can also help animals catch food. How does camouflage help protect this caterpillar from being eaten by a bird?

▲ Spring cankerworm

Some animals are the same color as their environment. So they are hard to see. Find the green praying mantis in the picture. The mantis matches the color of the leaves around it. This hides the mantis from birds that might eat it. It also helps the mantis hunt for insects to eat.

Other animals look like something else in their environment. Find the pink praying mantis on page 106. It has the color and shape of a flower. This disguise hides the mantis from insects it eats. What might happen to a butterfly that lands on this "flower"?

Some animals are different colors in different environments. This baby seal cannot swim. As a pup, it lives on ice and snow. Its white fur hides the pup from enemies. As the seal grows up, it is able to swim. Then its fur changes to brown. This color helps hide the seal in the dark waters where it swims.

▲ Costa Rican praying mantis

▼ Harp seal pup with mother

ACTIVITY

Explore Together

How does color help an animal survive?

Materials

Organizer 50 red, 50 blue, 50 green, and 50 yellow toothpicks · 1 sq m green cloth · timer

Procedure

Group A. Pretend that the green cloth is grass, the toothpicks are insects, and the Manager is a bird looking for insects.
1. Predict which color toothpick will be hardest to find. Explain your answer.

Investigator B. Place the cloth on the floor. Scatter the toothpicks on the cloth.

Manager C. Look for the "insects." You must collect as many toothpicks as you can in 15 seconds. Pick up the toothpicks one at a time.

Investigator D. Use the timer to tell the Manager when to stop.

Recorder E. Count how many toothpicks of each color were picked up.
2. Record the data.

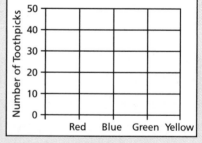

Investigator, Manager, Recorder F. Repeat steps **B** through **E** one more time.

Writing and Sharing Results and Conclusions

Group, Recorder
1. Plot your data on a bar graph like the one shown.
2. Which color toothpick was hardest to find?
3. Which color would hide an insect best in green grass?
4. Suppose the grass turns yellow during the winter. Predict which color would hide an insect best then.

Reporter 5. How do your results and conclusions compare with those of your classmates?

▲ **Bumblebee moth and bumblebee on a petunia**

What is mimicry?

Some animals survive because they look like dangerous animals. Look at the picture of the bumblebee and the bumblebee moth. Can you tell these two insects apart? The bumblebee gives a painful sting. So most animals stay away from it. Most animals also stay away from the harmless moth. The moth cannot sting. It is protected from enemies because it looks like the bumblebee. An adaptation in which an animal looks like a harmful animal is called **mimicry** (MIHM ihk ree).

Lesson Review

1. What is camouflage?
2. How can a body shape help to hide an animal in its environment?
3. How does mimicry help an animal survive?

Think! What kind of camouflage helps a polar bear catch the seals it eats?

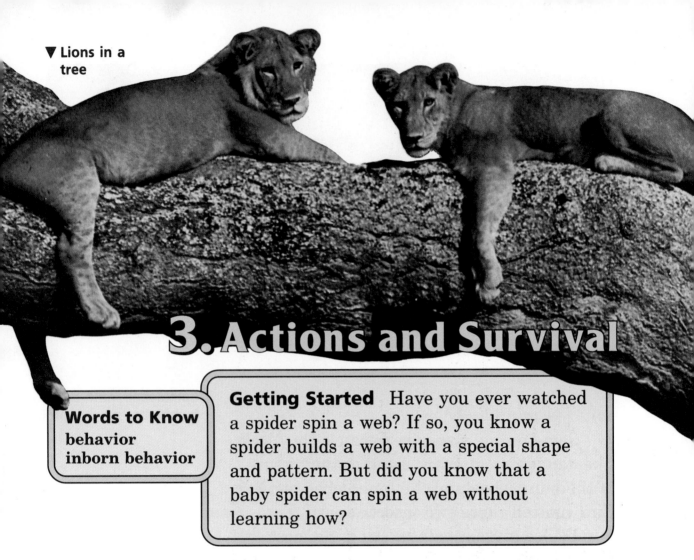

▼ Lions in a tree

3. Actions and Survival

Getting Started Have you ever watched a spider spin a web? If so, you know a spider builds a web with a special shape and pattern. But did you know that a baby spider can spin a web without learning how?

What is another kind of adaptation?

▼ Garden spider

An adaptation can also be something an animal does. The actions of an animal are called **behavior.** Animals have many behaviors. Dogs wag their tails, and cats purr. Birds build nests, and squirrels gather nuts. What behaviors do you see in the pictures? What is a behavior that you have?

Animals learn some behaviors. Fox pups learn how to hunt by watching their parents. But animals do many things without learning how. A behavior an animal is born with is **inborn behavior.**

What inborn behaviors help animals survive?

Some inborn behaviors are quick, automatic actions called reflexes (REE fleks ihz). Suppose something gets into your eye. Without thinking, you blink. Blinking is a reflex.

Reflexes help protect animals from harm. For example, many animals move away quickly when they hear a noise. Birds fly away. Frogs hop into the water. This behavior helps animals escape from enemies.

▲ Duck in flight

◄ Common frog

Other inborn behaviors are instincts (IHN stihngkts). Like reflexes, instincts help animals survive. One of these instincts is migration (MYE gray shun). Migration is the movement of animals from one place to another at certain times of the year. In some places the weather gets very cold during the winter. Food is hard to find. So, many animals migrate, or move to other places. When the seasons change, the animals return.

*Walking with wild birds and swimming with sea lions was only the beginning of a summer of fun for Hans. Find out what else he did when he got to a strange new place. Read **Galapagos** in Horizons Plus.*

111

Explore

What can you observe about the behavior of a goldfish?

ACTIVITY

Each August, salmon in the Pacific Ocean begin a long journey. Millions of fish swim toward rivers in North America. They swim up these rivers, jumping over waterfalls along the way. Finally the salmon reach the same streams where they hatched. There the females lay eggs and die. In the spring the eggs hatch. Then millions of tiny salmon return to the sea.

Materials
aquarium · goldfish · pencil · bell · fish food

Procedure
A. Use the pencil to carefully tap on the glass of the aquarium.
   1. Record any evidence that the goldfish hear the tapping.

B. Experiment to see if goldfish hear sounds. Sprinkle some fish food on the water at one end of the aquarium. Ring the bell as you put in the food. Repeat the experiment every day for a week.

C. After a week, ring the bell but do not put in any food.
   2. Observe how the goldfish behave.

Writing and Sharing Results and Conclusions
1. What evidence did you observe that the goldfish heard sounds?

2. Explain how goldfish might use hearing to survive.

3. How do your results and conclusions compare with those of your classmates?

Many animals travel great distances when they migrate. Monarch butterflies fly south to California and Mexico for the winter. In the spring they return north, as far as Canada. But some animals migrate only as far south as is needed to find food. The map shows where house wrens migrate. As winter nears, these birds fly south where there is food. Do house wrens spend the winter in your state?

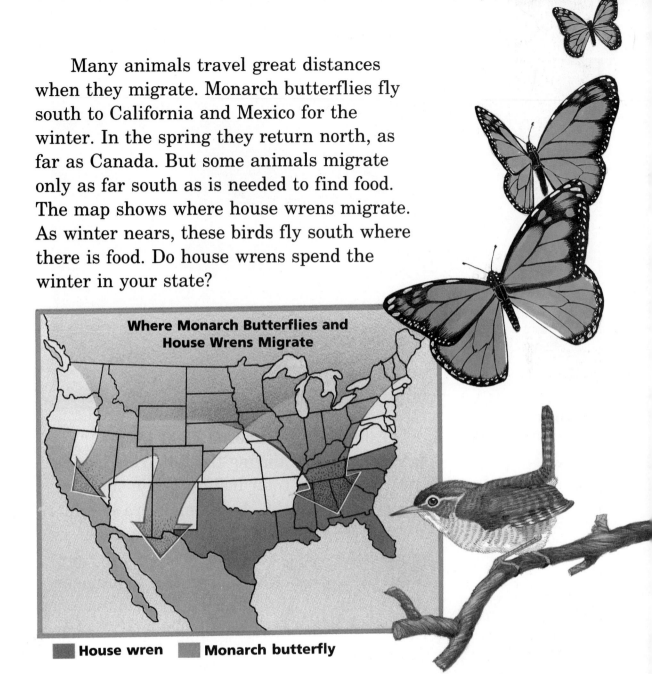

Where Monarch Butterflies and House Wrens Migrate

■ **House wren**   ■ **Monarch butterfly**

Some animals do not migrate in the winter. Another instinct helps them survive the cold and lack of food. These animals spend the winter in a long, deep sleep called hibernation (hye bur NAY shun). Woodchucks, ground squirrels, and chipmunks hibernate. Many bears and some bats do, too.

▲ Hibernating black bear with cubs

Animals that hibernate eat large amounts of food during the fall. This food is stored as fat in their bodies. When the weather turns cold, the animals crawl into a safe place, such as a cave or a deep hole. There they sleep and use the stored fat as food. Some animals, such as this black bear, wake up many times during the winter. Other animals, such as this squirrel, do not wake up until spring.

▲ Hibernating ground squirrel

Lesson Review

1. Define the term *behavior*.
2. Why is it hard for some animals to live in the same place all year round?
3. Name two instincts that help animals survive the winter.

Think! What reflex helps a bombardier beetle escape when it is attacked by an enemy?

THINKING

Skills

Using a hypothesis to explain things

You may have observed a certain kind of bird in the summer but not in the winter. You may explain what you observe by saying that certain birds move in the winter. This explanation is a hypothesis.

Practicing the skill

1. Look at the young insect in the drawing. This kind of insect builds a sac to live in. The young insects are like soft worms

2. You may think of the question "Why do insects of this kind build a covering to live in?"

3. Describe what the insect's sac is made of.

4. List ways that building a sac may help the insect.

5. Write a hypothesis that can explain why the insect builds a sac. The hypothesis should use what you have observed.

▲ Caddisfly larva

Thinking about the skill

How do you think the insect's sac is like your home?

Applying the skill

Can you see the fish in the picture? Write a hypothesis that can explain how it helps the fish to look like the ocean floor.

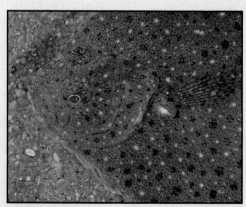

▲ Flounder

4. Learning and Survival

Words to Know
learned behavior

Getting Started Do you like to listen to music on the radio? You probably like to sing some of the songs you hear. How do you learn the words to your favorite songs?

What is another kind of behavior?

Think about things you learn how to do. You learn how to tie your shoes, write your name, and ride a bicycle. A behavior that is learned and not inborn is a **learned behavior.**

How do animals learn behaviors? Usually animals practice, or do an action over and over again. The pictures show how a chimpanzee learns to find insects to eat. The baby watches his mother carefully. She is poking a twig into a hole to pull out termites. Then the baby will try to do it. He may practice many times before learning how to use a twig as a tool.

How can learning help animals survive?

Many learned behaviors help animals get food. Squirrels learn how to crack open nuts. Lion cubs learn how to hunt. Think about the baby chimpanzee. Once he learns how to use a tool, he can get food on his own.

Learned behaviors also help animals survive when their environment changes. A long time ago, sea otters lived on land near the ocean. There the otters were hunted for their soft, warm fur. But otters learned how to live in the ocean, where hunters could not reach them. The otters survived in their new environment because they learned many things. They learned how to find food in the water and how to hide from enemies there. The picture shows another thing they learned. Otters wrap themselves in long strands of seaweed. This keeps the otters from floating toward land while they sleep.

▼ **Sea otter wrapped in kelp**

▲ Canada goose with goslings

Another kind of learned behavior helps some young birds survive. Imprinting is a special kind of learning in certain newborn animals. Soon after hatching, baby ducks and geese imprint on, or learn to follow, the first moving thing they see. Usually this is their mother. So the babies imprint on her. Then the young birds stay close to their mother and follow her everywhere. Notice that these young geese swim close to their mother. So she can protect them and lead them to places where they can find food.

Lesson Review

1. How do animals learn behaviors?
2. How were otters able to survive in a new environment?

Think! In a famous experiment, a scientist was the first moving thing that some baby geese saw. Predict what these goslings learned to do.

118

Chapter Connections

Draw the shapes of the graphic organizer on your paper. Try to fill them in without looking at the book. Compare your drawing with the organizer.

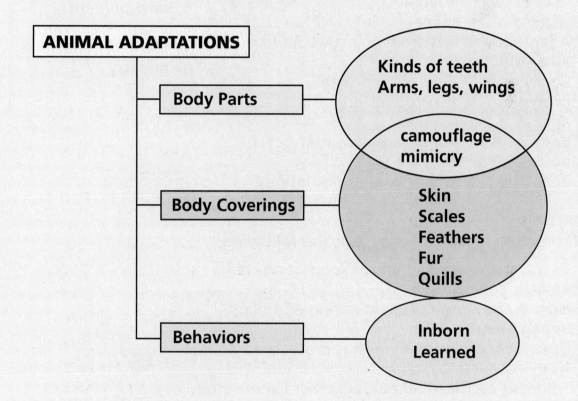

ANIMAL ADAPTATIONS

- **Body Parts**
  - Kinds of teeth
  - Arms, legs, wings
  - camouflage
  - mimicry
- **Body Coverings**
  - Skin
  - Scales
  - Feathers
  - Fur
  - Quills
- **Behaviors**
  - Inborn
  - Learned

Writing About Science • Describe

Use this form to write a riddle about an animal:

My body is covered with _____.
My teeth help me eat _____.
I move by _____.
To protect myself from enemies, I_____.
What am I?

Science Terms

Write the letter of the term that best matches the definition.

a. adaptation
b. behavior
c. camouflage
d. environment
e. inborn behavior
f. learned behavior
g. mimicry

1. Color or shape that helps an animal blend in with its environment
2. Actions of an animal
3. Adaptation in which an animal looks like a harmful animal
4. Behavior an animal is born with
5. Everything that surrounds and affects an animal
6. Body part, covering, or action that helps an animal survive
7. Behavior that is learned and not inborn

Science Ideas

Use complete sentences to answer the following.

1. Describe two ways in which adaptations help animals survive.
2. How do the teeth of meat-eating and plant-eating animals differ?
3. Describe a body covering that protects an animal from enemies.
4. Tell how each animal below survives the winter.

▼ House wren   ▼ Monarch butterflies   ▼ Ground squirrel

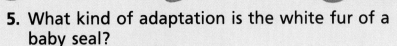

5. What kind of adaptation is the white fur of a baby seal?
6. How is a bumblebee moth protected from enemies?
7. Tell which of these behaviors is a reflex and which is an instinct: (a) migration and (b) blinking.
8. How does imprinting help young birds survive?

Applying Science Ideas

Use complete sentences to answer the following.

1. What adaptations protect the beetle and the land snail?
2. A skunk can spray a liquid with a very bad smell. This liquid can burn an animal's eyes, nose, and mouth. How is this behavior an adaptation?
3. Many jellyfish are transparent. You can see through their bodies. How does this clear color help jellyfish survive in the ocean?
4. Suppose you had to make a costume that would be camouflage in your classroom. What would your costume look like?

▲ Beetle

Using Science Skills

Look at the teeth of the killer whale and porcupine. Write down as many observations as you can about their teeth. What hypothesis can you make about the kinds of food that each animal eats?

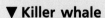

▲ Land snail

▼ Killer whale   ▼ Porcupine

Ecosystems

Forest Fires: Helpful or Harmful?

In 1950 a fire swept through Lincoln National Park in New Mexico. When it was over, park rangers found a tiny bear cub. He was holding on to a burned tree. His fur and paws were badly burned. The rangers looked for his mother, but she was nowhere to be found.

Firefighters kept the cub and named him Smokey, after the Smokey the Bear symbol. Smokey's motto is, "Only You Can Prevent Forest Fires." But some fires cannot be prevented, and others are difficult to stop.

In 1988 a fire spread through Yellowstone National Park. At first the forest rangers thought they should let the fire burn naturally. But then the rangers decided to stop the fire, and they were almost too late! It burned for about 100 days. More than 10,000 firefighters fought the blaze. When the fire was finally over, one million acres of the forest had been destroyed.

Sometimes it takes a forest about 100 years to grow back. And yet, scientists say that fires help to keep a forest healthy. How can a fire be good for a forest? Fires rid the forest of old or dead trees and thick bushes, letting more sunlight and water reach the forest floor. After a fire, black ashes, which are rich in minerals, cover the ground. Also, some seeds are released from cones only by the heat of a fire. These and other seeds begin to grow in the black ashes. The growing plants then provide food for the forest's animals to eat.

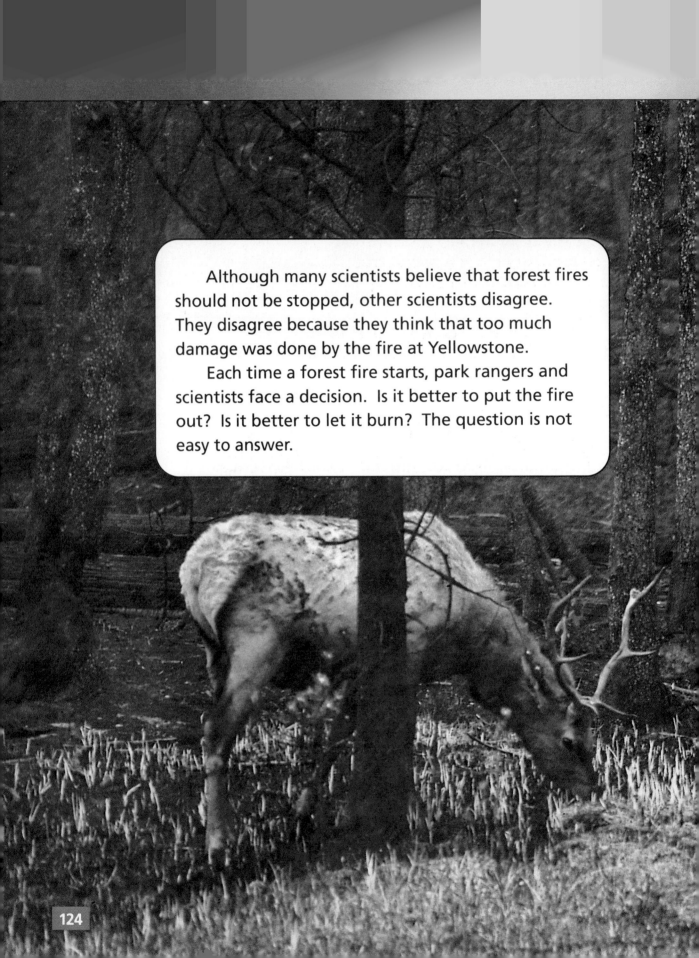

Although many scientists believe that forest fires should not be stopped, other scientists disagree. They disagree because they think that too much damage was done by the fire at Yellowstone.

Each time a forest fire starts, park rangers and scientists face a decision. Is it better to put the fire out? Is it better to let it burn? The question is not easy to answer.

Discover

How does fire help plants grow?

Materials   2 paper cups · potting soil · vegetable seeds · white construction paper · black construction paper

Procedure

After a fire, black ash covers the forest floor. Will the black ash absorb heat or reflect heat? Heat helps seeds on the forest floor sprout and grow. Do you think heat would help vegetable seeds sprout? Write down your prediction.

Fill the cups with potting soil. Plant your seeds according to the directions on the package. Cover one cup with white construction paper. Cover the other cup with black construction paper. Now place both cups in a sunny area. Which seeds will start to grow sooner? Which cup of soil is like the ash-covered forest?

In this chapter you will learn how plants and animals depend on each other. You will discover how each member of the community is affected by changes in other members.

1. The Living and Nonliving World

Words to Know
ecosystem

Getting Started Make a circle by touching the tip of your first finger to the end of your thumb. Hold the circle up to one eye and close the other eye. Look at a spot in your classroom or out a window. What living and nonliving things do you see?

What is an ecosystem?

Look at the fish tank. What living and nonliving things do you see? The living and nonliving things in the tank affect each other. The water, for example, has materials that the fish and plants need. Notice the bubbles of air in the water. Air contains oxygen. Fish take in this oxygen from the water. Then the oxygen combines with food, and energy is released. Without energy the fish could not

▲ Tropical fish tank

live. What would happen if all the oxygen in the water was used up?

As they breathe, fish give off a gas called carbon dioxide. The plants use this carbon dioxide to make food. Like animals, plants use energy from food to live and grow.

As you can see, the living things in the tank depend on the nonliving things. The living things also depend on each other. When plants make food, for example, they give off oxygen. How is oxygen used by the fish?

The fish tank is an example of an ecosystem (EK oh sihs tum). An **ecosystem** is a place where living and nonliving things affect each other. In an ecosystem, living things depend on each other and on nonliving things.

*Have you ever seen an osprey? Find out why there are so few of these beautiful birds left when you read **The Ospreys of Great Island** in Horizons Plus.*

127

An ecosystem can be small, like a fish tank, or large, like an ocean. A forest is a large ecosystem. This tree is a small ecosystem. What plants and animals live here?

▲ Blue jay feeding baby birds

What parts make up an ecosystem?

Plants and animals are parts of most ecosystems. Other living things are, too. These mushrooms belong to a group of living things called fungi. Fungi live in most ecosystems. Tiny living things called microbes also live in ecosystems. Microbes can only be seen with a microscope.

Most ecosystems also have three nonliving parts. These parts are soil, water, and air. Where might you find water in a forest?

▲ Fox squirrel

Lesson Review

1. What is an ecosystem?
2. List four kinds of living things found in most ecosystems.

Think! Can a puddle of water be an ecosystem? Explain your answer.

Skills

THINKING

Observing patterns

When you look at dogs, you see that they are alike in certain ways. Dogs walk on four legs and have fur. You are used to seeing things that have traits that are put together in about the same way. A pattern is a set of traits that are put together in a certain way.

Practicing the skill

1. The three drawings below show birds that can fly but that can also swim in water. What traits do the feet of all these birds have? This is the pattern of the feet of birds that swim.

2. Look at the bills of these birds. All of these birds eat small plants that grow in water. The bills also have a pattern. Write about the pattern of the bills of these swimming birds.

▲ Canvasback duck   ▲ Mallard duck   ▲ Canada goose

Thinking about the skill

How does having several birds to look at help you to find the patterns?

Applying the skill

Look at the drawings at the right of the page. Which of the birds has feet that fit the pattern of a swimming bird?

2. Living Parts of Ecosystems

Getting Started What happened to the dinosaurs? Some scientists think that an object from space hit the earth. Dust from the crash filled the air and blocked out sunlight for months. How would this have affected the ecosystems of the dinosaurs?

How do plants get energy?

Some plants and animals of a forest ecosystem are shown here. Like all living things they need energy to live and grow. The energy needed by most living things comes from the sun.

Plants use sunlight to produce, or make, food. A living thing that makes food using the sun's energy is a **producer** (proh DOOS-ur). Some of the food plants make is used for living and growing. The rest is stored in the plant. This stored food has energy that can be used by other living things.

How do animals get energy?

Unlike plants, animals cannot make food. Animals must consume, or eat, food to get energy. All animals are consumers (kun-SOOM urz). A **consumer** is a living thing that eats other living things.

Some animals, such as this rabbit, eat plants. They get energy that was stored in the plants. Some animals, like this bobcat, eat other animals. They get energy that was stored in those animals. Now suppose a bobcat eats a rabbit. The rabbit got its energy from plants. By eating a rabbit the bobcat gets energy that once came from plants. So, as you can see, all animals really depend on plants for energy. What would happen to the rabbit if the plants died? What might then happen to the bobcat?

▼ **Rocky mountain forest**

Explore Together

What do molds look like?

Organizer

Materials

water · bread · cheese · orange peel · 6 sealable plastic bags · hand lens

Procedure

Manager   A. Sprinkle enough water to moisten a piece of bread, a piece of cheese, and a piece of orange peel.

Investigator   B. Place the moist bread into a plastic bag. Then seal the bag.

Investigator   C. Repeat step **B** with the moist cheese and moist orange peel.

Investigator   D. Place a piece of dry bread into a bag. Seal the bag.

Investigator   E. Repeat step **D** with a piece of dry cheese and a dry orange peel.

Investigator   F. Place the six bags in a warm, dark place.

Group, Recorder   G. Use a hand lens to look at the food samples. **Caution:** *Some molds are harmful. Do not open the bags.* Do this every day for eight days. Make drawings of what you observe.

Writing and Sharing Results and Conclusions

Group, Recorder
1. What happened to the food samples in the plastic bags?
2. Did different kinds of molds grow on different foods?
3. Do you think molds grow better in dry or wet places? Explain your answer.

Reporter   4. How do your results and conclusions compare with those of your classmates?

▲ Decomposers in a forest ecosystem

▲ Soil microbes

How do other living things get energy?

Some living things get energy from dead plants and animals. Fungi, such as mushrooms and molds, get food from this dead tree. Microbes get food from it, too. Many fungi and microbes are decomposers (dee-kum POHZ urz). A **decomposer** is a living thing that gets energy by breaking down dead plant or animal parts.

Decomposers are an important part of an ecosystem. As they break down dead things, simple materials are left. These materials can be used again in the ecosystem. Look at the drawing. Which living things in an ecosystem use materials left by decomposers?

Producers, consumers, and decomposers — you can find them all as you try **Food Chains and Food Webs.**

Lesson Review

1. How do producers and consumers differ?
2. Why are decomposers important in ecosystems?

Think! Like plants, mushrooms grow in soil. Why do you think mushrooms are not classified as plants?

133

3. Nonliving Parts of Ecosystems

Words to Know

soil
water
air

water vapor changes
to liquid water
and falls to the
ground as rain

Getting Started Get some soil from outside your school. Spread out the soil on a
piece of paper. What things do you see?
How would you group the things that make
up soil? How does soil help plants live?

How does soil help plants grow?

Soil is the part of the ground where plants
grow. Soil is a mixture of materials. It is
made of bits of rock. It has leaves, twigs, and
other dead parts of plants and animals. Soil
also contains water and air.

Soil helps plants grow in two main ways.
First, soil helps to hold plants in place. Look at
the next page. Notice that a plant has roots
that grow into the soil. Second, soil contains
nutrients (NOO tree unts) that plants

need. Nutrients are materials that help living things grow and stay healthy.

How does water move through ecosystems?

One of the nutrients in soil is water. **Water** is a nutrient needed by all living things in an ecosystem. As the drawing shows, water moves back and forth between the parts of an ecosystem. Water in the air falls to the ground as rain. Some of the water goes into rivers, lakes, and oceans. Some water soaks into the soil. Water on or in the ground can then be used by living things. Look at the drawing. How is water taken in by plants and by animals?

Water goes back into the air when it evaporates from lakes and oceans. When water evaporates, it changes to a gas called water vapor. In the air, water vapor changes back to liquid water. What happens to this water then?

water evaporates

▼ **White-tailed deer drinking**

roots take in water

135

Explore

Which contains more carbon dioxide, air you breathe in or air you breathe out?

carbon dioxide

oxygen

Take a deep breath and breathe out slowly. Every time you do this, you add carbon dioxide to the air around you. But how can you tell that this is happening? Like other gases in air, carbon dioxide has no color and no smell. So try a simple test. Carbon dioxide makes clear lime water turn a milky color.

Materials

safety goggles · clear bottle · limewater · flexible plastic straw · inflexible plastic straw · modeling clay · timer

Procedure

Caution: *Wear safety goggles for this activity.*

A. Half fill the bottle with limewater.

B. Put a flexible straw and an inflexible straw into the bottle. Seal the bottle with clay. Make sure the flexible straw is below the water and the inflexible straw is above the water.

C. Blow through the flexible straw of the bottle for two minutes. Observe and record any changes in the limewater.

D. Suppose you pumped the air around you into a bottle of limewater. This air is the same air you breathe in. After two minutes there would be no changes in the limewater.

Writing and Sharing Results and Conclusions

1. Where did the air come from that you blew through the straw?

2. What changes did you observe in the limewater?

3. Which contains more carbon dioxide, the air you breathe in or the air you breathe out?

How do gases move through living things?

Almost all living things in an ecosystem need air. **Air** is a mixture of gases. Two important gases in air are oxygen and carbon dioxide. As the drawing shows, these gases move back and forth between plants, animals and the air. Animals take in oxygen from the air they breathe. The oxygen is used to get energy from food. As animals breathe they give off carbon dioxide. The carbon dioxide can be used by plants when they make food. As plants make food, they give off oxygen. Then this oxygen can be used by animals.

▼ How oxygen and carbon dioxide move between plants and animals

Lesson Review

1. List two ways that soil helps plants grow.
2. Why is water important in ecosystems?

Think! Suppose animals did not use plants as food. Would they still need plants to stay alive? Explain your answer.

Earth Science CONNECTION

Use reference books to find out about different types of soil. What types of soil can be found in your town?

4. Relationships in Ecosystems

Words to Know
community
predator
prey
parasite
host

Getting Started How many students are there in your classroom? Are there any plants in the room? Perhaps there are some animals, such as hamsters. How do the living things in your classroom affect each other?

How do living things affect each other?

The plants and animals shown here live together in a place called the tundra. The tundra is an ecosystem in northern Canada and Alaska. Notice that deerlike animals called caribou live there. Wolves and other animals also live there. What kinds of plants grow on the tundra? All the living things in an ecosystem make up a **community**

▼ Tundra

(kuh MYOO nuh tee). The members of a community live together in the same place and affect each other in certain ways.

The ways in which living things affect each other are called relationships. Look again at the caribou and the wolves. Notice that the wolves are following the caribou. Wolves are predators (PRED uh turz). A **predator** is an animal that hunts and eats other animals. Caribou are prey (pray) for the wolves. A **prey** is an animal that a predator hunts.

Relationships between predators and prey are important in ecosystems. Suppose the wolves of the tundra are killed by people. How might this affect the number of caribou in the tundra? Caribou eat the plants of the tundra. How might killing the wolves affect the tundra's plants?

Problem Solving
It Might Not Go Down Too Well

Have you have ever been hot and thirsty during a walk through the woods? If so, you may have thought about drinking the water from a cool pond. But pond water is not tap water. It is an ecosystem with a community.

How does pond water differ from tap water?

Observe some samples of pond water and tap water. What materials might help you? Make drawings of the living things you observe. How do tap water and pond water differ? Describe the community you observed in the pond water.

actual size

dog flea

Not all relationships in a community are between predators and prey. Look at the picture of the dog flea. Fleas are insects that live on dogs, cats, and other animals. Fleas get food by sucking blood from an animal's body. Like mosquito bites, flea bites are itchy and painful. Some fleas also carry diseases that make animals very sick.

Fleas are parasites (PAR uh syts). A **parasite** is a living thing that feeds on and harms another living thing. The living thing that is harmed is a **host**. A dog is a flea's host. Most parasites harm, but do not kill, the host. How does this help the parasite?

▲ Ants feeding on aphid honeydew

How can living things help each other?

In another kind of relationship, two kinds of living things depend on each other. Each living thing does something that is helpful to the other. Look at the picture of ants and very small insects called aphids (AY fihdz). The ants protect the aphids from predators. The ants also protect the aphids from cold weather. Before winter begins, the ants carry the aphids into nests underground.

The aphids make a sweet liquid called honeydew, which ants eat. When the ants touch the aphids with their feelers, the aphids give off drops of honeydew. Then the honeydew is collected and eaten by the ants.

Lesson Review

1. Why is a flea called a parasite?
2. How are ants and aphids helpful to each other?

Think! Can an animal be both predator and prey? Explain your answer.

141

5. Changes in Ecosystems

Words to Know
succession

Getting Started Have you ever moved a rock with a stick? If so, what living things did you see under the rock? What happened when you moved the rock?

What is succession?

Sometimes the living things in an ecosystem are affected by a sudden change. During the summer of 1988, fires destroyed forests in Yellowstone Park. Trees, shrubs, and grasses were burned. Many small animals died. After the fires many other animals could not find food or a place to live.

What happens in places where a community has been destroyed? It may take more than 100 years for the community to come back. During this time there are changes in the kinds of living things in the ecosystem. The changes in the communities of an ecosystem over many years are called **succession.**

▼ Field community

◄ Yellow-headed blackbird

▼ Deer mouse

How does succession take place?

Suppose a fire destroys a forest of oak and maple trees. The first community to appear after the fire is a field community. Grasses and weeds start to grow on the land. These plants provide food and a place to live for small animals. Which animals do you see?

▲ Fox

After a few years, larger plants start to grow. Shrubs and small pine trees sprout up. The animals change, too. Different birds build nests in the trees. Larger animals, such as foxes and deer, move onto the land. In about 20 years, a pine forest covers the land. The pine forest is the second community in succession.

As more time passes, the old pine trees slowly die. Oak and maple trees start to grow. These trees become the home for chipmunks, squirrels, and birds.

▲ Black bear

▲ Oak and maple forest

Finally, after about 100 years, the maple and oak trees have grown tall. The forest of oak and maple trees is the last community to live on the land. This forest is the home for many animals, such as bears, deer, raccoons, and porcupines. Many kinds of birds live in the trees. Fungi grow on dead trees. Microbes live in the soil. What other animals do you see in this forest?

Earth Science
CONNECTION

Volcanoes can cause large changes to ecosystems. Find out what changes were caused by the Mount St. Helens volcano.

Lesson Review

1. What is succession?
2. Name three communities that live on the land after a forest fire.

Think! What events besides a fire might affect the community of an ecosystem?

Chapter Connections

Choose five important words from the organizer.
Write your own definition of each word.

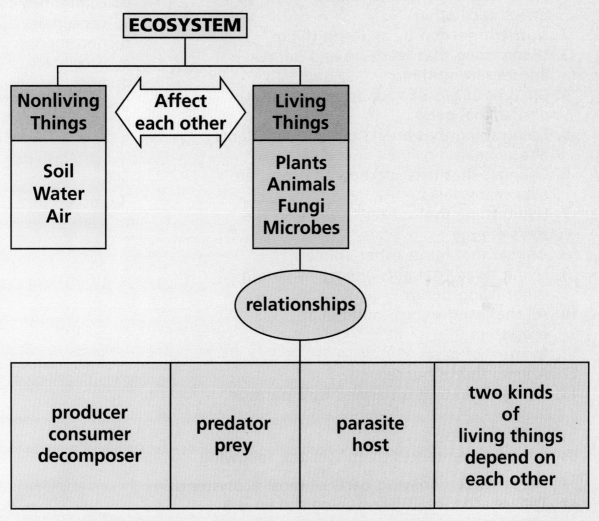

Writing About Science • Imagine

Imagine an ecosystem such as your back yard or your
school grounds. List living and nonliving things found
there. Write a paragraph about how the living and
nonliving things in the ecosystem affect each other.

Chapter 4 Review

Science Terms

Write the letter of the term that best matches the definition.

1. Place where living and nonliving things affect each other
2. Nutrient needed by all living things
3. Living thing that feeds on and harms another living thing
4. Mixture of bits of rock and dead plant and animal parts
5. Living thing that breaks down dead plants and animals
6. Changes that take place in an ecosystem over many years
7. Living thing that makes food using the sun's energy
8. Animal that hunts other animals
9. Living thing that gets energy by eating other living things
10. All the living things found in an ecosystem
11. Mixture of gases
12. Animal that is hunted
13. Living thing that is harmed by a parasite

a. air
b. community
c. consumer
d. decomposer
e. ecosystem
f. host
g. parasite
h. predator
i. prey
j. producer
k. soil
l. succession
m. water

Science Ideas

Use complete sentences to answer the following.

1. Name three nonliving parts of most ecosystems.
2. Tell whether each living thing shown is a producer, a consumer, or a decomposer.

mushroom

plant

cottontail rabbit

3. How does a consumer differ from a decomposer?
4. Which gas is given off when plants make food? How is this helpful to the animals in an ecosystem?
5. Name some living things that make up the community of the tundra.
6. Describe the kind of relationship between the flea and the dog shown.
7. What are two ways that fleas harm their host?
8. What are two ways that ants protect aphids?
9. Describe the first community that will live on land destroyed by a forest fire.

Dog and a flea

Applying Science Ideas

Use complete sentences to answer the following.

1. How would an ocean ecosystem differ from an ocean community?
2. Do you think your neighborhood is an ecosystem? Explain your answer.
3. Athlete's foot is a skin infection caused by fungi. The fungi grow between a person's toes and feed on skin. What kind of relationship is present between the fungi and a person with athlete's foot?
4. How do the movements of oxygen and carbon dioxide link consumers and producers in an ecosystem?
5. Do you think oxygen and carbon dioxide move between plants and animals in a water ecosystem? Explain your answer.

Using Science Skills

What is the pattern of the body of a fish? Make a drawing that shows this pattern. The picture on pages 126 and 127 can help you.

Unit 1 Wrap-up

Careers in Life Science

Forest-Fire Fighter

When Dave Poncin was 14 years old, he knew what he wanted to be when he grew up. He wanted to work in the mountains and be a fire fighter. Today, Dave is a **forest-fire fighter,** and he is still happy with his choice. "This job is exciting. It feels good to be a part of a hard-working team that protects forests, wildlife, and people," he says.

When Dave was growing up, he always liked the outdoors. He went fishing and hunting. He camped and hiked as a Boy Scout.

As a forest-fire fighter, Dave now works outdoors. His work includes different kinds of jobs. He has been a "smoke jumper." A smoke jumper parachutes into a burning area that cannot be reached in any other way. At another time, Dave was a "lookout." The lookout stays in a high tower in the middle of a forest and watches for fires.

Now, Dave plans how to put out big fires safely. He is the leader of a team of fire fighters. Each team member has a job. One plans how the fire should be controlled. This person decides when and where each team member will work. Another person is in charge of getting food, tools, and sleeping bags where they are needed. A third person must know where each team member and piece of equipment are at all times. Sometimes a fire suddenly changes the direction in which it is moving. Fire can trap people. Knowing where everyone is can save lives.

If you would like to be a forest-fire fighter, you first need to finish high school. You also need to take good care of your body. You must be in top shape for the hard work of fighting fires. If you are chosen for such a job, you will be trained in many ways to fight forest fires.

Connecting Science Ideas

1. On pages 122–125 you read about a fire in Yellowstone Park. Dave Poncin was there. What might he say is the hardest part of fighting a fire for 100 days? **Chapter 4; Careers**

2. You learned about two kinds of plant root systems. Which root system might keep a plant alive longer during a forest fire? **Chapter 1; Chapter 4**

3. What adaptations of reptiles protect the babies before they hatch? **Chapter 3; Chapter 2**

4. On pages 40–41 you learned about factory farms. A factory farm is like a small ecosystem. Describe how the farmer provides all the nonliving parts of that ecosystem. **Chapter 1; Chapter 4**

5. Factory farms grow crops. Could fish be grown in a "fish factory"? How could more fish be produced this way? **Chapter 1; Chapter 2**

Computer Connections

There are over 20,000 kinds of fish. Choose two kinds that are possible food sources. Use reference books to find out the description, location, and average weight of the two kinds. Enter the information into a class database. Have classmates enter information about other fish.

Trace a world map from an atlas. Use the class database to locate the different kinds of fish on the map. Write the name of each kind in the proper location. How are the fish from one location alike? How are they different?

Unit Project

Imagine a distant planet. Write a description of the planet. Invent a creature that could survive there. Write about five adaptations of the creature. Create a drawing or model of the creature in its environment.

from

McBROOM
Tells the Truth

SID FLEISCHMAN

Illustrated by Walter Lorraine

McBroom is one surprised farmer when he learns that the farm he bought is nothing more than an acre of muddy water. But he's in for an even bigger surprise when he plants some bean seeds. Can you guess what that surprise might be?

Well, there we stood gazing at our one-acre farm that wasn't good for anything but jumping into on a hot day. And the day was the hottest I could remember. The hottest on record, as it turned out. That was the day, three minutes before noon, when the cornfields all over Iowa exploded into popcorn. That's history. You must have read about that. There are pictures to prove it.

I turned to my children. "Will*jill*hester*chester*peter *polly*tim*tom*mary*larry*andlittle*clarindita*," I said.

"There's always a bright side to things. That pond we bought is a mite muddy, but it's wet. Let's jump in and cool off."

That idea met with favor, and we were soon in our swimming togs. I gave the signal, and we took a running jump. At that moment such a dry spell struck that we landed in an acre of dry earth. The pond had evaporated. It was very surprising.

My boys had jumped in headfirst and there was nothing to be seen of them but their legs kicking in the air. I had to pluck them out of the earth like carrots. Some of my girls were still holding their noses. Of course, they were sorely disappointed to have that swimming hole pulled out from under them.

But the moment I ran the topsoil through my fingers, my farmer's heart skipped a beat. That pond bottom felt as soft and rich as black silk. "My dear Melissa!" I called. "Come look! This topsoil is so rich it ought to be kept in a bank."

I was in a sudden fever of excitement. That glorious topsoil seemed to cry out for seed. My dear Melissa had a sack of dried beans along, and I sent Will and Chester to fetch it. I saw no need to bother plowing the field. I directed Polly to draw a straight furrow with a stick and Tim to follow her, poking holes in the ground. Then I came along. I dropped a bean in each hole and stamped on it with my heel.

Well, I had hardly gone a couple of yards when something green and leafy tangled my foot. I looked behind me. There was a beanstalk traveling along in a hurry and looking for a pole to climb on.

"Glory be!" I exclaimed. That soil was rich! The stalks were spreading out all over. I had to rush along to keep ahead of them.

By the time I got to the end of the furrow the first stalks had blossomed, and the pods had formed, and they were ready for picking.

You can imagine our excitement. Will's ears wiggled. Jill's eyes crossed. Chester's nose twitched. Hester's arms flapped. Peter's missing front teeth whistled. And Tom stood on his head.

"Will*jill*hester*chester*peter*polly*tim*tom*mary*larry* andlittle*clarinda*," I shouted. "Harvest them beans!"

Within an hour we had planted and harvested that entire crop of beans. But was it hot working in the sun! I sent Larry to find a good acorn along the road. We planted it, but it didn't grow near as fast as I had expected. We had to wait an entire three hours for a shade tree.

We made camp under our oak tree, and the next day we drove to Barnsville with our crop of beans. I traded it for various seeds—carrot and beet and cabbage and other items. The storekeeper found a few kernels of corn that hadn't popped, at the very bottom of the bin.

But we found out that corn was positively dangerous to plant. The stalk shot up so fast it would skin your nose.

Of course, there was a secret to that topsoil. A government man came out and made a study of the matter. He said there had once been a huge lake in that part of Iowa. It had taken thousands of years to shrink up to our pond, as you can imagine. The lake fish must have got packed in worse than sardines. There's nothing like fish to put nitrogen in the soil. That's a scientific fact. Nitrogen makes things grow to beat all. And we did occasionally turn up a fish bone.

But there were things we had to be careful about. Weeds, for one thing. My youngsters took turns standing weed guard. The instant a weed popped out of the ground, they'd race to it and hoe it to death. You can imagine what would happen if weeds ever got going in rich soil like ours.

We also had to be careful about planting time. Once we planted lettuce just before my dear Melissa rang the noon bell for dinner. While we ate, the lettuce headed up and went to seed. We lost the whole crop.

That's the entire truth of the matter. Anything else you hear about McBroom's wonderful one-acre farm is an outright fib.

Reader's Response

If you had the chance, what seeds would you plant on McBroom's farm? Why?

McBROOM
Tells the Truth

 Responding to Literature

1. Most of the things that happen in the story could not happen in real life, but McBroom does tell the truth about some things! What parts of the story might be true? How do you know?

2. Some plants grow and die in one season. Others take years to grow. Name some plants in each group.

3. The heat of the sun evaporated the water in McBroom's pond, drying it up. Discuss other examples of evaporation with your classmates.

4. Seeds are not just for planting. Many seeds are also good to eat. If you went to the supermarket, what kinds of seeds could you buy to eat? Make a shopping list of the seeds you would look for.

 Books to Enjoy

McBroom Tells the Truth by Sid Fleischman
If you read the rest of the book, you will learn how a squash seed comes to McBroom's rescue. Look in the library for more of McBroom's tall tales.

"Experiment 13" from Centerburg Tales
by Robert McCloskey
Dulcy is thrilled when he inherits some seeds. But when he and a friend plant the seeds in a greenhouse, they get some unusual results.

The Victory Garden Kids' Book by Marjorie Waters
Gardening is fun, and this book will show you how to grow fruits, vegetables, and flowers.

SCIENCE HORIZONS

PHYSICAL SCIENCE

Properties of Matter

Time for a Change

In October 1886 there was a big party in New York Harbor. The party was for the Statue of Liberty, a gift from the people of France to the United States. The statue was made of shiny copper, like a brand-new penny.

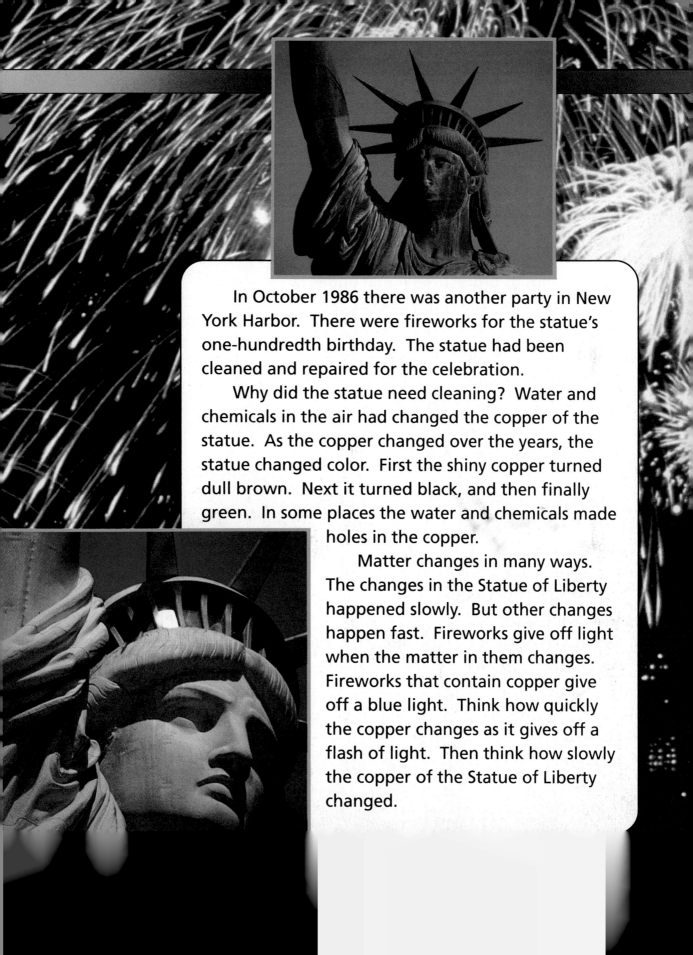

In October 1986 there was another party in New York Harbor. There were fireworks for the statue's one-hundredth birthday. The statue had been cleaned and repaired for the celebration.

Why did the statue need cleaning? Water and chemicals in the air had changed the copper of the statue. As the copper changed over the years, the statue changed color. First the shiny copper turned dull brown. Next it turned black, and then finally green. In some places the water and chemicals made holes in the copper.

Matter changes in many ways. The changes in the Statue of Liberty happened slowly. But other changes happen fast. Fireworks give off light when the matter in them changes. Fireworks that contain copper give off a blue light. Think how quickly the copper changes as it gives off a flash of light. Then think how slowly the copper of the Statue of Liberty changed.

Are you surprised that the green layer of the Statue of Liberty was not cleaned off? The green layer on the copper helps to protect the metal under it. The copper of the statue is only about 3 mm thick. This is a little thicker than the cover of your textbook. If the green layer had been completely washed off, the statue would have started to change color again. Each time the statue was cleaned, some of the metal would have been taken off. This would have made the copper covering thinner. So the people working on the statue decided to leave it green.

Some parts of the statue had to be patched. The patches were made of new, shiny copper. They would have looked strange next to the old, green copper. So workers used special chemicals to make the new copper look old. These chemicals caused the same changes that had turned the statue green.

ACTIVITY

Discover

How can you cause changes in a penny?

Materials safety goggles · piece of string · paper clip · penny from 1981 or earlier · 2 or 3 cotton balls · plastic jar with lid · graduate · 50 mL white vinegar · tape

Procedure

Tie a piece of string to one end of a paper clip. Put a penny between the loops of the paper clip.

Put three cotton balls in the bottom of a plastic jar. Add about 50 mL of vinegar to the cotton. Tape the end of the string to the lid and close the jar. The penny should hang just above the cotton balls.
Caution: *Do not open the jar.*

After 2 days, look at the penny. What happened to it?

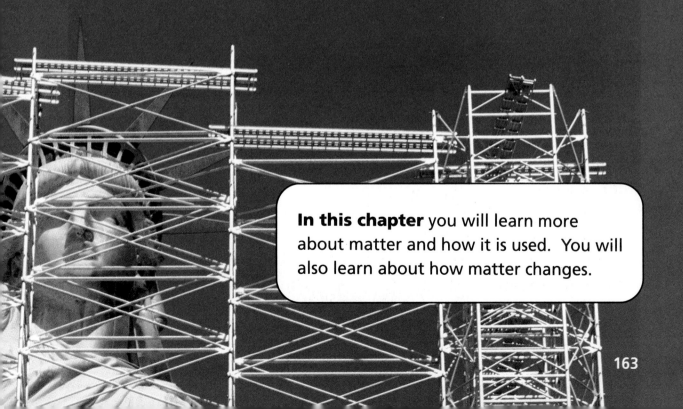

In this chapter you will learn more about matter and how it is used. You will also learn about how matter changes.

1. Matter

Words to Know
matter
mass
volume
particles of
matter

Getting Started Put a drop of perfume into a large balloon. Have your teacher blow up the balloon and knot it. Wave the balloon in the air a few times. What can you smell in the air near the balloon?

What are things made of?

Everything you see takes up space. Even things you cannot see take up space. Think of the air inside a balloon. How do you know the air takes up space?

Anything that takes up space and has mass is **matter.** Look at the things around you. They do not contain the same amounts of matter. **Mass** is a measure of the amount of matter in something. Things that contain more matter have greater mass. A bag that holds 20 marbles contains twice as much matter as one with 10 marbles. Which bag has greater mass?

▼ Matter around you

164

You can measure mass with a balance like the one shown. If objects with the same mass are placed on each pan, the pans will be level. If the objects have different masses, the pan with more mass will be lower. Which truck has greater mass? Which takes up more space?

How can you measure volume?

Suppose you want to measure an amount of milk for a recipe. You might use a measuring cup. When you do, you are measuring volume (VAHL yoom). **Volume** is the amount of space that matter takes up.

When scientists measure the volume of a liquid, they use a graduate. Like a measuring cup, a graduate is marked with units of measure. The graduate shown here is marked with very small units called milliliters (MIL ih leet urz). The symbol for milliliter is *mL*. Large volumes of liquid are measured in bigger units called liters (LEET-urz). The symbol for liter is *L*. One liter is equal to 1,000 milliliters.

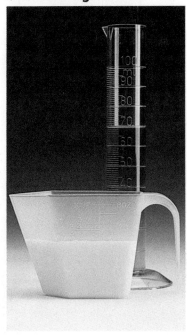

▼ Measuring volume

The volume of solids can also be measured. Suppose a solid has straight sides, like this box. The drawing shows that you measure the sides and calculate the volume.

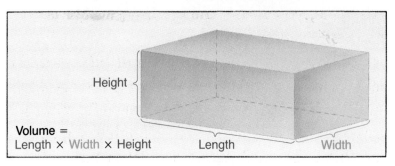

Volume =
Length × Width × Height

Height

Length   Width

But suppose you want to measure the volume of this rock. It does not have straight sides. So you must measure its volume in another way. Place the rock into a graduate partly filled with water. The rock displaces (dis PLAYS ehz), or takes the place of, some of the water. The volume of the displaced water is equal to the volume of the rock. Use a calculator to find the volume of this rock.

▼ Measuring the volume of a rock

What is matter made of?

Think about what happened when you put perfume in the balloon. Why did you smell perfume outside the balloon? To answer this, you must know what matter is made of.

Matter is made of very small bits, called **particles of matter.** These particles are too small to be seen even with a powerful microscope. In fact, they are small enough to get outside this balloon. But how do they get outside? The particles of matter are always moving. Some of the perfume particles are small enough to move through the balloon, so you can smell the perfume in the air.

◀ Testing for particles of matter

Lesson Review

1. What is matter?
2. How can you measure the mass of an object?
3. How can you measure the volume of a key?
4. What is matter made of?

Think! Suppose you put a tea bag into a glass of water. Why will the water begin to change color?

2. Properties of Matter

Getting Started Have you ever read a lost-and-found advertisement in a newspaper? The ad might tell the size, shape, and color of an object. Pretend you have lost a pet or a toy. Write an ad for it.

How can you describe matter?

You can describe matter the same way you described your lost object. How are the kinds of matter shown here different? You might say that the keys are hard. The rose is red. What else might you say?

Something that describes matter is called a property (PRAHP uhr tee) of matter. Color, smell, taste, and feel are physical (FIHZ ih kul) properties of matter. A **physical property** is one that can be observed or measured without changing the matter.

▼ Many kinds of matter

168

What properties of matter can you measure? Remember that you can measure the mass and the volume of matter. So mass and volume are physical properties of matter. This book has a size and a shape. Which property can you measure?

How do you measure density?

The balloons on this balance have the same volume. But, as you can see, their masses are not the same. The red balloon is filled with water and the blue with air. Which balloon has more mass?

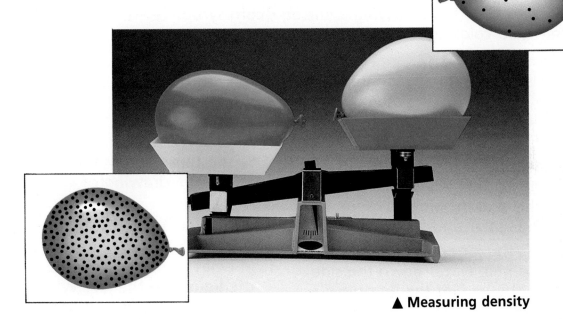

▲ Measuring density

The red balloon contains more particles of matter than the blue balloon. Scientists say that water has greater density (DEN suh tee) than air. **Density** describes the amount of matter packed into a given space. Like mass and volume, density is a property of matter that can be measured.

Alvin's act in the talent show was no ordinary act. But then, Alvin was no ordinary magician. Read about it in **Alvin's Magic** in Horizons Plus.

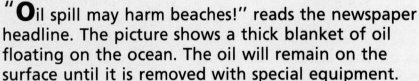
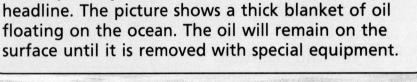

Explore

Are some liquids more dense than others?

ACTIVITY

"**O**il spill may harm beaches!" reads the newspaper headline. The picture shows a thick blanket of oil floating on the ocean. The oil will remain on the surface until it is removed with special equipment.

Materials

2 graduates · cooking oil · tall, clear plastic jar · water · blue food coloring · stirrer · corn syrup · red food coloring

Procedure

A. Use the graduate to measure 60 mL of cooking oil. Pour the oil into the tall, clear plastic jar.

B. Use the other graduate to measure 60 mL of water. Add one drop of blue coloring to the water and stir to mix.

C. Tilt the jar and slowly pour the blue water down the side of the jar. Set the jar on a table.

  1. Observe what happens to the liquids. Make a drawing of what you see.

D. Add one drop of red food coloring to 60 mL of corn syrup. Stir to mix well.

E. Tilt the jar again. Slowly pour the red corn syrup down the side of the jar. Set the jar on a table.

  2. Observe what happens to the three liquids in the jar. Make a drawing of what you see.

Writing and Sharing Results and Conclusions

1. In what order did you add the liquids to the jar? What was the final position of the liquids in the jar?

2. From your results, what can you conclude about the density of the liquids?

3. How do your results and conclusions compare with those of your classmates?

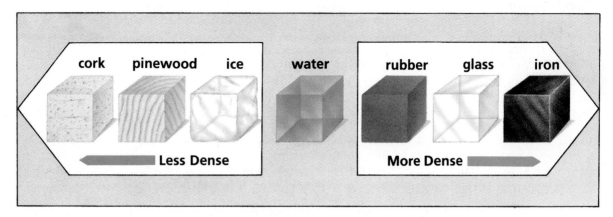

▲ Densities of some kinds of matter

You can compare the density of water with that of other kinds of matter. If an object is less dense than water, it will float in water. If an object is more dense, it will sink. Look at the drawing above. Suppose you put pieces of these solids in water. Which ones will float?

Now look at the blocks of matter in the picture. The yellow block is made of plastic. The other block is made of cork. Notice that they are floating at different levels in the water. Which block has greater density?

▼ Solids with different densities

Lesson Review

1. List three physical properties of matter.
2. Look at the lemon and the hairbrush. Describe 2 physical properties of each.

3. Define the term *density.*

Think! Suppose you put a birthday candle in a glass of water. Why will the candle float on top of the water?

Earth Science
CONNECTION

Density is a property that can be used to identify minerals. Find the density of quartz, talc, and gypsum.

171

Will a foam home be the house of the future?

Can you imagine building a house from a kit the way you build a model car? Believe it or not, you can do just that if you build a home with polystyrene walls. Polystyrene is the same foam material used to keep fast food hot. Keeping heat in is one of the properties of polystyrene foam. Another property is that the foam is less dense than other building materials, such as wood. Compared with a block of wood, a block of foam has a lot less matter packed into the same space. Although foam is not very dense, it is very strong.

Some people think foam homes are a good idea. The foam is good insulation. It keeps heat in during cold weather, and it keeps the house cool in hot weather. With good insulation, heaters and air conditioners are not used as often. This means that foam homes can use less electricity than other houses. Power plants would burn less fuel in making electric power for those homes. That would mean less pollution to the environment.

Other people think foam homes create problems. One problem is that making foam gives off chemicals into the air. These chemicals destroy the earth's ozone layer high above the earth. The ozone layer blocks some of the sun's harmful rays from reaching the earth's surface. Less ozone means that more of the sun's harmful rays will reach the earth. These rays could harm all the living things on the earth.

Another problem is that polystyrene foam is hard to get rid of. If foam is thrown away, it could take up space at a dump forever. It never breaks down. If foam is burned, it gives off harmful chemicals to the environment.

172

Will there be many foam homes in the future? People will have to decide whether the homes are more helpful to them than harmful to the environment.

Critical thinking

Decide for yourself whether foam houses are more helpful to people than they are harmful to the environment. Then use the facts to persuade a classmate with a different opinion to agree with you.

Using what you learned

Imagine you are entering an invent-a-home contest. First prize will go to the home that helps the environment most. Draw your home or make a model of it. Explain how your home helps the environment.

3. States of Matter

Words to Know

states of matter
solid
liquid
gas

Getting Started Think about ice and water. Are they the same kind of matter? Ice and water have some properties that are alike. How is ice different from water? Make a chart comparing the properties of ice with those of water.

What are the forms of matter?

You have learned that matter has properties such as size, smell, and shape. Another physical property of matter is its state, or form. Matter is found in three states. The **states of matter** are solid, liquid, and gas. Which states of matter can you find in this picture?

How do the states of matter differ? You learned that matter is made of moving particles. The spaces between these particles are not the same in solids, liquids, and gases. The way the particles move is also different. For these reasons, solids, liquids, and gases behave differently.

What are solids, liquids, and gases?

A **solid** is matter that has a definite volume and shape. As you can see in the drawing, particles in a solid are packed closely together. The particles move very little. They can only vibrate, or move back and forth, in a very small space. This is why a solid holds its shape. What solids can you name?

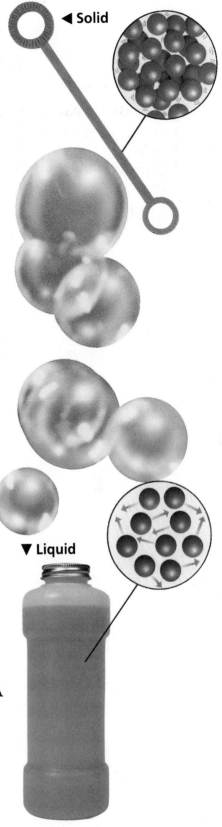

◀ Solid

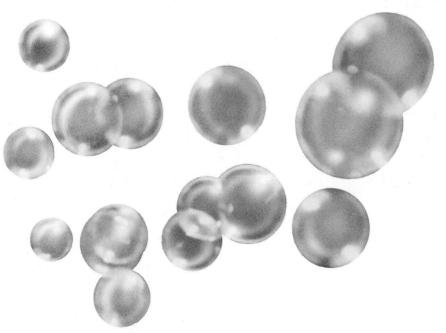

▼ Liquid

A **liquid** is matter that has a definite volume but no definite shape. For most materials, particles in the liquid state are not as close together as in the solid state. They can move and slide over each other. So a liquid flows and has no shape of its own. A liquid takes the shape of any container it is in. But its volume does not change. Suppose you pour milk from a full carton into four glasses. The milk changes shape. But its volume does not change. How do you know?

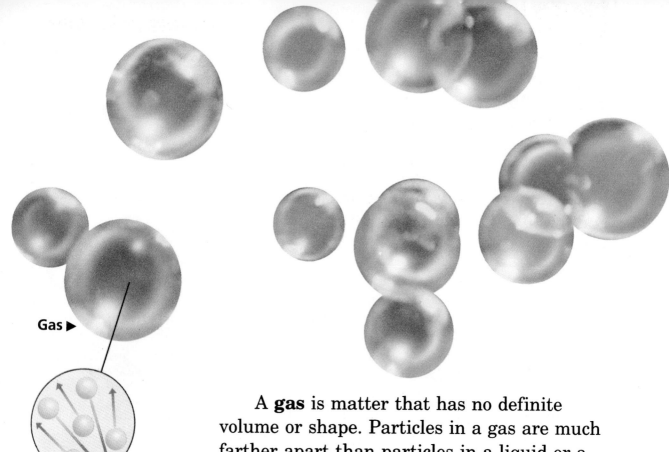

Gas ▶

A **gas** is matter that has no definite volume or shape. Particles in a gas are much farther apart than particles in a liquid or a solid. They also move faster than particles in a liquid or a solid. They bump into each other and move out in all directions. So the particles quickly spread out and fill any space they are in. What will happen to the gas in this bubble if the bubble bursts?

Lesson Review

1. What are the three states of matter?
2. Define *solid, liquid,* and *gas.*
3. How are the particles arranged in wood, milk, and air?
4. How do the particles move in solids, liquids, and gases?

Think! Suppose you pour juice from a small glass into a large pitcher. What would happen to the shape and volume of the juice?

Skills

THINKING

Interpreting a trend in data

Have you ever watched your shadow during the day? Early in the morning your shadow is long. As the morning passes, your shadow becomes shorter. At noon it is shortest of all. Then it grows long again in the afternoon. Every day the length of your shadow follows this trend. A trend is a series that remains constant or changes in a regular way.

Practicing the skill

1. The balloon data table shows how temperature affects the volume of one balloon.

2. The balloon volume is 1,450 mL at 17°C. The volume is 1,475 mL at 22°C.

3. What is the balloon volume at 27°C?

4. What is the balloon volume at 32°C?

 5. The data show a trend. Use a calculator to find how the volume changed as the temperature increased.

Temperature	17°C	22°C	27°C	32°C
Balloon Volume	1,450 mL	1,475 mL	1,500 mL	1,525 mL

Thinking about the skill

What did you do to find the trend in the data table?

Applying the skill

Think about the trend in the data table. What would happen to the volume of the balloon at 37°C? Would the balloon volume be 1,425 mL, 1,550 mL, or 1,675 mL? Use the trend to decide.

4. Changes in Matter

To learn more about how heat changes matter, you might enjoy reading **Sugaring Time,** page 246.

Getting Started After it rains you might see puddles of water. What happens to this water when the sun shines?[1] Now wipe a wet sponge across the chalkboard. Watch what happens to the moisture. Think about how water changes as the chalkboard dries.

Words to Know
physical change
melting point
evaporation
boiling point
freezing point
condensation
chemical change

What is a physical change?

Many kinds of matter can change from one state to another. When water freezes, it changes from a liquid to a solid. What change takes place when ice melts?

When water changes to ice, some of its physical properties change. But it is still water. It does not change into something different. When the ice melts, it tastes and looks like it did before it was frozen. A change in state is a physical change. A **physical change** is a change that does not form new kinds of matter.

How does matter change state?

Heat can cause matter to change state. Adding heat to this ice makes the particles move faster and slide over each other. The ice starts to melt and lose its shape. Melting is the change of state from solid to liquid. The temperature at which a solid changes to a liquid is called the **melting point.**

Think about what happens to a puddle of water as it dries. Some of the particles escape from the surface of the water into the air. These particles form a gas called water vapor. This kind of change of state from a liquid to a gas is called **evaporation** (ee vap uh RAY shuhn).

▲ Ice melting

Sometimes a great deal of heat is added to a liquid. Then bubbles of gas form in the liquid. This kind of change from a liquid to a gas is called boiling. The temperature at which a liquid boils is called the **boiling point.** In the picture, water is boiling. How can you tell?

Cooling can also cause a change in state. When water loses heat, the particles slow down and move closer together. The water begins to freeze. Freezing is the change of state from liquid to solid. The temperature at which a liquid changes to a solid is called the **freezing point.**

▼ Water boiling

▼ Water condensing

Cooling also causes a gas to change back to a liquid. The change from a gas to a liquid is called **condensation** (kahn dun SAY shun). Water vapor in the air cools and condenses when it touches a cold surface. Notice the drops of liquid water on this glass.

Problem Solving

Out of Sight

Have you ever made a cup of hot cocoa? If so, you may have mixed cocoa powder with milk or water. Think about what you did to make the powder dissolve.

How can you speed up the rate of dissolving?

Get some sugar cubes and a timer. Predict some ways that might speed up the rate at which sugar dissolves in water. Try some experiments that test your predictions. What ways did you find to speed up the rate of dissolving? Which way worked the fastest?

What are some other physical changes?

Changes in the size or shape of matter are also physical changes. Breaking a glass changes its size and shape. But the pieces are still glass. They do not change into another kind of matter. How is matter changing in this picture?

Another physical change takes place when something dissolves in water. Sugar and water are different kinds of matter. When sugar dissolves in water, the sugar particles mix with the water particles. But particles of sugar are still in the water. How do you know?

▲ Matter changing in size and shape

181

What is another kind of change?

You have learned about many physical changes in matter. But matter can change in another way. Burning causes wood to change into ashes and smoke. Ashes and smoke are different from wood. A change that forms different kinds of matter is called a **chemical** (KEM ih kul) **change.**

You can see both chemical and physical changes when you make these hamburgers. Making the patties causes a physical change. But cooking the meat causes a chemical change. The cooked meat is not the same kind of matter as raw meat.

Some chemical changes take place slowly. Rust on this bridge forms from a slow chemical change. Oxygen in the air joins with iron to form rust. How does paint stop rust from forming? Now think about what happened to the copper of the Statue of Liberty. What slow chemical change took place?

▲ Cooking—a chemical change

▼ Removing rust

ACTIVITY

Explore Together

What is one sign of a chemical change?

Organizer

Materials
safety goggles · 2 graduates · magnesium sulfate solution · 4 test tubes · calcium chloride solution · test tube-rack · filter paper · funnel

Procedure
Caution: *Wear safety goggles for this activity.*

Investigator **A.** Add 3 mL magnesium sulfate solution to one test tube. In another test tube add 3 mL calcium chloride solution.

Group, Recorder
  1. Observe the appearance of the two solutions.

  2. Predict what will happen if the contents of the two test tubes are mixed.

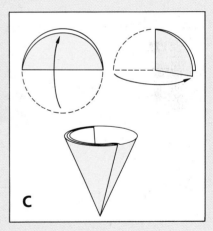

Investigator **B.** Pour the contents of the two test tubes together.

Group, Recorder
  3. Observe the mixture for 5 minutes.

Manager **C.** Fold a piece of filter paper as shown. Place the paper into the funnel. Place the funnel into a test tube.

C

Investigator **D.** Slowly pour the mixture into the funnel.

Writing and Sharing Results and Conclusions

Group, Recorder
1. What happened when you mixed together the contents of the two test tubes?

2. What evidence was there that a chemical change took place? Explain your answer.

Reporter **3.** How do your results and conclusions compare with those of your classmates?

▼ An explosion—a fast chemical change

Other chemical changes take place quickly. An explosion is a very fast chemical change. To launch this rocket, fuel and oxygen are burned in a controlled explosion. Heat and light are given off.

Another fast chemical change takes place when vinegar is poured on baking soda. One of the new kinds of matter formed is carbon dioxide gas.

▲ A new kind of matter forming

Lesson Review

1. Define *physical change*.
2. How does heating cause ice to melt?
3. How does evaporation differ from condensation?
4. Why does chopping wood cause a physical change?
5. What is a chemical change?

Think! When milk sours, a chemical change takes place. Do the physical properties of the milk change? Explain your answer.

Chapter Connections

Choose a kind of matter that you see on or in your desk. Describe this matter using the graphic organizer as a guide.

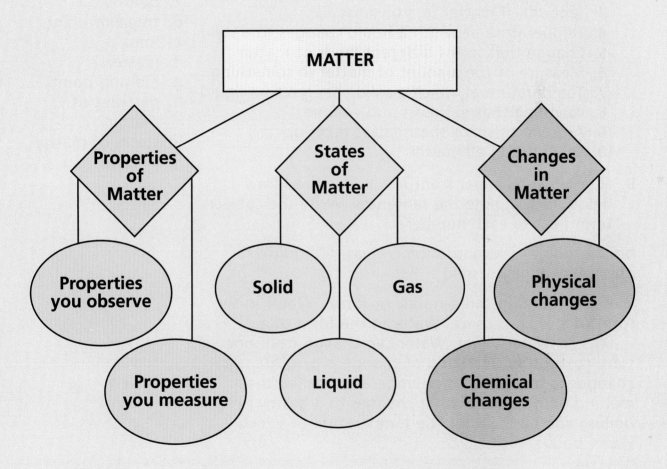

Writing About Science • Inform

Choose a kind of matter you know about. List some properties of this matter. What is its physical state? Describe one way to change the matter. Write a paragraph telling about the change.

Chapter 5 Review

Science Terms

A. Write the letter of the term that best matches the definition.

1. Change in state from a gas to a liquid
2. Solid, liquid, and gas
3. Amount of matter in a given space
4. Temperature at which a liquid changes to a solid
5. Change that forms different kinds of matter
6. Measure of the amount of matter in something
7. Temperature at which a solid changes to a liquid
8. Anything that has mass and volume
9. Amount of space that matter takes up
10. Small bits in all matter

a. chemical change
b. condensation
c. density
d. freezing point
e. mass
f. matter
g. melting point
h. particles of matter
i. states of matter
j. volume

B. Number your paper from 1 to 6. Use the terms below to complete the sentences. Write the correct term next to each number.

boiling point   evaporation   gas   liquid
physical change   solid

Water is found in three states, or forms. Water in the form of a ___(1)___ is ice. Water in the form of a ___(2)___ is water vapor. Water can change from one state to another. This kind of change is a ___(3)___. Ice changes to a ___(4)___ at a temperature called the melting point. Liquid water changes to a gas by boiling and by ___(5)___. The temperature at which water boils is the ___(6)___.

Science Ideas

Use complete sentences to answer the following.

1. How does mass differ from volume?
2. Why can you smell food when you walk past the school lunchroom?
3. Name a physical property that you can measure. Name one you can see.

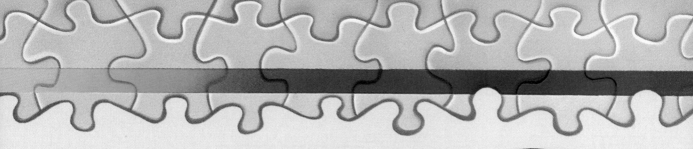

4. The drawings show the particles of matter in a rubber stopper and a cork stopper. Do the stoppers have the same volume? The same density? Explain your answers.
5. Why does a solid have a definite shape?
6. The melting point and the freezing point of water are the same. What does this mean?
7. Give an example of a slow chemical change?

▲ Cork stopper

▲ Rubber stopper

Applying Science Ideas

Use complete sentences to answer the following.

1. Ice is less dense than liquid water. How does this property help fish survive the winter in a Vermont lake?
2. In the kitchen many foods are changed before they are eaten. Read your favorite recipe. Describe the chemical and physical changes that you find.
3. List two properties of polystyrene foam.

Using Science Skills

Interpret the data table showing the mass of different volumes of water at room temperature. What trend can you find?

MASS OF DIFFERENT VOLUMES OF WATER	
Volume in milliliters	Mass in grams
200 mL	200 g
350 mL	350 g
410 mL	410 g
900 mL	900 g

6

Work and Energy

The Easy Way Out

Machines do a lot of things. But do you think they can make people laugh?

A man called Rube Goldberg invented machines to make people laugh. He drew cartoon machines. The machines were the inventions of the imaginary Professor Butts. The cartoons ran in newspapers for many years.

Rube Goldberg's machines were very strange. The one on this page is called the *Simple Shoe Shine*. It starts when you bend over to tie your shoes. When you bend, you pull a string. The string sets off other activities. What are some of the activities? Finally, polish drips on your shoes, and the puppy shines them. What easier ways can you think of to shine your shoes?

Simple Shoe Shine:
Professor Lucifer Gorgonzola Butts A.K. invents simple self-shining shoes—as passerby steps rudely on your shoes, you bend over, causing string **(A)** to pull open accordian **(B)**, sounding note **(C)**. Dancing mouse **(D)** starts waltzing and steps on spring **(E)**. Ball **(F)** disengages hook **(G)** and allows accordian gate that swings out **(H)** to shoot out, pulling cord **(I)** which opens inverted box **(J)**, dropping bone **(K)**. Pet dog **(L)** sees bone, wags tail, causing brush **(M)** to spread polish **(N)** which drops from hole in derby **(O)**.

Goldberg drew cartoons of many other machines. The machines could open a window or a garage door. They sharpened pencils. They found buttons. The machines used hammers and watering cans. Sometimes they used old boots.

Rube Goldberg's machines were not simple. In fact they were very complex. They were funny because they made very simple tasks very difficult.

What was Rube Goldberg making fun of? He made fun of labor-saving machines. These machines were supposed to save time and energy and make life much easier. But Goldberg's machines did not save energy. They needed more energy.

Rolling Up a Rug:
Place a piece of cheese **(A)** on a window sill **(B)**. When mouse **(C)** sneaks up to steal it, housemaid **(D)** falls back with fright into rocking chair **(E)** which tilts pedestal **(F)**, causing marble statue of diving girl **(G)** to dive into goldfish bowl **(H)** and splash water on plant **(I)** which grows and turns on switch **(J)** of radio **(K)** which plays old tune called "Oceana Roll." Little trick rolling circus elephant **(L)**, hearing tune, does his stuff and keeps rolling over and over until rug **(M)** is completely wrapped around him and floor is cleared for dancing.

Rube Goldberg knew a lot about machines. He went to school to become an engineer. But instead of being an engineer, he drew cartoons for newspapers. Readers could not wait to see what the next machine would be!

Rube Goldberg died in 1970, leaving dozens of strange and wonderful machines. People still use his name today when they see something simple done the hard way. They call it a "Rube Goldberg." What "Rube Goldbergs" can you think of around your school and at home? How would you change them to make them simpler?

ACTIVITY

Discover

How can you change a simple task into a difficult task?

Materials   paper · drawing supplies

Procedure

   Think of a simple task. Then think of the most difficult way to do that task. Show the task in a cartoon. Write a paragraph listing the steps in your cartoon. Explain to the class how your invention works. How many steps are needed to complete the task?

In this chapter you will learn more about the serious things Rube Goldberg looked at in a funny way. You will study work, energy, and machines.

H   I   J   K   L   M

1. Force and Work

Words to Know
force
work

Getting Started Have you ever watched or played a soccer game? If you have, you know that the players are almost always in motion. Make a list of some of the different actions of the players during a game. Write down whether each of these actions is a push or a pull.

What is a force?

In the picture of the girl playing soccer, the ball is moving through the air. It started moving because the girl kicked, or pushed, it with her foot. A force was used to start the ball moving. A **force** is a push or pull on an object, caused by another object. In this case the foot supplied the force on the ball.

▼ Children playing soccer

Now look at the picture of the boys playing soccer. You know that a force was used to move the ball. But the boys are also moving. What forces are affecting the motion of the boys?

Several things can happen to an object acted on by a force. A force can cause an object to start or stop moving. It can cause a

▲ Skier about to go downhill

moving object to go faster or slower. A force may also cause a moving object to change direction. How is the motion of the people in the pictures affected by forces?

▲ Children skating

As you may have noticed, not all forces are the same. Forces may differ in two ways. One difference is in the *strength* of the force. The other difference is the *direction* in which the force acts.

▲ Pushing on a door

▲ Pulling on a door

What is work?

Think about the word *work*. It can have many meanings. You may say, "My parents go to work." Or, "How does a computer work?" But work means something specific to scientists. To them, **work** is done only when a force moves an object.

Suppose a force is applied to an object, but it does not move. Then no work has been done on the object. Which of these pictures shows work being done?

Different amounts of work are done when different objects are moved. The amount of work done depends on the amount of force used and the distance the object moves.

A force was used to move each apple in the drawings. The first drawing shows an apple being lifted from the floor to a table. The second shows two apples being lifted.

▼ Lifting one apple from the floor to a table

▼ Lifting two apples

The apples in both drawings are moved the same distance. But the two apples weigh twice as much as one apple. So it takes more force to lift the two apples than it does to lift one apple. So more work is done.

Now look at the pictures of the trophy being lifted from the floor to two different shelves. One shelf is higher than the other. The force used to move the trophy to both shelves is the same. Why then is more work done moving the trophy to the higher shelf?

▲ Lifting a trophy to a higher shelf

Lifting a trophy to a shelf ▶

Lesson Review

1. What is another name for a push or a pull?
2. In what ways may a force affect an object's motion?
3. What is work?
4. What two things must you know to measure work?

Think! A weight lifter does work while lifting a barbell. But if the barbell is held without moving it, the lifter does no work. Explain why.

2. Work and Machines

Getting Started The picture here shows the Great Pyramid in Egypt. It was built about 3000 B.C. Each stone block weighs more than 2½ tons. How do you think the blocks were moved and lifted?

Words to Know
simple machine
effort
resistance
compound
  machine

What are simple machines?

The workers who built the Great Pyramid used ramps and pulleys. Ramps and pulleys are kinds of machines. Machines help make it easier to do certain tasks.

People use machines to do work. A **simple machine** is a device that changes the size or direction of a force. Like all machines, simple machines makes a task easier to do. There are four kinds of simple machines. They are inclined planes, wheels and axles, levers, and pulleys.

196

An example of each kind of simple machine is shown here. Name some other devices that are examples of each of these kinds of simple machines. For any of these machines to do a task, a force must be applied to the machine. Remember that a force is a push or a pull. You often use your muscles to push or pull on a machine. A force applied to a machine is called **effort.** Where do you think the effort is applied on the rope and pulley?

Just as force is applied to a machine, a machine applies a force to an object. Point to the place on the bottle opener where it moves the cap. This is where force is applied by the machine to the object. A force applied by a machine is called **resistance** (rih ZIHS-tuns).

▼ A pulley

▼ A lever

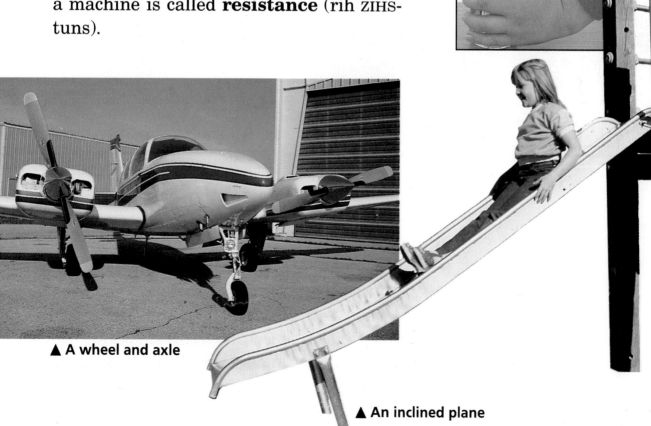
▲ A wheel and axle

▲ An inclined plane

Problem Solving

Rise and Shine!

Are there some mornings that you do not feel like waking up? Cartoonist Rube Goldberg solved that problem with an alarm clock similar to the one shown. As you may recall, Mr. Goldberg invented complex machines to do simple tasks. With this alarm clock, you would rise and shine each morning whether you liked it or not.

How can you make a machine to wake someone up?

Study the cartoon to find out how the clock works. Describe the simple machines used. Point to where the effort and resistance of each machine are applied. Then design a Rube Goldberg-style alarm clock of your own. Include a drawing to show others how your machine works.

How can you use simple machines?

A machine can make a task, such as moving an object, easier in at least one of three ways. A machine may change the distance that an object moves. A machine may also change the amount of force needed to move an object. And it may change the direction of the effort applied to the object.

Suppose your gym teacher asked you to lift a heavy box of sports equipment to the top of a platform. Using only your muscles, you must apply a large force to lift the box. But if you used a simple machine, this task would be easier to do.

For example, suppose you pushed the box up a ramp. The ramp is a simple machine. It is a type of inclined plane. By using the ramp, it would be easier to move the box to the top of the platform.

The inclined plane changed the distance that the box was moved. Also, less force was needed to move the box. But the same amount of work was done when the children in the pictures lifted the box straight up and when they used the ramp. The same amount of work was done because the box was moved to the same height.

▲ Lifting a box

▼ Using an inclined plane

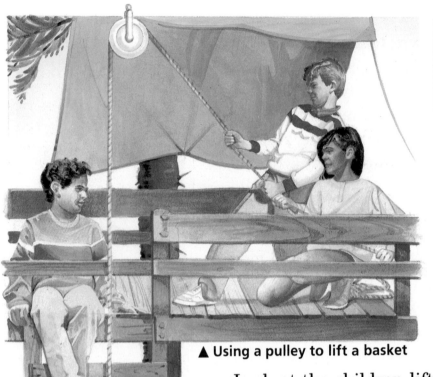

▲ Using a pulley to lift a basket

Look at the children lifting the basket in the drawings. The children on the right are trying to pull the basket straight up to the treehouse. But the children on the left are using a pulley. Instead of pulling straight up, the children using the pulley are pulling to the side. You can see that a pulley makes a task, such as lifting a basket of snacks, easier by changing the direction of the effort. Where is the effort being applied to the pulley?

What is a compound machine?

Remember that a machine is a device that makes a task easier to do. Cars and buses make the task of moving you from place to place easier. So cars and buses are machines. But they are not simple machines. Cars and buses are compound (KAHM pownd) machines.

A **compound machine** is a device made of two or more simple machines. Cars and buses are made of many simple machines put together. Other compound machines are shown in the pictures. What simple machines make up each of the compound machines?

A machine made of wings, wheels, and a bathtub? You can make it when you try **Creative Writer: Transportation Tales.**

▼ A scooter

▼ A can opener

Lesson Review

1. What is the term for any device that makes doing a task easier?
2. What are the four kinds of simple machines?
3. Draw a sketch of scissors being used to cut paper. Label the effort and the resistance of the scissors.
4. Compare a simple machine with a compound machine.

Think! Suppose you had to lift two blocks of the same mass to a height of 3 meters. You lift one block, using only your muscles. You lift the other block, using an inclined plane. One which block did you use more effort? Explain your answer.

▲ An egg beater

201

3. Energy

Words to Know
kinetic energy
potential energy

Getting Started Energy is needed to do work. For a machine to do work, it must have a source of energy. Look at the simple machines shown on page 197. Where do you think the energy for each machine comes from?

▼ Swimmers with potential energy

What are kinetic energy and potential energy?

An object that has energy can do work. A moving object can do work. The energy of a moving object is called **kinetic** (kih NEHT-ihk) **energy.** The diver in the picture is moving. So he has kinetic energy.

Now suppose an object is not moving but has the ability to do work. That object's energy is stored. Stored energy is called **potential** (poh TEHN shul) **energy.** Why do the swimmers in the picture have potential energy?

▲ A diver with kinetic energy

It is usually easy to see if an object has kinetic energy. Whenever an object moves, it has kinetic energy. A car moving down a street has kinetic energy. When you run, you have kinetic energy, too.

It is not always so easy to decide if an object has potential energy. A wind-up toy can have potential energy. Energy is stored in the wound spring of the toy. When the spring is wound, the toy has only the *ability* to move. But it does not move as long as the spring stays wound. When you release the spring, the toy moves. So the potential energy is changed to kinetic energy.

▼ Potential energy

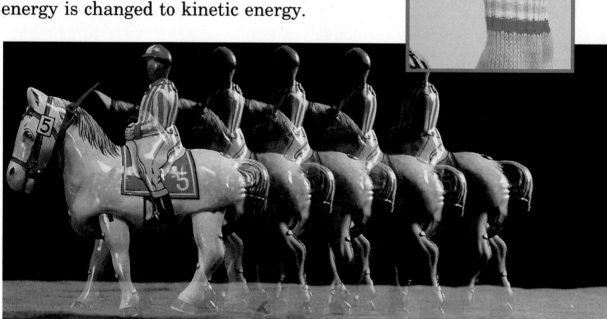

▲ Kinetic energy

Coal has chemical potential energy. The energy is stored in the particles of matter that make up the coal. You know that fuels such as coal give off heat when burned. Heat is a form of energy. To give off energy, fuels must first have stored energy.

Explore Together

ACTIVITY

How can the potential energy of an object be increased?

Materials

Organizer

2 pieces of string · 2 rectangular blocks of wood · masking tape · long sheet of white paper · meterstick · pencil

Procedure

Manager

A. Tape one end of each string to opposite ends of one block. Tape the other ends of the strings to the edge of a desk, as shown. The block should hang just above the floor.

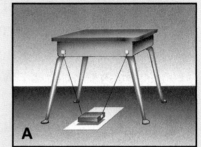

B. Tape the sheet of paper to the floor, under the block. Make a pencil line across the paper, under the center of the block.

Investigator, Recorder, Group

C. Pull back the block on the strings so that the bottom of it is 10 cm above the floor. Place the other block on the line on the paper. Let go of the block on the strings.
   1. How far did the block on the floor move?
   2. Predict what will happen to the block on the floor if the other block were let go from a greater height.

Group, Investigator, Recorder

D. Repeat step **C**, pulling the block on the strings 20 cm, 30 cm, 40 cm, and 50 cm above the floor.

Writing and Sharing
Results and Conclusions

Group, Recorder

1. When did the block on the strings have the greatest potential energy? How do you know?

Reporter

2. How did your results compare with those of others in your class?

How can potential energy and kinetic energy change?

Potential energy can change to kinetic energy. And kinetic energy can change to potential energy. Look at the gymnast on the high bar. When he is in position 1, he is not moving. At that moment the man has only potential energy. When the man swings toward position 2, his potential energy begins to change to kinetic energy. But some of his energy is still stored.

The faster the man moves, the more of his potential energy is changed to kinetic energy. At point 2, the man is moving the fastest. The man has the most kinetic energy and least potential energy at that point. As the man swings toward point 3, he begins to slow down and move higher. So his kinetic energy begins to change back to potential energy.

Changing kinetic energy ▶ to potential energy

1

3

2

You already know that the faster an object is moving, the more kinetic energy it has. Look at the car and the truck in the picture. Both are moving at the same speed. But they do not have the same amount of kinetic energy.

▲ A car and a truck moving at the same speed

When objects move at the same speed, the one with more mass has more kinetic energy. The truck has more mass than the car does. So the truck has more kinetic energy. Suppose the car and the truck were both about to roll down a hill. Which do you think would have more potential energy?

Physical Science
CONNECTION

As you know, you eat food to obtain energy. Is the energy found in food potential energy or kinetic energy? Explain your answer.

Lesson Review

1. What is needed to do work?
2. What do you call the energy of a moving object?
3. What is the stored energy of an object called?

Think! Which would have more kinetic energy when going the same speed, a bicycle or a car? Explain your answer.

Skills

Identifying variables

Think of a softball game. Each batter may hit the ball a different distance. The distance that the ball flies changes. Anything that can change is called a variable. Sometimes a variable does not change. For example, each batter stands in the same place on the field. Where the batter stands is a variable that does not change.

Practicing the skill

1. Observe the child in the two pictures. The child is doing an experiment. In both pictures, the child is going to drop a ball and see how high it bounces.

2. The type of surface that he drops the ball on is a variable. In this case, the type of surface is a variable that does not change. Write down another variable that does not change.

3. Find a variable that changes. Write it down.

Thinking about the skill

What question do you think you could answer with this experiment?

Applying the skill

The picture shows things to be used in an experiment. The experiment is to find out which rubber band stretches the most. The mass will be hooked on each rubber band. Name a variable that will change. Name another variable that will not change.

4. Changes in Energy

Getting Started Think about sound, heat, and light. You use different senses to hear sound, to feel heat, and to see light. But each of these has something in common. Sound, heat, and light are all forms of energy. What are some other forms of energy?

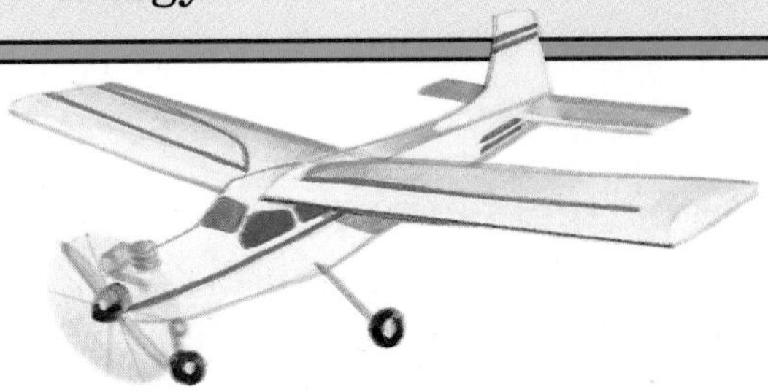

▼ Different forms of energy

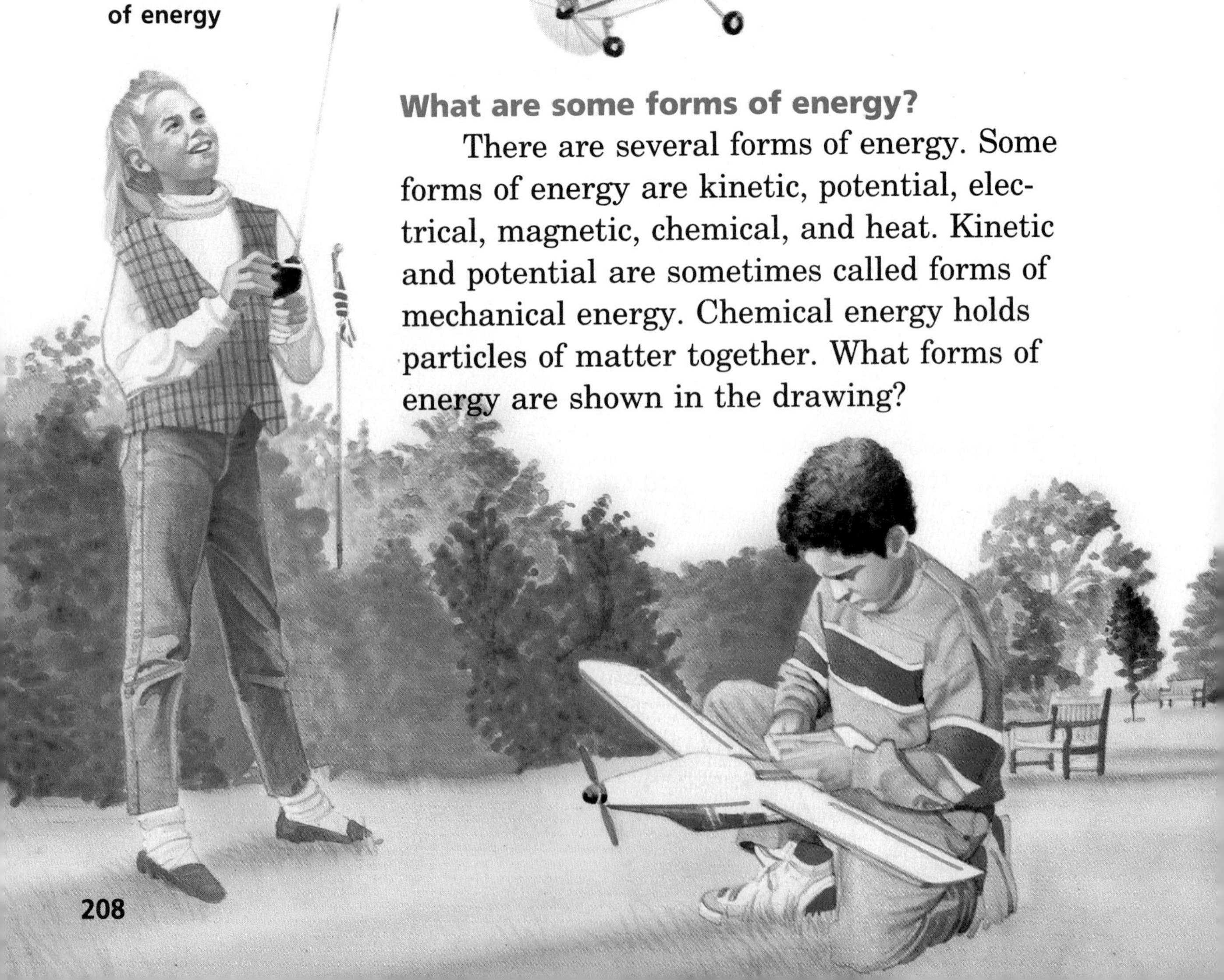

What are some forms of energy?

There are several forms of energy. Some forms of energy are kinetic, potential, electrical, magnetic, chemical, and heat. Kinetic and potential are sometimes called forms of mechanical energy. Chemical energy holds particles of matter together. What forms of energy are shown in the drawing?

208

An **appliance** (uh PLYE uns) is a device used to change energy from one form to another. A light bulb is an appliance. A light bulb is used to produce light. A light bulb changes electrical energy to light energy. Make a list of appliances that you can find in your home and classroom.

What form of energy other than light is given off by the light bulb? If you said "heat," you were correct. The electrical energy was changed to at least two other forms of energy. The bulb changes electrical energy to both light and heat energy.

Electrical energy is not the only form of energy that can be changed to other forms. All forms of energy can be changed to other forms. The chemical energy of the batteries in the drawing is changed to electrical energy when the batteries are used. What other energy changes are shown in the drawing?

Changing energy from one form to another ▼

209

How is energy changed to other forms?

Energy is often changed from one form to another to make the energy useful. A pile of coal has chemical energy. But for most people to use it, the chemical energy of the coal must be changed to electrical energy.

The drawings show how the chemical energy in coal is changed to electrical energy at a power plant. (1) The coal is burned. This changes the coal's chemical energy to heat energy. (2) The heat energy of the coal is transferred to the water, changing it to steam. (3) The energy of the steam is changed to mechanical energy in the generators. (4) The generators change the mechanical energy to electrical energy. (5) Power lines carry this energy to homes where it can be used.

You have learned that a light bulb changes some electrical energy to heat energy. In fact, more of the electrical energy is changed to heat energy than to light energy. Yet, light is the useful energy. Heat is the energy that is not useful.

▼ Changing energy from one form to another

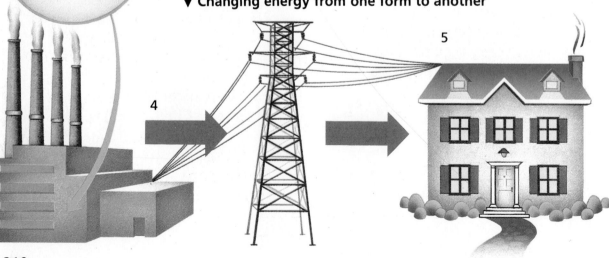

Explore

How can chemical energy be changed to another form of energy?

Suppose some special mittens were invented to keep your hands warm. The mittens would have a pouch of chemicals inside them. These chemicals would give off heat for hours. In this activity, you will find out how mittens like these might work.

Materials

safety glasses · graduate · water · thin, tall jar · thermometer · balance · calcium chloride · stirrer

Procedure

A. Put on your safety glasses. Use the graduate to measure 20 mL of water. Pour the water into the jar.

B. Copy the table. Measure the temperature of the water and record it in the table.

C. Use the balance to measure 3 g of calcium chloride. Pour it into the jar of water. Stir the mixture with the stirrer.

D. Measure and record the temperature of the mixture.
1. Predict what will happen to the temperature in 30 seconds.

E. Repeat step **D** until the temperature no longer changes.
2. Can you still see the calcium chloride?

Time	Temperature
water without chemical	
water with chemical	
water after 30 seconds	
water after 60 seconds	
water after 120 seconds	

Writing and Sharing Results and Conclusions

1. What form of energy did the calcium chloride have before it was added to the water?

2. What form of energy was given off by the calcium chloride in the water?

3. Make a graph of the time and temperature information in your table.

▼ An electric mixer

The heat energy from the light bulb flows into the matter around it. The same thing happens to other forms of energy that are not useful. The energy still exists. Energy can never be destroyed. But often it cannot be used again.

In almost all energy changes, at least some of the energy is changed to heat energy. In most cases the heat energy is not useful. Look at the pictures shown here. Which forms of energy are not useful?

▼ A bicycle pump

▲ A stove burner

Lesson Review

1. List six forms of energy.
2. Why is a toaster called an appliance?
3. Why is energy often changed from one form to another?
4. What happens to the energy that is changed to a form that is not useful?

Think! A fluorescent light that is turned on usually feels cool. But a plain light bulb may feel very hot. Which kind of light gives off more energy that is not useful? Explain your answer.

Chapter Connections

Find or draw pictures of machines that help to make a task easier. Use the graphic organizer. Talk about the machines, the forces, and the objects that are affected in your pictures.

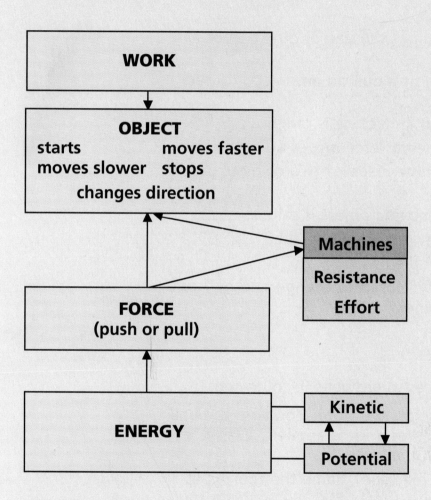

Writing About Science • Inform

Write the word *work* in the center of your paper. Around it list examples of work you do every day. Be sure to use the term *work* as a scientist would.

Science Terms

Copy the sentences below. Choose the word below that best completes each sentence.

appliance   compound machine   effort   force
kinetic energy   potential energy   resistance
simple machine   work

1. A device that changes the size or direction of a force is called a _____.
2. A _____ is a push or a pull on an object, caused by another object.
3. A force applied to a machine is called _____.
4. _____ is done when a force moves an object.
5. A _____ is a machine made of two or more simple machines.
6. The energy of a moving object is called _____.
7. A force applied by a machine is called _____.
8. Stored energy is called _____.
9. An _____ is a device used to change energy from one form to another.

Science Ideas

Use complete sentences to answer the following.

1. A ball is rolling across the floor. You stop the ball with your finger. Was a force applied? Was work done? Explain your answers.
2. What is a simple machine? Name the four types of simple machines.
3. Classify the following as having either potential energy or kinetic energy. (a) a person walking slowly down a hallway (b) a toy truck being held at the top of a ramp (c) a gas-powered lawn mower about to be turned on

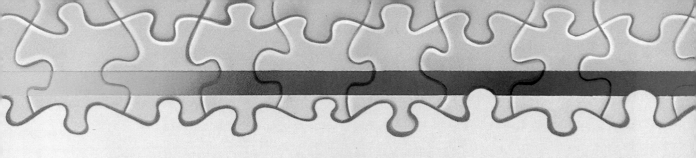

4. How do kinetic energy and potential energy differ?

5. Name four forms of energy. Give an example of each form of energy you name.

6. When a toaster is used to toast bread, electrical energy is changed to heat and light energy. Which is the useful energy? Explain why.

Applying Science Ideas

Use complete sentences to answer the following.

1. Suppose you had to push a box up two ramps. Both are the same height. But one ramp is straight and the other spirals. Would you do more work pushing a box up one ramp or the other? On which one would you use the most effort?

2. Give an example of each of the four types of simple machines. What task is made easier by each of the examples you gave?

3. Name three appliances that can be found in your home or at school. Explain why each example is an appliance.

4. Suppose an adult lights a match. Did the match have kinetic or potential energy before it was lighted? What form of energy did the unlighted match have? What form of energy did that change to when the match was lighted?

5. Is a bicycle a compound machine? Explain why or why not.

Using Science Skills

Suppose a high jumper wants to rate which of two mats is softer. She jumps three times from the same distance and height onto each mat. What are the variables? Which stay the same? Which change?

Chapter 7

Heat

SEEING HEAT

Everything gives off heat. Your body gives off heat. The earth does, too. Computers can be linked to scanners that sense heat. The scanner measures the temperature of an object. The computer shows different temperatures as different colors in a picture on a computer screen. Such a picture is called a thermogram (THUR moh gram).

The shape that you see in a thermogram is the shape of the object. But the colors you see are not the colors of the object. In most of these pictures, the hottest parts of the object look white, red, or yellow. Cooler parts look green or blue. The coolest parts look black.

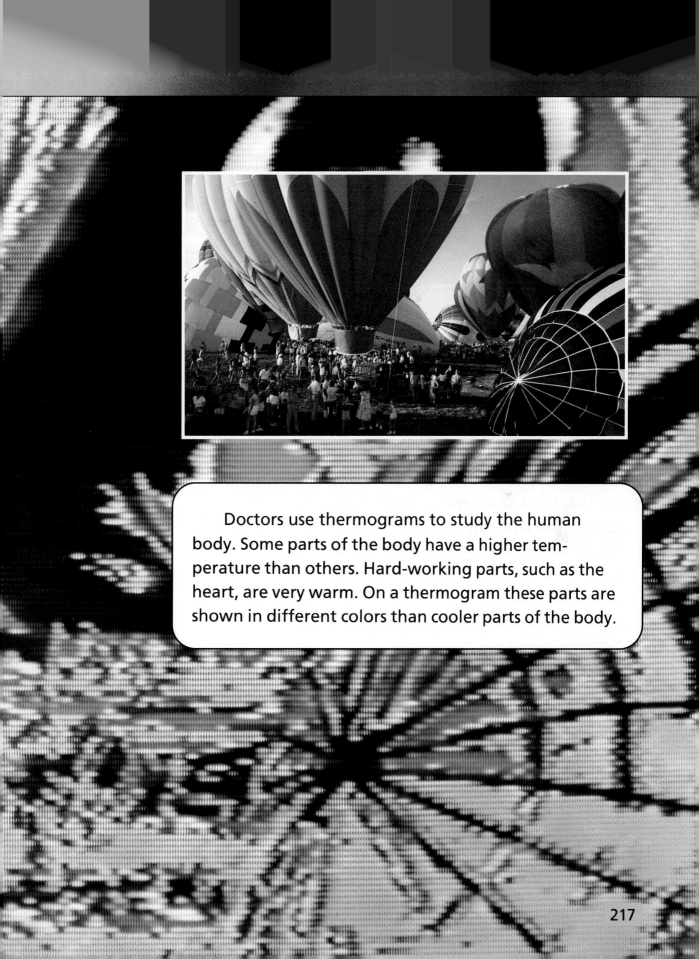

Doctors use thermograms to study the human body. Some parts of the body have a higher temperature than others. Hard-working parts, such as the heart, are very warm. On a thermogram these parts are shown in different colors than cooler parts of the body.

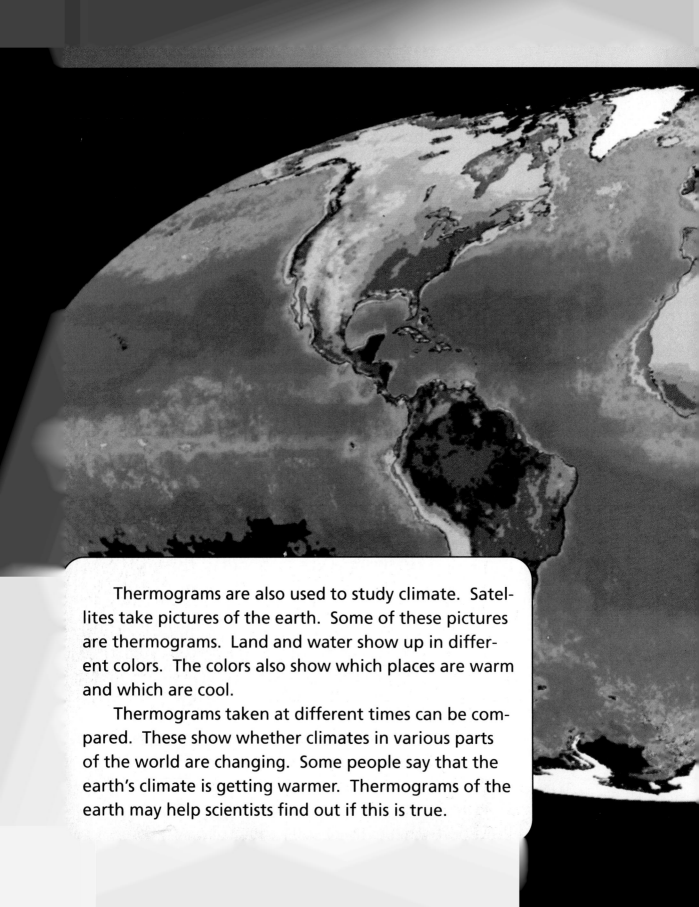

Thermograms are also used to study climate. Satellites take pictures of the earth. Some of these pictures are thermograms. Land and water show up in different colors. The colors also show which places are warm and which are cool.

Thermograms taken at different times can be compared. These show whether climates in various parts of the world are changing. Some people say that the earth's climate is getting warmer. Thermograms of the earth may help scientists find out if this is true.

Discover

How do thermograms show heat loss?

Materials   pencil · paper

Procedure

Thermograms have been used to help people find out where their houses are losing heat. Think about the parts of a house—the walls, roof, windows, doors. Make a list of parts of the house that you think have the most heat loss. Then list the parts that have the least heat loss.

Look at the thermogram of a house. Which parts of this house have the most heat loss? Which parts have the least heat loss? How did this house compare with your predictions?

apter you will learn more about
how it is measured. You will see
travels. And you will see ways in
t can be used.

Stepping on hot sand ▶

1. Heat and Matter

Getting Started Look at the picture of the people at the beach. How could the people in the picture find out if the sand is hot? Could they tell if the sand was hot by looking at it?

How is warm matter different from cold matter?

What makes a greenhouse warm? Maggie and Jan accept a challenge to discover the answer. You can find out, too, in **Summer in January** in Horizons Plus.

You can feel warmth when you step on hot sand. You can feel that the sand is much hotter than your feet. You feel heat that has moved from the sand to your feet. **Heat** is energy that moves from warmer matter to cooler matter. The more heat energy something has, the hotter it is.

You can feel heat. But you cannot see it. Very hot matter, such as burning wood, may give off light. But you still cannot see the heat.

The people in the picture cannot tell that the sand is hot by looking at it. Hot sand and cool sand look the same. But they are different in one important way.

Grains of sand, like all matter, are made of tiny particles. These particles **vibrate,** or move back and forth. When sand gets hot, the particles vibrate faster. So the particles in a grain of hot sand vibrate faster than those in a cool grain.

▼ **Particles in hot and cool grains of sand**

particles in a hot grain of sand

particles in a cool grain of sand

▼ Heated balloon

▼ Balloon at room temperature

▼ Cooled balloon

How does heat change the size of matter?

Most kinds of matter expand, or take up more space, as they are heated. Look at the top and center balloons in the drawings. Both were blown up to the same size. Then the top one was heated. As you can see, that balloon has expanded, or gotten bigger.

▲ Warm balloon　　▲ Cold balloon

Why does matter expand when heated? Look at the particles of air in the balloons in the drawings. As the air is heated, the particles begin moving faster. The particles also move farther apart. Because the particles of the air move farther apart, the air expands.

Now look at the balloon that was cooled. As the air loses heat, or cools, the particles slow down and move closer together. The air contracts, or takes up less space, when cooled. The size of the balloon shrinks.

Solids and liquids also expand when heated. But they do not expand as much as gases do. Look at the railroad track in the picture. There is a space between the rails. The space is needed to give the rails room to expand when they become warmer. How do you think heat could cause damage to the rails if there were no spaces?

▲ Space between rails of a railroad track

Lesson Review

1. What is heat?
2. What change would there be in particles of water as it became warm?
3. A balloon is seen to have increased in size after being left by a sunny window. Explain what has caused the change in size.

Think! A metal lid is stuck on a glass jar. After the lid is held under hot water, it screws off easily. Why does the hot water make it easier to remove the lid?

Earth Science
CONNECTION

Sometimes water gets into the cracks of large rocks. How can this water help to break apart the rocks?

2. Measuring Temperature

Getting Started In the picture, hot gold-colored wax is being poured into molds. The wax is used to make crayons. Use the word *temperature* to describe the wax. Now use the word *heat* to describe it.

How are heat and temperature different?

People often use the word *temperature* when talking about how hot something is. But heat and temperature are not the same. Heat causes the particles in matter to move faster. **Temperature** is a measure of how fast the particles in matter are moving. But temperature does not measure how much heat matter contains.

▼ Filling a bucket with melted wax

▼ Wax being   poured into molds

Look at the hot wax pouring from the pail. The wax still in the pail and the wax in the molds have the same temperature. This means that the particles of wax in the pail are moving as fast as the particles of wax in the molds. But there is now more wax, or matter, in the molds than in the pail. So the wax in the molds has more heat than does the wax still in the pail.

The amount of heat in matter depends on: (1) how fast the particles of matter are moving, or the matter's temperature and (2) the amount of matter. Two different amounts of matter can have the same temperature. But the larger amount of matter will have more heat. It has more particles of matter in motion.

*Find how heat changes sap into a tasty treat by reading **Sugaring Time**, page 246.*

▼ **The crayons made of cooled wax**

ACTIVITY

Explore Together

What is the difference between heat and temperature?

Organizer

Materials
2 jars, same size · water · 2 thermometers · graduate · tape

Procedure

Recorder A. Copy the table shown on a separate piece of paper.

Manager B. Half-fill both jars with tap water at room temperature. Be sure to put the same amount of water into each jar. Label one jar A and the other jar B.

Investigator C. Measure the temperature of the water in each jar.

Recorder D. Record the temperatures in the table.

Step	Water Temperature (°C)	
	Jar A	Jar B
B		
D		
E		

Manager, Recorder E. Measure 50 mL and 150 mL of hot tap water. Record the temperatures.

Investigator, Recorder F. Pour 50 mL of the hot water into jar A. Pour 150 mL of the hot water into jar B. Measure and record the water temperatures in jars A and B.

Writing and Sharing Results and Conclusions

Group, Recorder 1. What was the temperature of the water in jars A and B in step C? Do the jars have the same amount of heat?

2. What were the water temperatures in step E?

3. What were the water temperatures of jar A and jar B in step F? Why were they different?

Reporter 4. What is the difference between heat and temperature?

226

How is temperature measured?

The faster particles of matter vibrate, the higher is the temperature of the matter. A thermometer is an instrument that is used to measure temperature. The pictures show some kinds of thermometers and their uses.

▼ **Digital thermometer**

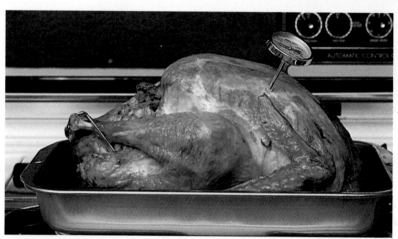

▲ **Dial thermometer**

Thermometers such as the one on the right contain a liquid. The liquid is sealed in a thin glass tube. The liquid in the thermometer rises as the temperature of the matter being measured goes up. But why does the liquid rise as temperature increases?

Recall that most kinds of matter expand as they are heated. As the liquid in a thermometer becomes warmer, it expands. When the liquid expands, it can only rise in the narrow tube. What would happen to the particles of the liquid as the temperature decreased?

◄ **Mercury thermometer**

Look at the picture of the two thermometers. Both thermometers contain the same amount of liquid. But the liquid level is higher in one than in the other. Which glass has the water with the higher temperature? Why is the liquid higher in one thermometer than in the other?

What scales are used to measure temperature?

Look at the temperatures shown in the picture on the next page. The numbers are not the same. But they show the same temperature. The temperature on the top is shown on the Fahrenheit (FER un hyt) scale. The temperature on the bottom is shown on the Celsius (SEL see us) scale.

On the **Fahrenheit scale**, temperature is measured in degrees Fahrenheit. The symbol for degrees Fahrenheit is °F. This scale is used mostly in the United States. The air temperature in weather reports may be given in this scale. If your refrigerator has a thermometer, it may use this scale. And when a doctor takes your temperature, it may be measured on this scale.

On the **Celsius scale**, temperature is measured in degrees Celsius. The symbol for degrees Celsius is °C. This scale is used by scientists all over the world to measure temperature. It is also used by most countries in the world. The Celsius scale is becoming more widely used in the United States, also.

▼ **Temperature in degrees Celsius and in degrees Fahrenheit**

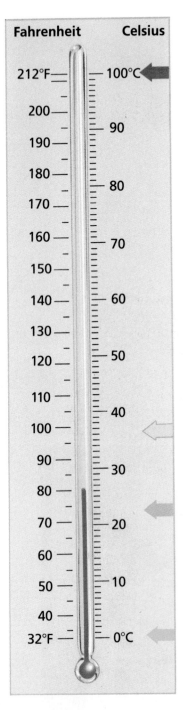

Fahrenheit   **Celsius**

212°F — — 100°C
200 —
190 — — 90
180 —
170 — — 80
160 — — 70
150 —
140 — — 60
130 —
120 — — 50
110 —
100 — — 40
90 —
80 — — 30
70 — — 20
60 —
50 — — 10
40 —
32°F — — 0°C

➡ boiling point of water
➡ normal body
    temperature
➡ room temperature
➡ freezing point of water

Look at the drawing on the left. It compares the Fahrenheit scale with the Celsius scale. At what temperatures do the scales show that water freezes? At what temperatures do the scales show that water boils? In the pictures below, what would be the temperatures on the Celsius scale?

Lesson Review

1. How is heat different from temperature?
2. Why does a large lake have more heat than does a small pond though both have the same temperature?
3. What is a thermometer? How is it used to measure temperature?
4. Identify the temperatures at which water freezes and boils on the Fahrenheit and Celsius scales.

Think! A change in temperature of 5°C is equal to a change of 9°F. Use a calculator to find what a change of 10°C would be in degrees Fahrenheit.

THINKING

Skills

Measuring temperature with a thermometer

Pretend you are going to make a home for a tropical fish. You must make sure the water is the right temperature (24°C) for the fish. You can mix warm and cool water. You can use a thermometer to measure the temperature of the water.

Practicing the skill

1. First, half fill a cup with warm water. Measure the temperature with a thermometer. Make sure the water is warmer than 50°C. Next, put cold water into another cup. Make sure it is colder than 5°C.

2. Put the thermometer into the warm water. Add small amounts of cold water to the warm water. Stop when the warm water has cooled to 24°C. About how much cold water did you add?

Thinking about the skill

What helped you decide how much cold water to add at a time?

Applying the skill

You are given warm water and an ice cube. You want to cool the water as much as possible. You can let the warm water cool awhile and then add the ice. You can also add the ice right away. Try both ways and measure the water temperature after the ice melts.

How much testing should be done on new products?

Imagine that you are outside on a sunny July day and you are feeling very hot. Now imagine putting an ice cube on your forehead. What happens? Heat from your skin moves to the ice. As the cube soaks up heat, the ice melts. The ice takes heat away from your forehead, so your forehead feels cooler.

What if you had on a T-shirt that soaked up heat from your skin and made you feel cool? Scientists have invented such a T-shirt. They have made a new chemical called PEG, which is added to cloth.

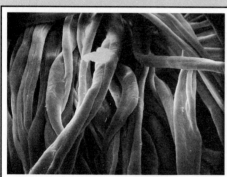

▲ Without PEG

▲ With PEG

Heat moves from your skin to the PEG in the clothing. The tiny particles of PEG absorb the heat. They soften a little. PEG particles are like tiny ice cubes cooling you down, except that they do not drip.

PEG can also be used to warm you on cold days. Indoors the PEG in clothing soaks up heat. Then when you go outside into the cold air, the PEG particles harden, just as water freezes into ice. As PEG particles harden, they release heat, and this heat warms you up.

You cannot buy PEG clothes yet. Scientists are still testing PEG. They are trying to make it give off more heat for a longer period of time. Scientists also want to be certain that PEG is safe for everyone to use.

Critical thinking

Mark thinks we should be able to wear PEG T-shirts now. Jenny thinks we should first be sure PEG is safe. Do you agree with Mark? Why? How could PEG make our lives easier if we could use it right now? Do you agree with Jenny? Why?

Using what you learned

Think of things that could be made with PEG cloth for use in hot and cold places. With some classmates, write those things on a chart, listing ways in which PEG would make each thing better.

3. The Movement of Heat

Getting Started Think about the last time you ate a bowl of hot soup. Did you use a metal spoon? How did the spoon handle feel after the spoon was left in the soup for awhile?

Words to Know
conduction
convection
radiation
insulator

How does heat move in solid matter?

Heat always moves from matter that is warmer to matter that is cooler. Heat does not move from cooler matter to warmer matter. If hot soup is left out on a table, it will get cooler. Heat moves from the hot soup to the cooler air.

Heat will also move to a cool metal spoon left in the hot soup. Heat will move from the hot soup to the cooler spoon. First the tip of the spoon in the soup will get hot. Then the whole spoon will become hot.

How does heat move from the tip along the rest of the spoon? Look at the drawing. As the tip of the spoon gets hotter, its particles vibrate more. They bump into particles farther along the spoon. The particles that get bumped vibrate more and bump into still other particles. Soon all the particles in the spoon are vibrating faster. Recall that the faster particles of matter vibrate, the higher the temperature of the matter is.

The metal spoon is a solid. Heat moves through other solids in the same way it moves through the spoon. The movement of heat through matter as particles bump each other is called **conduction** (kun DUK shun). What are some examples of conduction that you can find at school or at home?

▼ **Particles of matter in the spoon**

▼ **Heat moving by conduction**

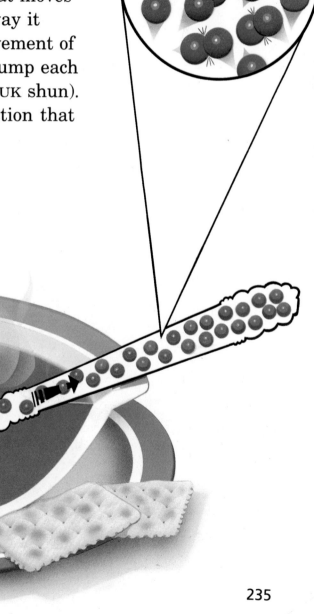

How does heat move through liquids and gases?

Heat does not move by conduction as well in liquids and gases as it does in solids. The particles in liquids and gases are farther apart than those in solids. So they do not bump into one another as often.

Look at the picture of the wood-burning stove. The top of the stove is very hot. As cooler air comes in contact with the hot stove top, that air is warmed by conduction.

Warm air is less dense than cool air. So the cool air moves in toward the stove and pushes up the warm air. The warm air cools as its heat moves into the air around it. As the warmed air cools, it becomes more dense. So it sinks. Then more cool air moves toward the stove. And it pushes up the warmer air.

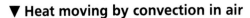

▼ Heat moving by convection in air

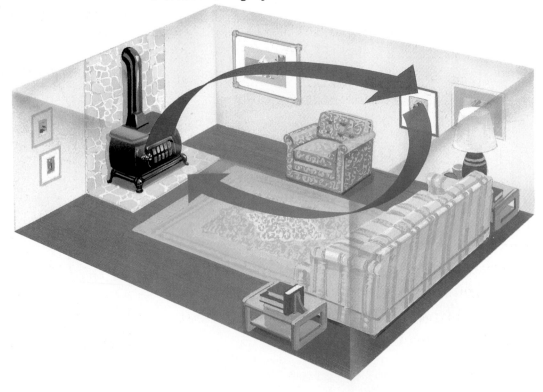

The rising and sinking air sets a current of air in motion. The air current carries heat through the whole room. The movement of heat through liquids and gases by currents is called **convection** (kun VEK shun).

◄ **Water being heated by convection**

In the drawing, heat is moving through the water by convection. Water at the bottom of the pan is heated by the burner. The heated water rises. Cooler water from the top sinks and replaces it. The water keeps rising and sinking as it is heated and cooled.

How does heat move in empty space?

Have you ever seen food being warmed by heat lamps such as those shown in the picture? Energy moves from the lamps to the food. The energy moves in the form of invisible waves. The movement of energy in the form of waves is called **radiation** (ray-dee AY shun). The energy changes to heat when it is absorbed by matter.

▼ **Food being heated by radiation**

The sun, stoves, and all warm objects give off radiation. Most radiation cannot be seen. Radiation can move without the presence of matter. It moves through empty space where there is almost no matter.

When the waves do strike matter, some waves are absorbed. The energy of the waves causes the particles of matter to move faster. So the matter becomes warmer. Heat has been transferred by the waves to the matter.

What is an insulator?

Look at the picture of the person taking a hot pot out of the oven. The potholders keep the person's hands from being burned. The particles of matter in a potholder are far apart. Heat cannot move easily by conduction from particle to particle. Notice that the material of the potholder is fluffy.

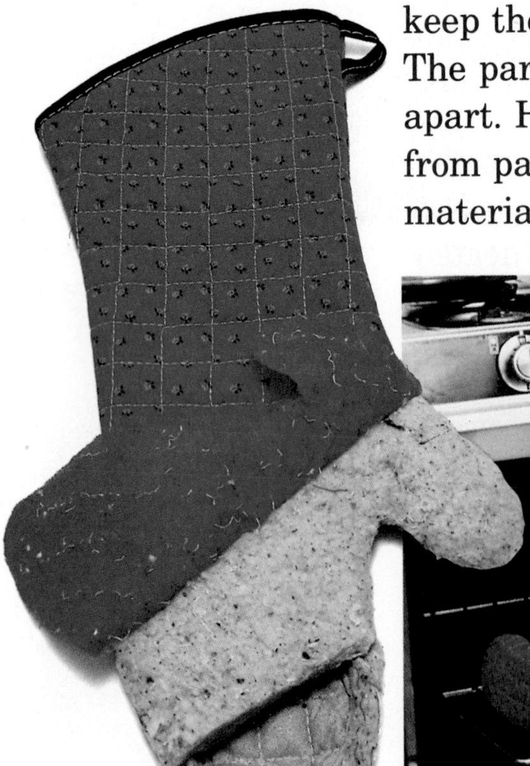

Problem Solving

Keep Your Cool

Have you ever watched how grocery clerks handle frozen food? They often put frozen food in a plastic bag or a thick paper bag with foil lining. You might guess that such bags keep food cold. But how do they work?

How can you design a way to keep things cool?

Suppose you have three cubes of frozen matter—an ice cube, a cube of frozen milk, and a cube of frozen apple. Will all three absorb heat at the same rate? Which do you predict will thaw first at room temperature? Design a way to keep each cube from thawing for the longest time possible. Will the same method work for all the cubes?

Matter through which heat does not move easily is called an **insulator** (IHN suhlayt ur). The potholders are insulators. Often, the particles of matter in insulators are far apart. Also, these materials trap much air in them. Heat does not move easily by conduction through air. You may remember that most conduction occurs in solid matter. Some materials that are good insulators are shown in the picture. What are some other things in your classroom and at home that are also good insulators?

▼ Insulators

▲ Insulator used
in buildings

As you read on page 216, a thermogram shows different temperatures as different colors. You can see in this thermogram that heat escapes from certain parts of the house. The heat escapes from places where there are no insulators. The insulators used in buildings slow the movement of heat. So insulators keep heat inside buildings when it's cold outside. And they keep heat out when it is hot outside. The material used as insulators in buildings has many air spaces. How is the movement of heat slowed by this insulator?

▼ Thermogram

Life Science
CONNECTION

Down is the name given to small feathers found on birds. How does goose down insulate a goose?

Lesson Review

1. What would happen to the temperatures of hot tea and iced tea if they were left out on a table?

2. Describe the three ways that heat moves.

3. What is an insulator? Give some examples.

Think! Why do you feel cooler in the shade on a hot day?

Chapter Connections
Write a paragraph about a main idea in this chapter.
Use the graphic organizer as a guide.

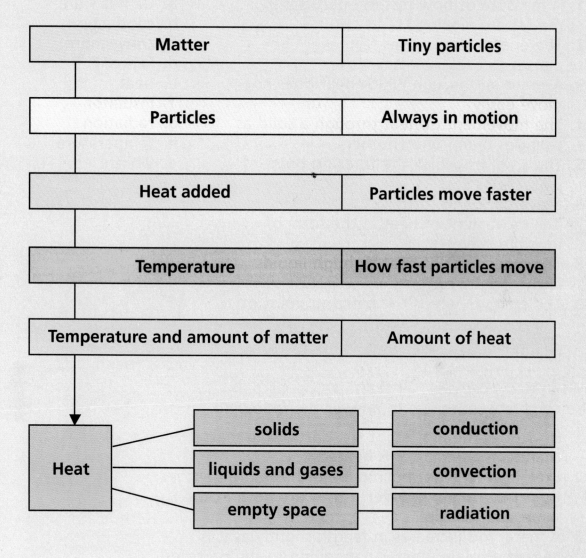

Matter	Tiny particles
Particles	Always in motion
Heat added	Particles move faster
Temperature	How fast particles move
Temperature and amount of matter	Amount of heat

Heat	solids	conduction
	liquids and gases	convection
	empty space	radiation

Writing About Science • Classify
Find objects around your home that act as insulators.
Describe what they are and how they work.

Science Terms

Write the letter of the term that best matches the definition.

1. A measure of how fast the particles in matter are moving
2. The energy that moves from warmer matter to cooler matter
3. A material through which heat does not move easily
4. The movement of heat through a solid as particles bump one another
5. The scale on which the freezing point of water is 32°F
6. Move back and forth
7. The movement of heat in the form of invisible waves
8. The movement of heat through liquids and gases by currents
9. The scale on which the freezing point of water is 0°C

a. Celsius scale
b. conduction
c. convection
d. Fahrenheit scale
e. heat
f. insulator
g. radiation
h. temperature
i. vibrate

Science Ideas

Use complete sentences to answer the following.

1. How does the motion of the particles in matter change as the matter is heated?
2. Explain why 3 L of boiling water has more heat than 1 L of boiling water if they are both at the same temperature.
3. A metal rod increases in length slightly as it is heated. Explain what is happening to the particles that make up the rod.
4. How would you measure the speed of the vibrating particles in each of several samples of water?

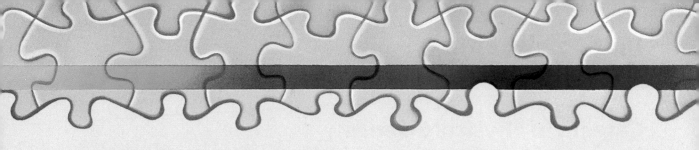

5. Compare the temperatures at which water boils and freezes on the Fahrenheit scale with those on the Celsius scale. Which scale more easily measures small changes in temperature?

6. As cold juice warms, how does the amount of heat in the juice change?

7. A scientist is using tongs to heat a sample of matter in a flame. Explain why the handle of the tongs becomes hot after awhile.

8. Explain how the water in a pot becomes heated all the way through when only the bottom of the pot is heated.

Applying Science Ideas

Use complete sentences to answer the following.

1. A camper heats equal amounts of water in two pails by placing a hot rock from the campfire in each pail. The camper selected two rocks with the same temperature but different sizes. Ten minutes later the camper finds that the water in one pail is much hotter than the water in the other. Explain how this happened.

2. Two different liquids expand at different rates when heated. Suppose both are heated equally. Liquid A expands more than liquid B. Which liquid would be more useful in a thermometer? Explain your answer.

3. What kinds of athletes might want PEG-treated uniforms? Explain your answers.

Using Science Skills

Measure and record the temperature of warm water with a thermometer every two minutes. The water's temperature will go down. When does the temperature go down the fastest?

Careers in Physical Science

Energy Auditor

When Gwendolyn Hawkins was young, she lived where it was very cold. So she thought a lot about keeping warm. She still does. But now it's her job to do so.

Gwendolyn is an **energy auditor** (AW diht ur) in Washington, D.C. She inspects houses. Then she tells people what they can do to save energy — and to keep warmer in cold weather.

Gwendolyn's work is like that of a detective. She spends about 3 hours at each house. She pokes into corners in the basement. She checks for drafts near windows and doors. She inspects the furnace and insulation in the house. She even checks the temperature of the water in the water heater. "Lowering the temperature from 160°F to 120°F can save lots of energy," Gwendolyn says.

Because of the work they do, energy auditors do not dress up to go to work. "You have to climb into dusty attics and damp crawl spaces," Gwendolyn says. So she wears jeans and work boots. And she takes along tools such as a flashlight, a screwdriver, and a ladder for climbing.

When the inspection is done, Gwendolyn suggests ways to keep heat from escaping the house. She also gives out information about appliances that use less energy.

How did Gwendolyn get her job? First, she finished high school. Then she took a 2-week class at a college and passed an energy auditor's test. Next came training on the job. Now, Gwendolyn trains other energy auditors.

Gwendolyn likes her job. "It's important to show people how to save energy." But she also likes getting to know the people she helps. "I've kept up friendships with many of them," she says.

Connecting Science Ideas

1. On pages 216–219 you read about thermograms. How could thermograms be used by an energy auditor such as Gwendolyn?   **Careers; Chapter 7**

2. Look back at the picture of fireworks on pages 160–161. Recall what you learned about changes in energy. What two forms of energy are given off when fireworks explode?   **Chapter 5; Chapter 6**

3. You read about a new kind of matter called PEG on pages 232–233. Changes in PEG particles were described. Which are these changes — physical or chemical?   **Chapter 7; Chapter 5**

4. Read again the description of foam houses on pages 172–173. Imagine a thermogram of a foam house next to one of a regular house. What would you expect to see?   **Chapter 5; Chapter7**

5. List all the sources of heat energy in your home. For each source, describe how the heat moves away from the source.   **Chapter 5; Chapter 7**

6. To change a solid to a liquid you add heat. What does heat do to the particles of solid matter? How can you measure this change?   **Chapter 5; Chapter 7**

Unit Project

You have learned that liquids with less density float on top of liquids with greater density. Try to float layers of salt water on top of fresh water. Add different amounts of salt to several cups of water. Use food colors to color each cup of salt water. Try to drip the different solutions into a test tube so that you can see layers of color.

from

SUGARING TIME

WRITTEN BY KATHRYN LASKY◆PHOTOGRAPHS BY CHRISTOPHER G. KNIGHT

It takes skill and a lot of hard work to make maple syrup. First, holes are drilled into maple trees. Next, spouts are hammered into the holes, and buckets hung under the spouts to collect the sap. Then, the sap is brought to the sugarhouse to be boiled. Finally, the best part comes, tasting the fresh, warm maple syrup. Read how Alice and Don Lacey and their three children work together at sugaring time.

There is a time between the seasons. It comes in March when winter seems tired and spring is only a hoped-for thing. The crystalline whiteness of February has vanished and there is not yet even the pale green stain in the trees that promises spring. It is a time out of time, when night, in central Vermont, can bring a fitful late winter storm that eases, the very next day, into sunshine and a melting wind from the southeast.

Many people complain about this time of year. Snow cannot be counted on for sledding or skiing; cars get stuck in muddy roads; clothes are mud-caked and hard to clean; and the old folks' arthritis kicks up. Everyone, young and old, gets cranky about staying indoors.

But for a few people, this time is a season in its own right. For them it is *sugaring time,* when the sap begins to flow in the maple grove or sugarbush, as it is called. It is a time that contradicts all farming calendars that say crops are planted in the spring, cared for in the summer, and harvested in the fall. This crop, maple sap, is harvested in March, and that is part of the specialness of sugaring time. It is special, too, because young people have a reason to go outside, snow or no snow, mud or no mud, and older people have a reason to believe in the coming spring.

Alice and Don Lacey and their three children live on a farm that has a small sugarbush. They have been waiting almost two weeks for the sap to start running.

Outside, the wind freshens, the sky grows bluer, and puffy white clouds sail over the ridge. But inside the sugar-house it is different weather. The maple fog grows thicker. There are a few slivers and slats of light from the cracks between the boards of the walls. The fire thrums in the arch, and while Jeremy sleeps the others become more watchful for the telltale signs of sap turning to syrup. They must be alert now, for the temperature of the sap is rising. Sap turns to syrup at 218 degrees Fahrenheit. Things can move fast, too fast. The sap can turn to syrup, then to cream, within a few seconds and a few degrees, then burn in the pans. Hot syrup burns rapidly and can even explode.

Jonathan and his father are dipping the thermometer in frequently now as the temperature rises. There are other signs that the sap is about to turn. It becomes darker, taking on a golden amber tone. The bubbles look different, too. Near the end, just before the sap turns to syrup, the bubbles become very fine, then suddenly grow quite huge and explosive looking. And finally, when the liquid "aprons" or "sheets," the Laceys know that it is syrup. They use a tool similar to the skimmer to test for sheeting. If the liquid drops off in rapid little droplets it is not sheeting, but if it gathers along the edge of the scoop slowly and does not immediately dribble off in separate drops, then it is said to sheet. Only syrup sheets, not sap.

"Two hundred fifteen degrees, Dad," Jonathan says, and two minutes later, "Two hundred sixteen, Dad," and then, "Two hundred eighteen!"

"Is it sheeting?" Alice asks.

"Not quite," says Don. "Let's let it go to 219."

In another minute, Don exclaims, "We've got syrup!" Cheers rise in the maple fog. "We're ready to draw off."

They place a bucket under the drain-off spigot and a golden stream begins to run.

In this first drawing off there are nearly three gallons of syrup. They all work quickly now. Jonathan fetches the hydrometer, an instrument for checking the specific gravity, or density, of the liquid. Syrup should weigh eleven pounds per gallon. This is the weight at which it keeps best. If it is too heavy, it may crystallize; if it is too thin, it may ferment. The hydrometer will float at the red line marked 31.5 if the syrup is the proper weight. When the 31.5 mark sinks below the surface, they close the spigot and wait for more sap to turn to syrup.

"Clear the way! Hot syrup!"

Max and Jeremy back away. Being scalded by syrup could be a real disaster. Don carries the bucket to the filtering tank, where he pours it through felt funnels lined with heavy paper. This is the final step in cleansing the syrup and making sure it is crystal clear. The solid matter has been skimmed off, but traces of niter can remain. Filtering strains out these traces.

"When can we taste? When can we taste?" the children ask.

Don measures out a small cup of syrup for each child and puts them on a shelf to cool. "No drinking yet," he warns. "You'll burn your tongues."

When the cups have cooled and the children have tasted the first sap there are immediate cries for "More! More! More!"

Reader's Response

What do you think is the best part about making maple syrup? Explain why.

Selection Follow-up

SUGARING TIME

 ## Responding to Literature

1. How is temperature important in making sure the syrup turns out just right?
2. Imagine that you are with the Laceys in the sugarhouse. Discuss with classmates what you would see, smell, hear, and feel.
3. How can you tell when the sap is ready to turn into syrup? Tell how you might feel at that moment.
4. Make a list of some of the tools you need to make maple syrup, and tell how each is used.

 ## Books to Enjoy

Sugaring Time by Kathryn Lasky
You can find out much more about sugaring time by reading the book from which this selection was taken.

Kitchen Chemistry by Robert Gardner
Use the stove, refrigerator, counter, sink, and materials commonly found in the kitchen to help you experiment with some scientific principles.

The Magic Tree Nickolai Osipov
You can learn more about trees and other plants by reading this collection of 28 short stories that tell about the natural world.

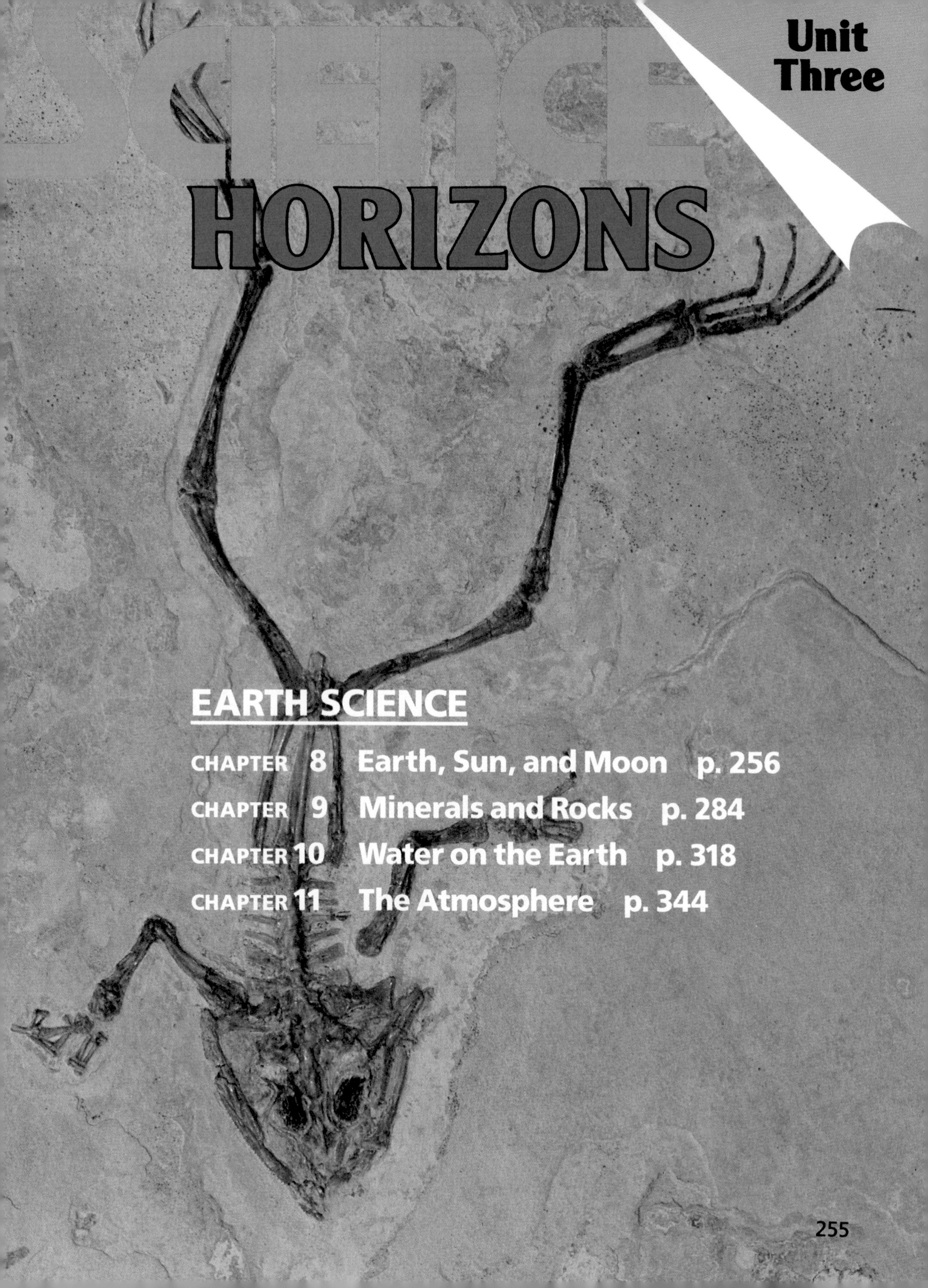

HORIZONS

EARTH SCIENCE

Earth, Sun, and Moon

Cloudy With a Chance of Sunspots

Astronomers have been seeing spots before their eyes for years. But they are not rushing to the eye doctor. The spots they see are called sunspots. Sunspots are the dark areas that show up on the surface of the sun. Every 11 years or so, the spots show up in large numbers. Then the spots mysteriously disappear.

Scientists are beginning to learn about sunspots and what causes them. Sometimes violent storms happen near sunspots. The storms shoot flames, called solar flares, thousands of kilometers into space.

The flares give off large amounts of energy. Earth's atmosphere filters out some of this energy. But the energy that does reach Earth can give you a bad sunburn. Space has no atmosphere to filter out some of the energy. So the energy from solar flares is dangerous to astronauts in space.

Some solar flares can damage satellites flying in space. The energy from a very large flare can heat up Earth's atmosphere. The warm air slows down satellites that fly through it. They may even fall from their orbit.

During the last cycle of sunspots, a satellite named Skylab slowed down and fell to Earth. Scientists were afraid that Skylab would fall on an area of land where people live. Fortunately, Skylab broke apart and fell into the ocean near Australia.

Today, many satellites are in orbit around Earth. Scientists think that the sunspots and flares during the present cycle will be the largest in 250 years. What do you think will happen to the satellites?

Scientists who study weather also study sunspots and their cycles. Some of them think that when the number of sunspots increases, winters are warmer. Others think that sunspots cause droughts.

Sunspots and solar flares can cause other problems on Earth. They can interrupt long-distance telephone calls. They can cause power outages. They can even cause static on your favorite radio stations. When that happens, remember, you are listening to the sun 150 million km (93 million mi) away!

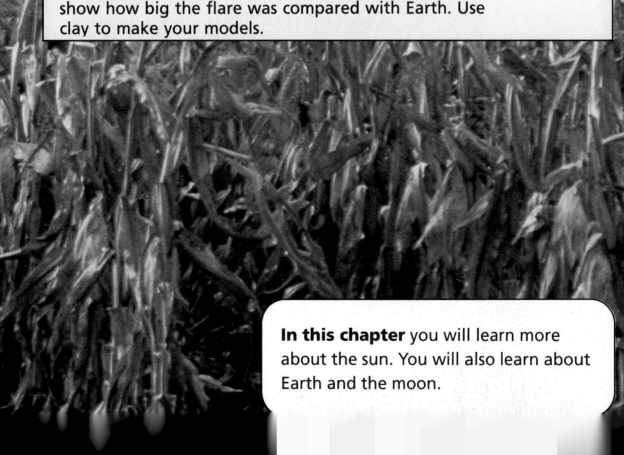

Discover

How can you compare the sizes of very large things?

Materials   metric ruler · clay

Procedure

Comparing the sizes of very large things is not always easy. That is why scientists often use models to compare the sizes of objects in space. On July 25, 1988, astronomers photographed a large solar flare. The flare was about 128,000 km (76,800 mi) long! The flare was ten times longer than the length of Earth at its diameter. Make a model to show how big the flare was compared with Earth. Use clay to make your models.

In this chapter you will learn more about the sun. You will also learn about Earth and the moon.

1. Earth, Moon, and Sun

Getting Started Describe for a classmate how to get to your house from school. Name some places or things near your home. Tell the distances between your home and nearby places. Can your classmate locate your house?

Where is Earth located in space?

You can describe the location of Earth as you would describe the location of your house. You can name objects near Earth. You can give the distances from Earth to these objects.

A **planet** (PLAN iht) is a body in space that moves in a regular path around the sun. Earth is a planet. It is one of nine planets that move around the sun.

▼ The sun and the nine planets

Sun

Jupiter

Venus

Mars

Mercury

Earth

260

Look at the drawing of the planets. You can see the order of the planets outward from the sun. Locate Earth in the drawing. In what position is Earth from the sun?

Just as planets travel around the sun, smaller bodies travel around planets. Earth and most other planets have moons traveling around them. Earth's moon is the nearest body to Earth in space. Together the planets, their moons, and other objects moving around the sun make up the solar system.

Of course, you know that Earth is closer to the moon than it is to the sun. Earth is about 150 million km (93 million miles) from the sun. But Earth is only 384,000 km (240,000 miles) from the moon. Suppose that the distance from Earth to the sun is 215 metric-ruler lengths. On this scale, the distance to the moon is only about half a ruler length.

To win a trip to watch a space shuttle launch, Bernardo has to solve five riddles. See if you can solve the riddles as you read **Bernardo and the Billion-Year Sunburn** in Horizons Plus.

Saturn

Uranus

Neptune

Pluto

▲ Earth

▲ The moon

In the picture of Earth, you can see that Earth looks like a ball. A ball-shaped object is called a sphere. But Earth is not a perfect sphere. Earth bulges around the equator (ee KWAYT ur). The equator is an imaginary line that divides Earth halfway between the North and South poles. Earth's bulge is too small to see in pictures. Now look at the moon. You can see that it is also a sphere.

▼ Earth's axis

What are the movements of Earth?

Earth has two main movements within the solar system. One of these movements is rotation (roh TAY shun). **Rotation** is the turning of an object on its axis (AK sihs). The **axis** is an imaginary line through the center of an object, around which that object turns.

Look at the picture of the globe. The rod going through the globe shows the axis of Earth. It takes about 24 hours, or one day, for Earth to make one rotation.

As Earth rotates, it also revolves. **Revolution** (rev uh LOO shun) is the movement of one body on a path around another body. The path one body follows around another is called an **orbit** (OR biht). Earth takes one year to make one complete revolution around the sun.

What are movements of the moon?

Like Earth, the moon rotates on its axis. The moon also revolves around Earth. One rotation and one revolution both take about a month to complete. Because of the rates of these two motions, the same side of the moon always faces Earth.

In the drawing, "X" marks a spot on the moon. Follow the "X" as you trace the moon's orbit around Earth. Notice that for each quarter turn the moon makes in its rotation, it also moves one-quarter of the way through its revolution.

▼ **The moon revolving around Earth**

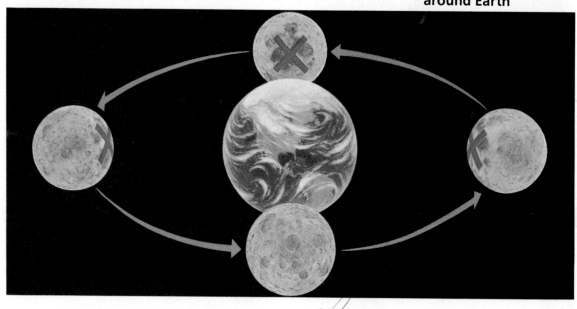

▲ New moon

▲ First quarter moon

▲ Full moon

▲ Last quarter moon

▲ The phases of the moon

The side of the moon facing the sun reflects sunlight. The side of the moon facing away from the sun is dark. From Earth you can see only the lighted part of the moon.

As the moon orbits Earth, you see different amounts of the lighted side of the moon. Because you can see different amounts of the lighted side at different times, the moon seems to change shape. The changing shapes seen from Earth are called phases. The moon phase you see depends on the positions of the moon, Earth, and the sun.

Lesson Review

1. Draw the solar system. Label the sun, the moon, and Earth.
2. How far away is Earth from the sun and the moon?
3. Describe Earth's rotation and revolution.
4. Design a model showing why the same side of the moon always faces Earth.

Think! Why would the second planet from the sun have a shorter year than Earth does?

THINKING

Skills

Putting things in a sequence

A person may eat breakfast in the morning, lunch at noon, and supper in the evening. Meals are eaten in a sequence. The sequence of meals is arranged by the time of day. Other things can be put into a sequence by time of day or by some other trait.

Practicing the skill

1. The three drawings were all made on the same afternoon.
2. Observe the positions of the sun and the length of the shadows.
3. Write the letters of the drawings to show a sequence, using what you observe.

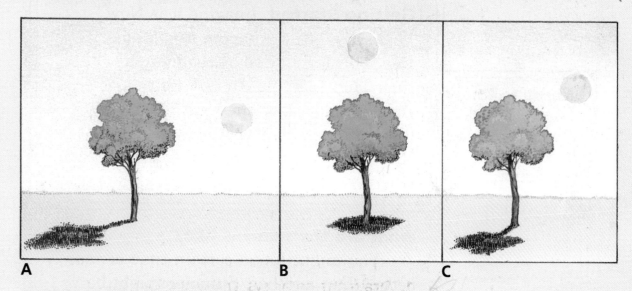

A   B   C

Thinking about the skill

What did you look for in the drawings to put them in sequence?

Applying the skill

Think about the sequence that you made with the drawings. Imagine another drawing that could be added to the sequence. What would it look like? Describe and then draw a picture to add to the sequence.

265

▲ Spring

▲ Summer

2. The Seasons

Getting Started Imagine it is New Year's Eve! Now imagine it is Memorial Day. This is followed by the Fourth of July, then Thanksgiving. In different parts of the United States, the weather is very different on each of these holidays. What is the weather like on each of these holidays where you live?

Words to Know
season
direct rays
indirect rays

What are the seasons like?

You might like a certain time of year better than another. Summer might be your favorite time because it is warm and you can go swimming. Winter might be your favorite because you like to ice-skate or ski. Different things can be enjoyed during different seasons. A **season** (SEE zuhn) is one of four periods of the year. The seasons are spring, summer, autumn, and winter.

◀ Autumn   ▲ Winter

In some places in the United States, the four seasons are very different from one another. Leaves change color and fall from trees in autumn. It snows and is very cold in winter. In spring the temperature gets milder. In summer it may be very hot.

In other places the four seasons are very much alike. In some states it is hot in the spring and autumn as well as summer. Winter is mild with little or no snow. There are no great changes in temperature. What are the seasons like where you live?

What causes the seasons?

Sometimes, Earth is closer to the sun than at other times. Many people believe that it is summer when Earth is closest to the sun. But this idea is false. Earth is *farthest* from the sun when it is summer in the United States. And when it is summer in the United States and the rest of North America, it is winter in South America!

To help you understand how this is possible, look at the drawing of Earth below. Because the earth's surface is curved, the sun's rays strike different parts of the surface at different angles. In some places the sun's rays strike the surface with very little slant. Rays that strike the earth's surface at almost no slant are **direct rays**. Rays that strike the earth's surface at a slant are called **indirect rays**.

In the drawing on the right, the two beams of light represent a direct ray and an indirect ray. Both rays have the same amount of energy. But you can see that the energy of the indirect ray spreads over a larger area than that of the direct ray.

▼ **Earth's surface receiving direct and indirect rays**

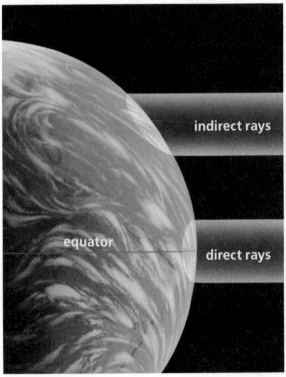
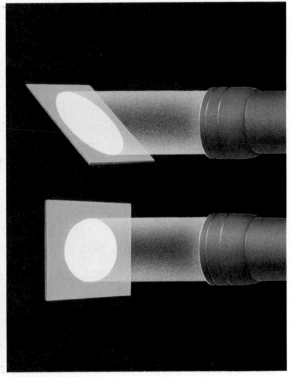

ACTIVITY

Explore Together

How do direct and indirect rays from the sun affect temperatures?

Organizer

Materials
sticky dot · 2 aluminum pie pans · 2 thermometers · soil · 2 textbooks · 2 gooseneck lamps · timer

Procedure

Investigator

A. Put a sticky dot on the side of one pan. Fill each pan with potting soil.

Investigator

B. Place a thermometer into each pan so that the bulb is just covered by the soil.

Investigator, Manager

C. Use the two books to prop up the pan with the dot. Place the other pan flat on the table next to the first pan. Place the gooseneck lamps so they shine directly on the two pans. The thermometer on the tilted pan should not cast a shadow.

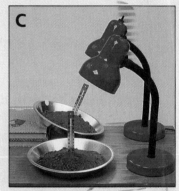

Recorder

1. Which pan receives the direct rays of light?

Group, Recorder

D. Record the starting temperatures. Read and record the temperature of each pan every minute for 8 minutes.

2. What was the highest temperature reading for each pan?

Writing and Sharing Results and Conclusions

Group, Recorder

1. How do the temperatures in the pans compare?

2. Which rays, direct or indirect, provide the most energy?

3. What do you think the seasons are like in places that receive mostly direct rays all year?

Reporter

4. How do your results and conclusions compare with those of your classmates?

269

Because the energy is more spread out, the places in the larger area receive less energy. This is why places receiving indirect rays from the sun may be cooler than areas receiving direct rays.

Now look at the drawing of the orbit, or path, of Earth around the sun. Notice that Earth's axis is tilted in relation to its orbit. Earth's axis is always tilted in the same direction no matter where it is in its orbit.

Because Earth's axis is tilted, direct rays strike different parts of Earth as it revolves. Whether more direct or more indirect rays strike a place on Earth at a certain time determines the season in that place.

▼ **The positions of Earth during the four seasons in the northern hemisphere**

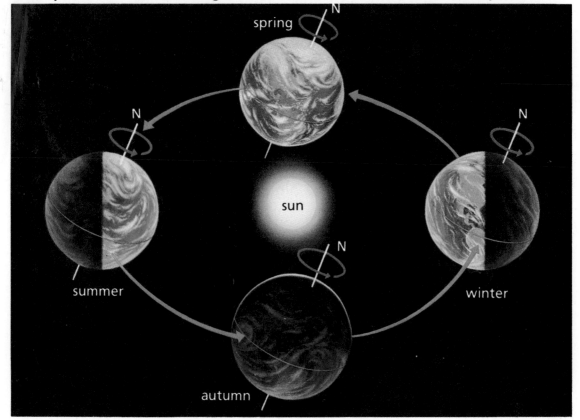

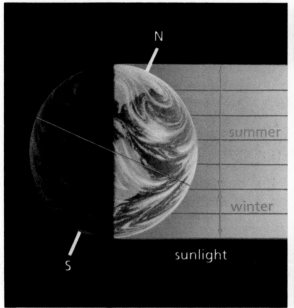

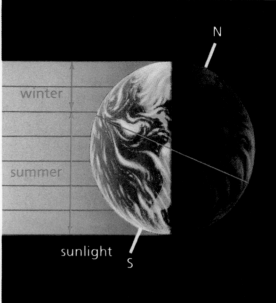

▲ North Pole tilted toward the sun   ▲ North Pole tilted away from the sun

On the drawing, point to the position of Earth in which the North Pole is tilted toward the sun. In this position the half of Earth north of the equator receives the most direct rays. So it is then summer north of the equator.

In the same position the half of Earth south of the equator receives more indirect rays. So, at that same time, it is winter south of the equator. When the South Pole is tilted toward the sun, it is winter north of the equator. What season is it at this time south of the equator?

Lesson Review

1. Describe the causes of seasons.
2. Describe the difference between direct rays and indirect rays.

Think! If Earth is closest to the sun in January, why is it winter in the United States then?

Life Science
CONNECTION

How does the behavior of animals change with changes in seasons?

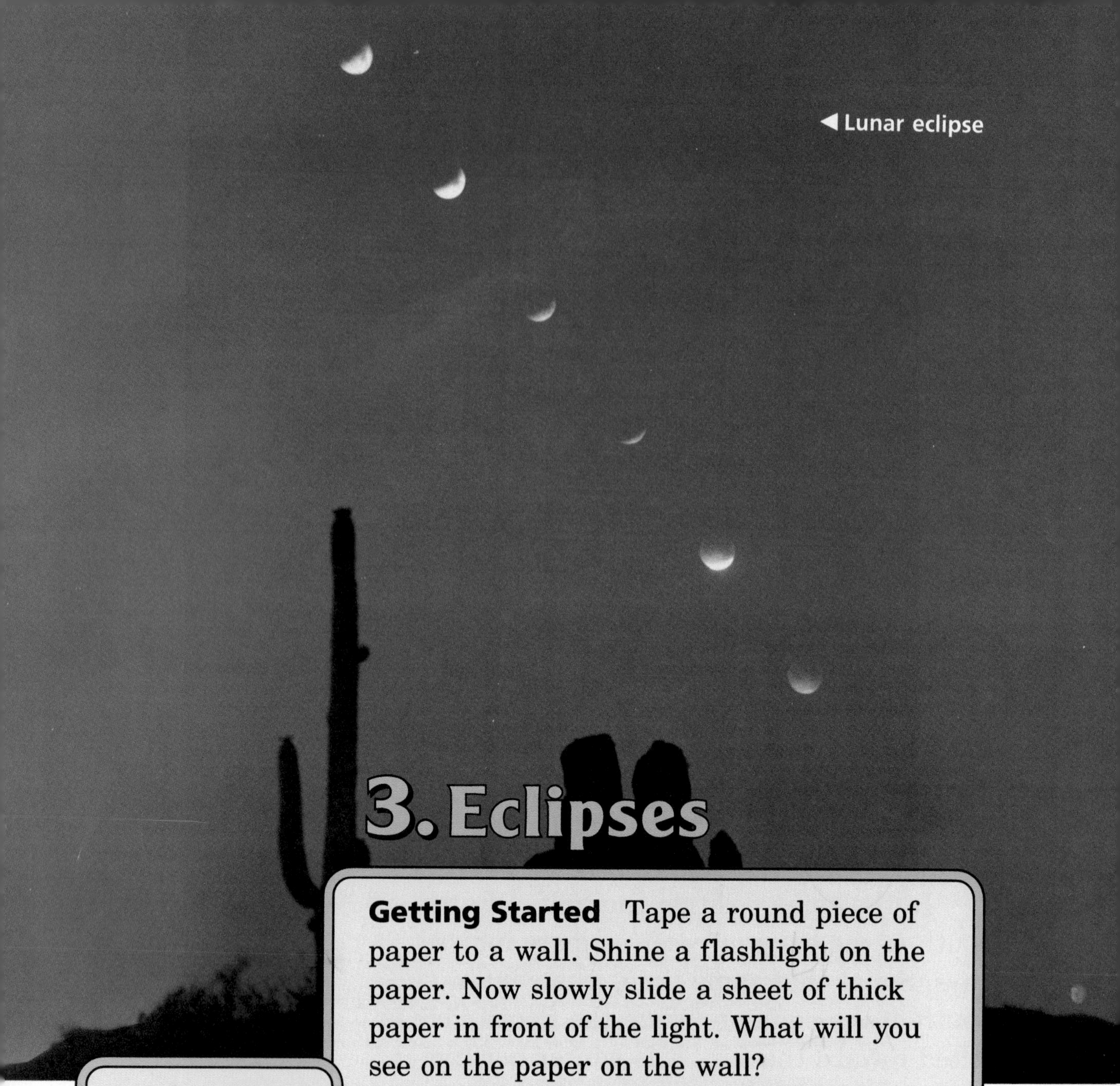

◀ Lunar eclipse

3. Eclipses

Getting Started Tape a round piece of paper to a wall. Shine a flashlight on the paper. Now slowly slide a sheet of thick paper in front of the light. What will you see on the paper on the wall?

Words to Know
lunar eclipse
solar eclipse

What causes a lunar eclipse?

At the new moon and full moon phases, the moon, Earth, and sun can be in a straight line with one another. When the three are lined up, eclipses take place. An eclipse is the blocking out of the view of the sun or moon from Earth.

A **lunar eclipse** (loo nur ih KLIHPS) occurs when Earth blocks the sun's light from the moon. This happens when Earth is directly between the sun and moon. At what moon phase can a lunar eclipse occur?

Look at the drawing below of the sun, Earth, and moon. You can see that a lunar eclipse occurs when the moon is in the shadow of Earth. As the moon slowly moves into Earth's shadow, the moon looks rust or copper colored.

▼ **Position of the moon and Earth during a lunar eclipse**

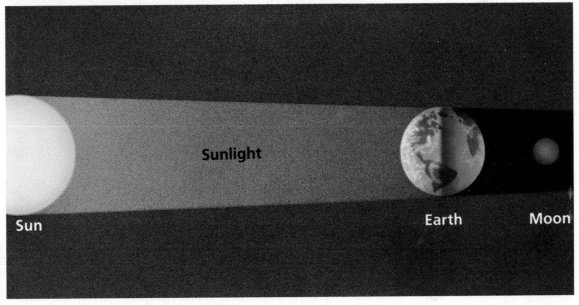

Most lunar eclipses can be seen from any place on the nighttime side of Earth. Lunar eclipses occur two to five times a year. Eclipses like the one shown in the picture on page 272 last about 3½ hours from the time Earth's shadow first touches the moon. But the moon is totally dark for about 2 hours.

Problem Solving

By the Light of the Silvery Moons

Some planets have more than one moon. Each moon has a different orbit around the planet. Imagine trying to fall asleep with three full moons reflecting light through your window. Now imagine an eclipse of all three moons at the same time! How could it happen?

How can the moons of a planet with three moons all eclipse at the same time?

Design a demonstration showing a three-moon eclipse. Plan on using a globe, three tennis balls, and a flashlight. Create an eclipse problem of your own about a different planet and its moons. See if others can show how your eclipses might occur.

What causes a solar eclipse?

Daylight turns to darkness, but it is not nighttime. Stars can be seen in the dark sky, but it is not nighttime. What do you think is happening? It is a solar eclipse (soh lur ih-KLIHPS). A **solar eclipse** occurs when the moon blocks some or all of the sun's light from a place on Earth.

▼ **Position of the moon and Earth during a solar eclipse**

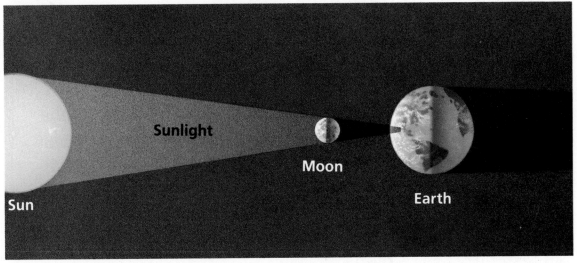

A solar eclipse happens when the moon moves directly between Earth and the sun. The moon's shadow falls on a small part of Earth's surface, blocking the sun's light. So, from that part of Earth, the view of the sun is cut off. A solar eclipse happens very quickly. The sun's light is blocked totally for only 7½ minutes at the most. At what moon phase can a solar eclipse occur?

Lesson Review

1. Draw the positions of the moon, the sun and Earth during a solar eclipse.
2. What happens during a solar eclipse?
3. Draw a picture of how the sun, Earth, and the moon are arranged in space during a lunar eclipse.
4. What happens during a lunar eclipse?

Think! Why would you have to be on the daylight side of Earth to see a solar eclipse?

4. Tides

Words to Know
tides
high tide
low tide

Getting Started Imagine you are at an ocean shore. You place your towel a few meters from the water. After 2 hours, the water has moved up the beach to the edge of your towel. Later in the day, the water moves back down the beach. What have you been observing?

What are tides?

The regular rise and fall of Earth's water is called **tides** (tydz). Tides occur in all bodies of water. But tides are seen best at ocean shores like the one in the picture.

When the ocean water level rises, the edge of the water moves toward land. It is **high tide** when the water reaches its highest point on land. When the ocean water level falls, the edge of the water moves toward the ocean. It is **low tide** when the water reaches its lowest point on land.

What causes tides?

Usually there are two high tides and two low tides each day. These four tides all occur during a period of 24 hours and 50 minutes. The tides are caused mainly by the pull of gravity between the moon and Earth. But the pull of gravity between the sun and Earth also affects the tides.

The pull of the moon's gravity causes two bulges in Earth's water. The drawing shows the two bulges. At each place within a bulge, there is a high tide. One high tide is on the side of Earth closest to the moon. The other high tide is on the opposite side of Earth. Low tides occur in places between the bulges. Locate these places in the drawing.

▼ **The two bulges in Earth's water**

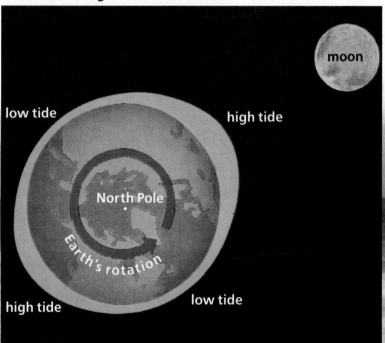

As Earth rotates, all places on Earth pass through the water bulges each day. They also pass through the areas between the bulges. So all places experience high and low tides each day.

Tides around Earth differ. The sizes and shapes of the coasts make differences in the number of tides and their heights. In some places there is almost no difference in height between the high tide and the low tide.

In places, such as the Bay of Fundy near Nova Scotia, the difference in the height of high tide and low tide is very large. The pictures show the great change in the height of the bay's water.

▼ Bay of Fundy at high tide

▼ Bay of Fundy at low tide

Explore

How does the time of high and low tide change each day?

Many kinds of fish can be caught at an ocean shore. Some fish are easier to catch at high tide. Others can be caught best at low tide. But the time of high and low tide changes from day to day. So, before going fishing, people often check a table of high and low tides.

Materials

sheet of graph paper · red pencil · green pencil · calculator

Procedure

A. The table shows the heights of the water level at an ocean beach. Use the data in the table to make a bar graph on your graph paper.
   1. What pattern can you find in the changing height of the water level?

B. Use the red pencil to color the bars showing the lowest daytime and lowest nighttime water levels.
   2. What is shown by the red bars?

C. Use the green pencil to color the bars showing the highest daytime and highest nighttime water levels.
   3. What is shown by the green bars?

Writing and Sharing Results and Conclusions

1. How much time was there between the two high tides? How much time was there between the two low tides?

2. From your graph, predict the time of the next low tide and high tide.

3. How much time is there between the first high tide of one day and the first high tide of the next day? Use a calculator to find out.

Time	A.M.		P.M.	
	2:00	8:12	2:25	8:37
Tide Height	12M	15M	10M	18M

279

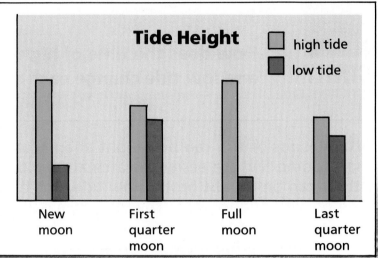

Tide Height

□ high tide
■ low tide

New moon | First quarter moon | Full moon | Last quarter moon

How does the sun affect the tides?

The pull of gravity between the sun and Earth can affect the tides. The sun, like the moon, causes Earth's water to bulge on opposite sides of Earth. The bulges caused by the pull of gravity of the sun are somewhat smaller than those caused by the moon, but still large enough to affect the tides.

As you read, find the tides described on the graph. During a full and new moon, the bulges caused by the sun and moon are in the same place. So the high tides are much higher than the low tide. During a first and last quarter moon, the bulges caused by the sun are between the bulges caused by the moon. So there is a very small difference in the heights of high tide and low tide.

Physical Science
CONNECTION

Find out how the tides can be used to provide electrical energy.

Lesson Review

1. What is a high tide? What is a low tide?
2. What causes two high tides on opposite sides of Earth?

Think! Why do ships enter ports at high tide?

Chapter Connections

Explain to a partner what causes seasons, eclipses, and tides. Use the graphic organizer to help you.

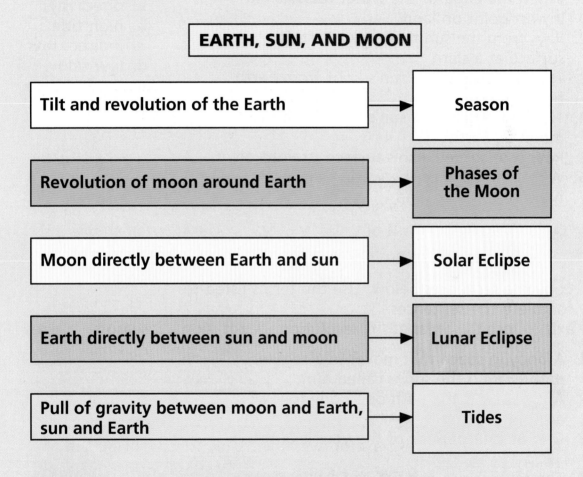

EARTH, SUN, AND MOON

Tilt and revolution of the Earth	Season
Revolution of moon around Earth	Phases of the Moon
Moon directly between Earth and sun	Solar Eclipse
Earth directly between sun and moon	Lunar Eclipse
Pull of gravity between moon and Earth, sun and Earth	Tides

Writing About Science • Create

Long ago, people did not understand the causes of eclipses. When they saw an eclipse, they made up stories to explain what was happening. These stories often had monsters, imaginary creatures, and fantastic events. Work with a partner to create a story that would explain an eclipse. Share your story with the class.

Chapter 8 Review

Science Terms

A. Write the letter of the term that best matches the definition.

1. When the edge of the water reaches its lowest point on land
2. Rays from the sun that strike Earth's surface at a slant
3. The blocking of the sun's light from Earth by the moon
4. The blocking of the sun's light from the moon by Earth
5. Rays that strike Earth's surface straight on
6. When the edge of the water reaches its highest point on land

a. direct rays
b. high tide
c. indirect rays
d. low tide
e. lunar eclipse
f. solar eclipse

B. Copy the sentences below. Use the terms listed to complete the sentences.

axis   orbit   planet   revolution   rotation   season   tides

1. A body in space that moves in a regular path around the sun is called a(n) _____ .
2. A(n) _____ is the path one body follows around another.
3. One of four periods of the year is a(n) _____ .
4. The regular rise and fall of Earth's water level is called _____ .
5. A(n) _____ is the movement of one body in a path around another body.
6. A(n) _____ is the turning of an object on its axis.
7. A(n) _____ is an imaginary line through the center of an object around which that object turns.

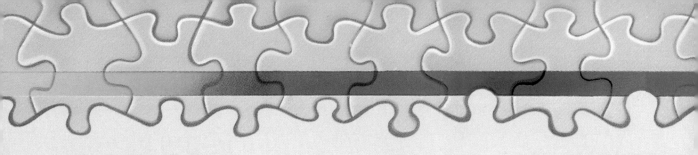

Science Ideas

Use complete sentences to answer the following.

1. What is the difference between rotation and revolution?
2. Describe how a lunar eclipse occurs.
3. Why do all places along the ocean shore have high and low tides each day?
4. Describe Earth's position in the solar system in relation to the moon and the sun.
5. Describe the positions of Earth during summer and winter in the Northern Hemisphere.

Applying Science Ideas

Use complete sentences to answer the following.

1. How much of the moon is lighted by the sun at the first quarter moon phase? Explain your answer.
2. Suppose you had to schedule the launch of a space station that would orbit Earth. Why is it important for you to know about the cycle of sunspots?

Using Science Skills

Look at the three pictures of the moon. The pictures are in a sequence. Draw the next picture in the sequence.

Minerals and Rocks

GOING FOR THE GOLD

Look at the pictures on these pages. What do all of these things have in common? The flame on the statue is covered with gold. The treasure is gold. And a very thin layer of gold is on the astronaut's helmet.

People have valued gold for many years. Egyptian kings were buried with gold jewelry and cups. Over 2,000 years ago, people made gold into coins.

Today, gold is used in many ways. It has even traveled to the moon and back. The thin gold film on astronauts' helmets protects their eyes from the sun. Gold is also used in computers. Thin gold wires are used in making computer chips.

Builders use gold on buildings and statues. When the Statue of Liberty was 100 years old in 1986, she received a gift of gold. Builders covered her flame with a thin sheet of gold. The gold will shine brightly for many years.

Glassmakers use gold to make a special kind of window. These windows save energy. The gold reflects the sun's rays. It keeps heat out in summer and it traps heat inside during winter.

Gold is also a modern medicine. Doctors give gold to people who have a disease called arthritis. Gold is also used to treat some forms of cancer. Many dentists use gold to fill cavities. Gold fillings fit snugly and last a lifetime.

Gold is special for many reasons. It is rare and beautiful. It is found in nature in almost pure form. Gold is soft, so it can easily be made into different shapes. It does not rust or change color with age. And it lasts almost forever.

Gold is found in the ground. Sometimes it is close to Earth's surface. Sometimes it even washes into streams. Long ago people collected gold from the streams in metal pans. Today some people still use metal pans. In other places people dig gold from the ground with just a pick and shovel. But in most places, gold is deep underground. People dig mines through rock to find gold. One reason gold is so valuable is that it is hard to find. Another reason is that there is not much gold on Earth.

Discover

How can you separate a mixture?

Materials mixture of salt, sand, and iron filings · other materials

Procedure

Mixtures can be separated in many ways. The best way depends on what is in the mixture.

How would you separate a mixture of salt, sand, and iron filings? Think about the properties of each of these materials. What things might help you separate them? Develop a plan. Show it to your teacher, and then try it.

In this chapter you will learn more about gold and other minerals. You will also learn about different kinds of rocks.

1. Minerals

Words to Know
mineral
luster
streak
hardness

Getting Started You have read that gold is useful because of its properties. Gold can be hammered and shaped. It is used to make jewelry. What might be some properties of the materials in the pictures that make them useful?

▲ Graphite

Halite ▶

▲ Gold

What are minerals and their uses?

Gold is a kind of mineral. A **mineral** is a natural solid substance found in the earth's crust. Minerals have many uses. The part of a pencil that is used for writing is made with the mineral graphite. Table salt comes from the mineral halite. The mineral quartz is used to make glass.

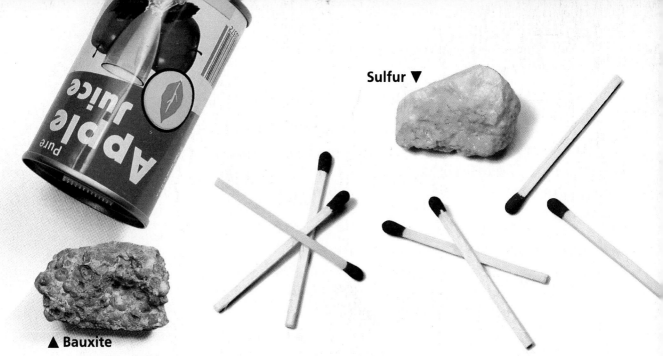

Sulfur ▼

▲ Bauxite

A useful mineral that is removed from the earth and sold for profit is called an ore. The pictures show different ores and the useful products made from them. What is something you used today that was made from an ore?

How are minerals identified?

The properties of a mineral result from two things. One is the kinds of particles making up the mineral. The other is the way the particles are arranged.

Particles in minerals are arranged in certain patterns. The pattern formed by their particles gives minerals a certain crystal shape. The crystal shape of minerals is one property that is used to identify them.

Minerals have other properties that are used to identify them. One of these properties is a mineral's luster. **Luster** is the way light reflects from a mineral's surface.

▼ Aquamarine crystals

▲ Pyrite crystals

Explore Together

How can you grow mineral crystals?

Materials

Organizer

cup · stirrer · water · alum · saucer · thread · tape · jar with lid · 250 mL beaker · pan · hot plate

Procedure

Investigator

A. Half-fill a cup with very hot tap water. While stirring, slowly add alum to the water. Stop when no more alum will dissolve.

Investigator, Recorder, Group

B. Pour the solution into the saucer. Leave it overnight. Look at the saucer the next day.

1. What happened to the solution?

Manager

C. Remove a large, single crystal. Tie a thread around it. Tape the other end of the thread to the jar lid.

Investigator

D. Put the 250 ml of water in the pan and add about 6 teaspoons of alum.

Caution: *Step E should be done by the teacher.*

Teacher

E. Heat, but do not boil, the solution. Remove the pan from the heat. Stir in 1 teaspoon of alum at a time. Stop when alum settles to the pan bottom.

Investigator, Recorder, Group

F. Fill the jar with the solution. Replace the lid on the jar so that the crystal is in the solution.

2. Predict what will happen to the crystal after four days.

Group, Recorder

G. Look at the crystal every day for four days. Write down any changes in the crystal.

Writing and Sharing Results and Conclusions

Group, Reporter

1. What happened to the crystal?
2. How did the amount of time affect the crystal size?

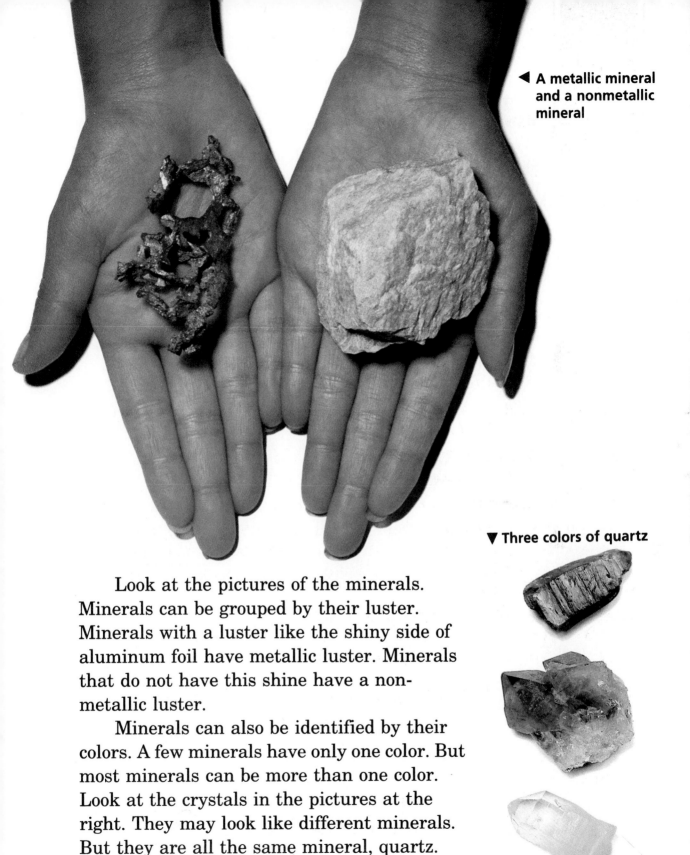

◀ A metallic mineral and a nonmetallic mineral

▼ Three colors of quartz

Look at the pictures of the minerals. Minerals can be grouped by their luster. Minerals with a luster like the shiny side of aluminum foil have metallic luster. Minerals that do not have this shine have a non-metallic luster.

Minerals can also be identified by their colors. A few minerals have only one color. But most minerals can be more than one color. Look at the crystals in the pictures at the right. They may look like different minerals. But they are all the same mineral, quartz.

Another way to identify a mineral is to crush the mineral into a powder. One way to do this is to rub the mineral on a hard tile plate. The mineral leaves a colored streak. **Streak** is the color of a powdered mineral. The picture shows the streak of a mineral. In this case, the streak is almost the same color as the mineral. Many minerals produce a streak that has a different color than that of the mineral itself.

1	2	3	4	5
softest Talc	Gypsum	Calcite	Fluorite	Apatite

A property that can be used to identify minerals is their hardness. **Hardness** tells how easy it is to scratch a mineral. Harder minerals cannot be scratched as easily as softer ones.

Ten minerals are used to make a hardness scale. The minerals are numbered from 1 to 10, in order of their hardness. The softest mineral is number 1. The hardness of any mineral can be measured using this scale.

*Can you tell the difference between real gold and "fools gold"? Learn how when you read **Rivers of Gold** in Horizons Plus.*

A mineral's hardness is measured by scratching it with minerals from the scale. A harder mineral will scratch a softer one. The hardness number is based on which mineral in the scale can scratch the mineral tested.

Suppose a mineral is scratched by fluorite but scratches calcite. That mineral has a hardness between 3 and 4. Two minerals have the same hardness if neither one scratches the other.

▼ **The scratch test**

| 6 | 7 | 8 | 9 | 10 | |
| Feldspar | Quartz | Topaz | Corundum | Diamond | **hardest** |

Lesson Review

1. What is a mineral?
2. Name three minerals and a use for each one.
3. What are the two luster groups for minerals?
4. Why is color not the best way to identify minerals?
5. How can you tell if one mineral is harder than another?

Think! Suppose you are given two cube-shaped metallic mineral crystals. Propose two tests you could do to tell if they are different minerals or the same minerals.

Life Science
CONNECTION
Find out what minerals are part of a balanced diet.

2. Rocks

Words to Know

crust
rock
mantle
core

Getting Started Imagine that you could travel to the center of the earth. Predict what you might see. What might you want to bring with you?

What are the layers of the earth?

The earth can be divided into three layers. You can see these layers in the drawing. The outer layer of the earth is called the **crust.** The crust is made mostly of rocks. A **rock** is a solid that is made of one or more minerals.

As you can see in the drawing, the crust is the thinnest of the earth's three layers. If you compare the earth to a boiled egg, the crust is like the shell of the egg.

The layers of the earth▼

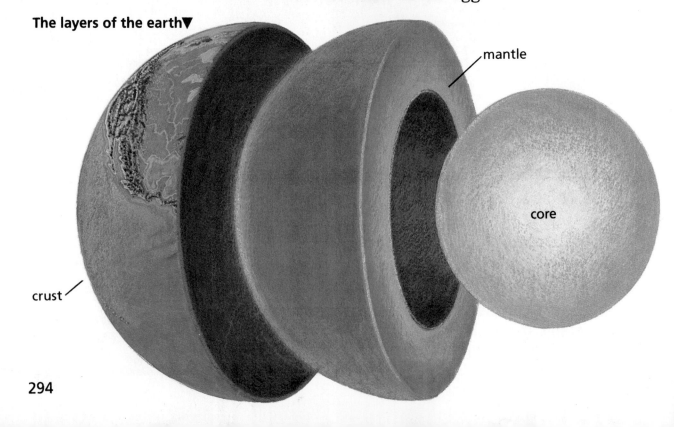

mantle

core

crust

294

The **mantle** is the layer just beneath the crust. The mantle is about 2,900 km (1,740 miles) thick. That is about the distance between Los Angeles, California, and Kansas City, Kansas. Even though the inside of the earth is very hot, most of the mantle is solid. The mantle could be compared to the white of the boiled egg.

Beneath the mantle, at the earth's center, is the layer called the **core.** The core is like the yolk of the egg. The earth's core has about the same diameter as two moons.

The core is divided into an outer core and an inner core. The outer core is liquid. It is thought to contain iron and nickel. Scientists think that the inner core is solid. It may be made of the same materials as the outer core.

▼ **The thickness of the mantle**

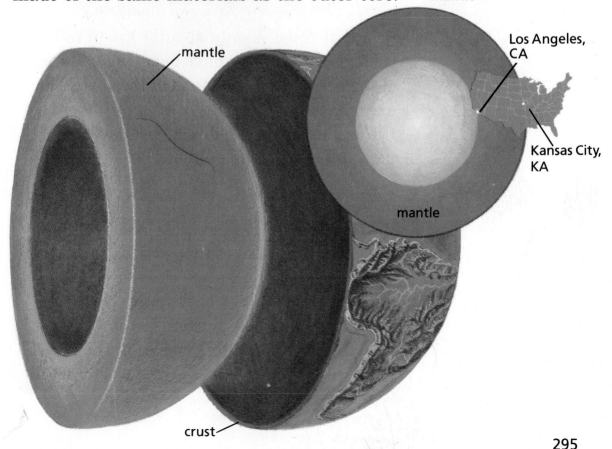

mantle

crust

Los Angeles, CA

Kansas City, KA

mantle

Problem Solving

A Closer Look

You can tell a lot about something just by looking at it. For example, even though the rocks in the picture are not labeled, you still might be able to tell what kind they are by looking at them.

What are some characteristics of the three groups of rocks?

Examine the rocks in the picture carefully. What characteristics can you observe? Use these characteristics to decide to which rock group each rock belongs.

The crust is the thinnest of the three layers of the earth. At some places in the ocean floor, the crust is only about 7 km (4 miles) thick. Deep oil wells have been drilled in parts of the ocean floor. Yet none of these wells have ever reached all the way through the crust to the mantle. Thus, no direct observations of the mantle have ever been made.

How are rocks classified?

You know that the crust is made mostly of rocks. The rocks of the crust can form in different ways. Rocks are classified into three groups based on how they form. There are many kinds of rock in each group. A kind of rock from each group is shown in the pictures on the next page. How is each rock different from the others?

▲ Igneous rock

▲ Sedimentary rock

◄ Metamorphic rock

Melted rock hardens to form igneous (IHG nee us) rock. Hardened sediments form sedimentary (sed uh MEN tur ee) rock. Sediments are bits of rock or minerals, shells, and plant or animal remains. Rocks changed by heat and pressure form metamorphic (meh tuh MOR fihk) rock.

Lesson Review

1. Describe the crust, the mantle, and the core of the earth.
2. What is a rock?
3. List the three groups of rocks.

Think! Suppose a new drill could reach twice as far into the crust as a drill can today. How might this affect the supply of useful rocks?

Physical Science
CONNECTION

Use reference books to find out the temperature of the center of the earth. How much hotter is that than the temperature at the earth's surface?

3. Igneous Rock

Getting Started Many outdoor monuments and buildings are made from igneous rock. Igneous rock is very hard. So it lasts a long time. Try to find places in your area that are made of igneous rock.

Words to Know
magma
lava
igneous rock

How do igneous rocks form?

Some spots inside the earth are so hot that the rock there melts. Melted rock is called **magma.** Magma that reaches the earth's surface is called **lava.**

Igneous rock is rock formed from melted rock that has cooled and hardened. Magma can form igneous rock beneath the earth's surface. Lava can form igneous rocks on the earth's surface. Devil's Tower, in Wyoming, formed from lava that hardened inside a volcano.

298

What minerals are in igneous rocks?

You can tell what kinds of minerals are in igneous rocks by looking at their color. These minerals can be grouped as being either light colored or dark colored. Different groups of minerals form different kinds of rocks.

Devil's Tower is formed from dark-colored igneous rock called basalt (buh SAWLT). Another kind of igneous rock, called granite (GRAN iht), is light colored. Compare the kinds of minerals they are made of. Notice that the minerals in granite are mostly light colored. The minerals in basalt are mostly dark colored.

The Minerals in Granite

Potassium feldspar

Quartz

Other

Sodium feldspar

Biotite

The Minerals in Basalt

Pyroxene

Olivine

Plagioclase

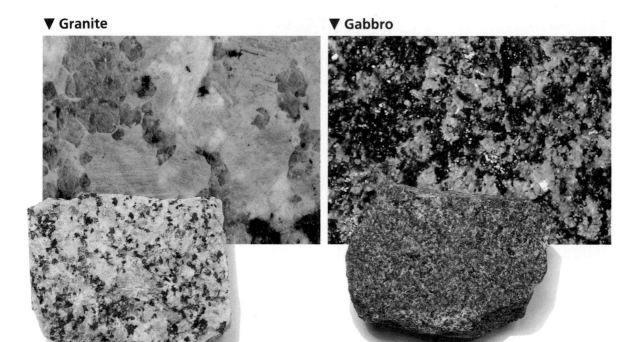

▼ Granite

▼ Gabbro

How are igneous rocks classified?

Igneous rocks can be classified by the kinds and sizes of their mineral crystals. Some igneous rocks have large crystals. Others have very tiny crystals. The size of the crystals depends on where the igneous rock formed.

Look at the pictures of the igneous rocks granite and gabbro (GAB roh). They form from hardened magma. You can see that the mineral crystals of gabbro and granite are large. Igneous rocks formed from magma have large mineral crystals. Large crystals form when rock cools slowly. The crystals have time to grow, or get larger.

Both gabbro and granite form below the earth's surface. But they are not the same kind of rock. Gabbro and granite are made of different minerals. How can you tell that their minerals are not the same?

▼ Rhyolite

▼ Basalt

Now look at the pictures of the rocks called rhyolite (RYE uh lyt) and basalt. Rhyolite and basalt form on the earth's surface. Notice that rhyolite is light colored like granite. Basalt is dark colored like gabbro.

Rhyolite is made from the same minerals as granite. And basalt is made of the same minerals as gabbro. But even though these rocks are made of the same minerals, they are not the same kind of rock. They are different because the mineral crystals in granite and gabbro are large. But the crystals in rhyolite and basalt are very small. You would need a microscope to see them!

Most igneous rocks that are formed from lava have very small mineral crystals. The crystals are small because the rock cools very fast. Melted rock cools faster on the earth's surface than it does under the ground. The crystals do not have time to grow as large.

◄ Pumice

Obsidian ►

Some lava cools so fast that there is no time for crystals to form at all. Rocks formed this way look like glass. The igneous rock called obsidian (ub SIHD ee un) is like this. Obsidian is usually black.

Other igneous rocks form when lava cools so quickly that gases are trapped in it. These gases form bubble holes in the rock. The rock called pumice, shown in the picture, forms this way.

Lesson Review

1. Compare the size of the crystals in a rock that formed on the earth's surface with those of a rock that formed beneath the surface.
2. How does a rock like granite form? How does a rock like rhyolite form?

Think! A rock has large crystals you can see. What does this tell you about its cooling time?

THINKING

Skills

Choosing materials for an investigation

When you do an activity, you decide which materials you will need. Suppose you want to put a plant in a new pot. You would get the new pot, soil, small rocks, gardening tools, and the plant. When you do an investigation in science, you need to decide what materials to use.

Practicing the skill

1. Imagine that you want to investigate how lava flows. You could make a model of a volcano and its lava.
2. A volcano has a cone shape. How could you make a cone for the volcano?
3. What can you find in a grocery store that would flow like lava?
4. What could you use to catch the flowing liquid?
5. What other materials could you use to make the model volcano realistic?

Thinking about the skill

What did you picture in your mind about a volcano that helped you select materials?

Applying the skill

Suppose you were in a place where lava had flowed several times. What materials could help you investigate whether the lava was the same in each flow?

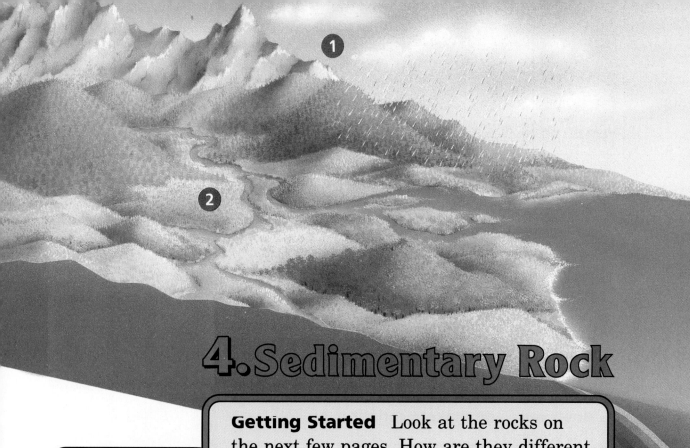

4. Sedimentary Rock

Getting Started Look at the rocks on the next few pages. How are they different from the igneous rocks you have seen?

Words to Know
sedimentary
 rocks
fossil

How are sedimentary rocks formed?

Rocks that form when sediments become cemented together are called **sedimentary rocks.** Many sedimentary rocks form from broken up rocks. (1) Water, wind, and ice break up rocks into sediments. (2) Often, streams move the sediments. (3) Then they are deposited, usually at the bottom of a lake or ocean.

Most sedimentary rocks form in layers such as the ones shown. Layers of sediments are deposited on top of one another. The top layers push down on the lower ones. This squeezes the sediments closer together until they harden. Tiny mineral crystals may form that cement the sediments together.

If you want to know more about fossils, read **If You Are a Hunter of Fossils,** page 374.

Sediments other than bits of rock can form sedimentary rocks. When water evaporates, minerals in the water are left behind. Sedimentary rocks can form from these minerals. The remains of plants and animals that have died can also form sedimentary rocks.

▼ Sedimentary rock

3

How are sedimentary rocks classified?

Sedimentary rocks can be classified by the way they form. One group of sedimentary rocks forms from bits of broken rock or minerals. These bits can be many different sizes. Sedimentary rocks made from bits of rock are named by the size of the bits.

Look at the rock called conglomerate (kun GLAHM ur ayt). It is made of bits of rock the size of gravel. The rounded, gravel-sized bits of rock are held together by tiny particles of minerals.

▲ Conglomerate

Explore

How does a conglomerate form?

Imagine you are walking on a pebble-covered beach. As you step into the waves, you feel your feet sink into soft mud. It is on this type of beach that the sedimentary rock conglomerate can form. The waves mix the pebbles with mud. The mud and pebbles dry and are covered by many layers of sediments. The layers squeezed the mud and pebbles so much that they have hardened into rock.

Materials

3 paper cups · spoon · pebbles · sand · 1/4 cup white glue · 1/4 cup water · pencil · sheet of waxed paper

Procedure

A. Add spoonfuls of sand and pebbles until one cup is half full. Mix well.

B. Use the pencil point to poke 5 or 6 small holes in the bottom of the cup.

C. In another cup, mix and stir the glue and water.

D. Pour the glue mixture into the cup of sand and pebbles. Let it drain back into the third cup as shown.

E. Repeat step D. Then set the cup of sand and pebbles on a piece of waxed paper and let it dry overnight.

F. Peel the paper cup. Draw the "rock" you have made.

D

Writing and Sharing Results and Conclusions

1. Of what is your "rock" made?

2. Why is the mud needed for conglomerate to form?

3. What kind of rock would form if there were no pebbles on the beach?

Another kind of sedimentary rock is called sandstone. It is made of mainly sand-sized bits of rock. The bits are usually made of the mineral quartz. Another sedimentary rock, shale, is made of bits that are so small you cannot see them. The materials in shale are usually made of quartz and clay minerals.

▲ Sandstone

▼ Layers of sandstone and shale

▲ Shale

▲ Gypsum

You know that not all sedimentary rocks are formed from bits of rock. One group of sedimentary rocks forms from minerals left by water that evaporates. Gypsum and rock salt form in this way.

Another group of sedimentary rocks forms from plant and animal material. Coal formed from plants that lived long ago. The plants died and were buried. As they became pressed together, they hardened.

▲ Coal

▼ Limestone

Look at the rock in the picture. Rocks like this were made of the shells and other remains of plants and animals that lived in the ocean. These rocks are called limestone.

How do fossils form in sedimentary rock?

Sedimentary rocks like limestone often contain fossils. A **fossil** is the remains or traces of living things preserved in rocks. Most fossils are found in sedimentary rocks. The way sedimentary rocks form helps to save the remains of living things.

When an animal dies, its soft parts such as skin often are destroyed. But the hard parts of living things can be buried in sediment. These hard parts include shells, bones, or teeth. The hard parts can be preserved in the rock and become fossils.

▼ Dinosaur bones

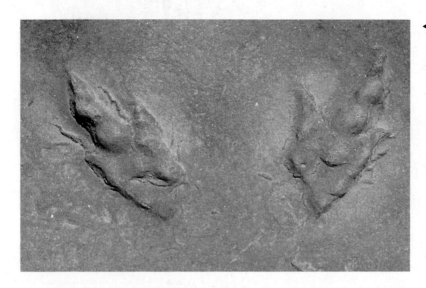

◀ Dinosaur footprints

Sometimes just a print of a plant or animal remains in the rock. Look at the fossil print of the fish. Sometimes plants or animals leave marks in the sediment. These marks become preserved in the rock and are also fossils. Dinosaur footprints are an example of this type of fossil.

▲ Fossil print of a fish

The fossil in the picture below formed when sediments were pressed around the leaf of a plant. Later the leaf was destroyed. But its print remained in the sediment. Sediment filled the leaf print and hardened. The hardened sediment made a fossil that looks like the original leaf!

Lesson Review

1. What is a fossil?
2. How are sedimentary rocks that form from bits of rock named?
3. Describe the particles that make up sandstone, limestone, and shale.

Think! Why would you probably not find fossils in igneous rock?

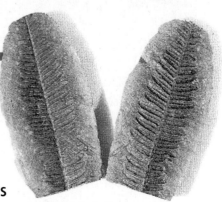

▲ Plant fossil

309

Can sound help us "see" underground?

How big was the biggest dinosaur? It may have been 33 m (about 110 ft) long. That is about as long as three big buses. Most likely, it was as tall as a five-story building. Scientists are now studying the bones of this giant dinosaur. They call it *Seismosaurus,* or "earth shaker."

How was Seismosaurus found? A hiker was in the mountains of New Mexico. He found some bones of Seismosaurus. Scientists then dug out some of the bones. But most are still buried. They are under meters of soil and rock.

Scientists often need years to get bones out of the ground. They cannot see where all the bones are. They must dig up a big area very carefully. But there is a new process that can speed up the job. Scientists can now use sound waves to find buried objects.

Sound moves at different speeds through different kinds of matter. For example, sound moves through fossil bones at 3,800 m (12,500 ft) per second. It moves through soil much more slowly.

310

STS

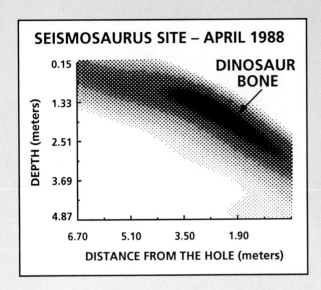

SEISMOSAURUS SITE – APRIL 1988

DINOSAUR BONE

DEPTH (meters)

0.15
1.33
2.51
3.69
4.87

6.70   5.10   3.50   1.90

DISTANCE FROM THE HOLE (meters)

To find buried objects, scientists put microphones into holes in the ground. Then they fire a special sound gun into the ground. Computers record how long the gun sound takes to reach each microphone. Scientists can then tell what kinds of matter the sound has passed through. The computer draws a map of the underground area, showing where bones and other buried objects are.

Critical thinking

1. Explain how sound waves make digging up dinosaur bones easier and faster.
2. Why might it be important to dig up fossils quickly?

Using what you learned

Scientists often must use clues to learn about things they cannot see. Write a scientific riddle for a classmate to solve. Think of an event that might happen on or under the earth's surface. Choose five words that describe the event. The words should not form a sentence. Trade riddles with a classmate and solve each other's riddle.

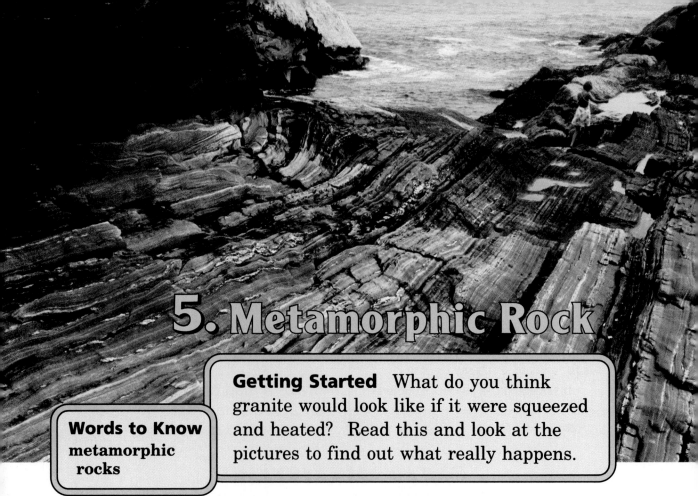

5. Metamorphic Rock

Getting Started What do you think granite would look like if it were squeezed and heated? Read this and look at the pictures to find out what really happens.

Words to Know
metamorphic rocks

What is a metamorphic rock?

Metamorphic rocks form from rocks that are changed by heat and pressure inside the earth. Sedimentary, igneous, or other metamorphic rocks can be changed to form new metamorphic rocks. The heat and pressure change the rocks but do not melt them. They remain solid. What kind of rock would form if the rocks melted and cooled?

Heat and pressure can change the size and the shape of the mineral crystals. They can also change the minerals in the original rock to other minerals. The picture on page 313 shows some metamorphic rock that was formed when the minerals in granite were changed by heat and pressure.

granite

gneiss

shale

slate

schist

When heat and pressure act on the igneous rock *granite,* it can be changed to a metamorphic rock called gneiss (nys). What differences do you see between the granite and the gneiss?

Look at the picture of the sedimentary rock *shale.* Shale can be changed to the metamorphic rock called slate. This happens when heat and pressure in the earth act on shale.

Slate breaks into smooth, thin slabs. Table tops and sidewalks can be made from slate. Even though slate is already a metamorphic rock, it can be changed more by heat and pressure. It forms another metamorphic rock called schist (shihst).

limestone

marble

sandstone

quartzite

The sedimentary rock *limestone* can be changed to the metamorphic rock called marble. Marble is often used to make buildings and statues. The sedimentary rock *sandstone* is changed to the metamorphic rock called quartzite. The surface of quartzite looks like sugar. The quartz particles in this rock have been pushed tightly together.

Lesson Review

1. Give three examples of a metamorphic rock and the rock that each forms from.
2. What metamorphic rock looks like granite with thin lines of black minerals?
3. What is the name of the rock that is made of the mineral quartz and looks like sugar?

Think! You know that metamorphic rocks can form from all three types of rocks. How could a sedimentary or igneous rock form from metamorphic rock?

Chapter Connections

Make a copy of this organizer, but leave out some of the words and phrases. Exchange papers with a classmate. Fill in the missing words.

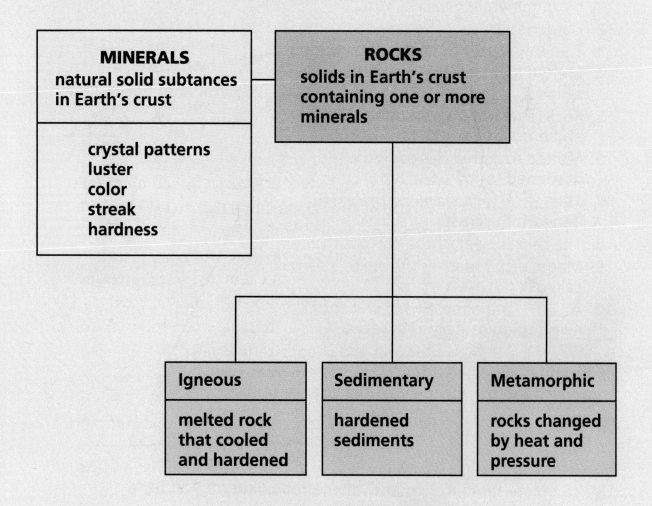

MINERALS
natural solid subtances in Earth's crust

crystal patterns
luster
color
streak
hardness

ROCKS
solids in Earth's crust containing one or more minerals

Igneous	Sedimentary	Metamorphic
melted rock that cooled and hardened	hardened sediments	rocks changed by heat and pressure

Writing About Science • Research

Gemstones and gems used in jewelry are really minerals that have been cut and polished in special ways. Read about how these stones are mined and cut. Write a paragraph about what you learned.

Chapter 9 Review

Science Terms

A. Write the letter of the term that best matches the definition.

1. A _____ is a solid that is made of one or more minerals.
2. Hardened layers of sediments form _____.
3. The outer layer of the earth is the _____.
4. Melted rock below the earth's surface is called _____.
5. Rocks that have been changed by heat and pressure form _____.
6. Melted rock that has cooled and hardened forms _____.
7. The _____ is the layer of the earth beneath the crust.
8. The center layer of the earth is the _____.
9. Magma that reaches the earth's surface is called _____.
10. A _____ is the remains or traces of a living thing preserved in rocks.

a. core
b. crust
c. fossil
d. igneous rocks
e. lava
f. magma
g. mantle
h. metamorphic rocks
i. rock
j. sedimentary rocks

B. Write a paragraph that uses the science terms listed below. The sentences must show that you understand the meaning of the science terms.

hardness   luster   mineral   streak

Science Ideas

Use complete sentences to answer the following.

1. Name three minerals and their uses.
2. Describe the different properties that can be used to identify a mineral.
3. What are the three main layers of the earth?
4. How are rocks classified? What are the three major groups of rocks?

5. Describe the two ways igneous rock can form.
6. You have three kinds of sedimentary rocks made of sediments. How would you classify them?
7. How are metamorphic rocks formed?

Applying Science Ideas

Use complete sentences to answer the following.

1. Mineral A scratches apatite but can be scratched by quartz. Mineral B can be scratched by both apatite and quartz. Which mineral is softer, A or B?
2. The two rocks shown here are igneous rocks. Identify each as one of the following: gabbro, granite, rhyolite, or basalt. Explain your choice.

3. The formation of the three types of rocks from one another can be described as a cycle. Make a chart or drawing that illustrates this concept.
4. Copy the chart below. Then fill in the answers for each of the minerals.

Rock Name	Kind of Rock	Size of particles or crystals	Kinds of particles or crystals
Granite			
Marble			
Sandstone			

5. How might the method used to find seismosaurus be used to help clean up buried toxic waste more quickly?

Using Science Skills

Imagine you want to know what happens to lava that flows into the ocean. What materials would help you to find the answer to this problem?

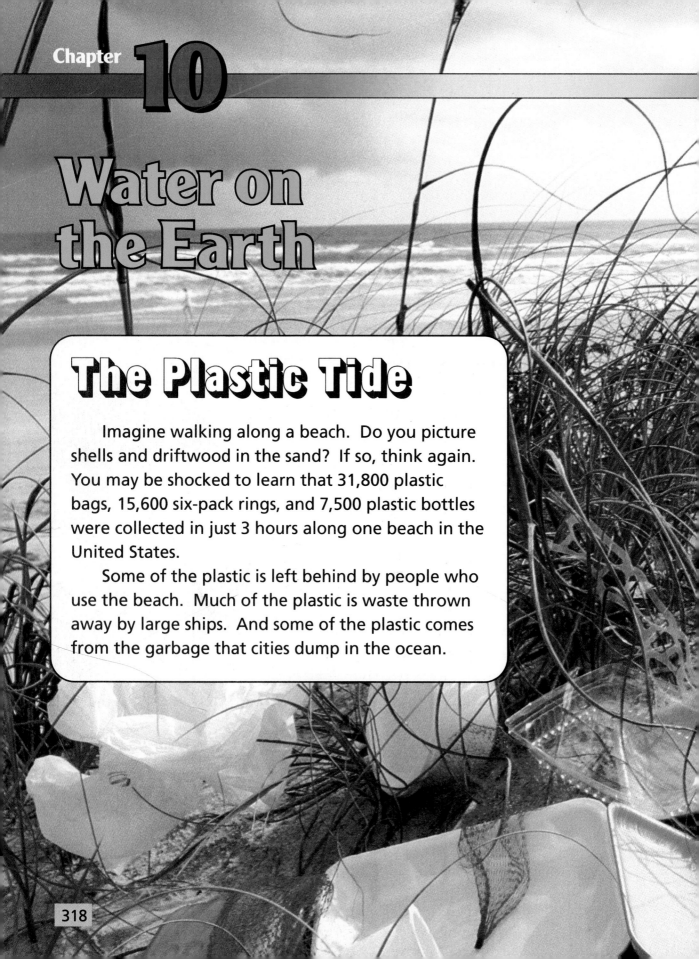

10

Water on the Earth

The Plastic Tide

Imagine walking along a beach. Do you picture shells and driftwood in the sand? If so, think again. You may be shocked to learn that 31,800 plastic bags, 15,600 six-pack rings, and 7,500 plastic bottles were collected in just 3 hours along one beach in the United States.

Some of the plastic is left behind by people who use the beach. Much of the plastic is waste thrown away by large ships. And some of the plastic comes from the garbage that cities dump in the ocean.

Do you think this plastic garbage is ugly? It is much worse than that. The plastic that is dumped in the ocean is dangerous to living things. Gulls and other sea birds have been choked by the plastic rings from six-packs of soft drinks. The birds dive into the water to get food. As they dive, they can get caught in the rings.

Sea turtles eat jellyfish in the water. Many of the turtles have eaten plastic bags. Scientists think that to a turtle, the bags look like jellyfish. The bags block the turtle's digestive system. Often this kills the turtle.

Plastics in garbage are a problem for many reasons. One reason is that people use so many things made of plastic. Most of these things are made to be thrown away after being used just once.

Throwing away this much of anything would be a problem. But plastics do not rot, or break down. They do not dissolve in the water. They just drift from place to place.

Scientists are looking for ways to make plastics that will break down. Some new plastics are made of materials that will rot. Other plastics break down when they are in the sunlight. Many kinds of plastic can be recycled. This plastic is melted down and used again. It does not get dumped in the garbage.

You can help, too. Try to use less plastic. Also be aware of what you throw away. Before you throw away the plastic rings from a six-pack of soft drinks, cut through the rings. Also tear plastic bags into small pieces.

Discover

How can you reduce the number of plastic items you throw away?

Materials   pencil · paper

Procedure

For five days keep a record of every plastic item you use and then throw away. Study your list. What plastic items do you use most often?

Think of a plan to reduce by one half the number of plastic items you throw away. Test your plan. How did you do? Can you reduce the new amount by one half?

In this chapter you will learn about some other problems caused by garbage in the ocean. You will also discover how water moves in the ocean. You will study the water in lakes and ponds, too. Maybe you will think of some new ways to keep Earth's water clean!

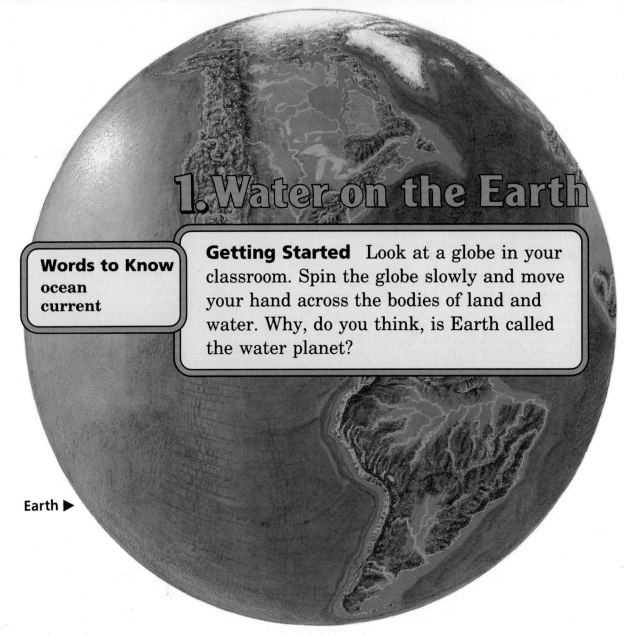

1. Water on the Earth

Earth ▶

Words to Know
ocean
current

Getting Started Look at a globe in your classroom. Spin the globe slowly and move your hand across the bodies of land and water. Why, do you think, is Earth called the water planet?

Where is water on the earth?

Look at the drawing and at circle graph *A* on this page. They show that water covers almost three fourths of the earth's surface. Now look at circle graph *B*. Notice that water on the earth is either fresh water or salt water. How much of circle graph *B* is fresh water? The water you drink is fresh water. So is the water that is used for bathing, growing crops, and cooking food.

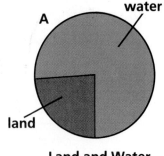

A

water

land

Land and Water on the Earth

Look again at circle graph *B*. How much of the circle is salt water? Have you ever swallowed salt water? If so, you know it is too salty to drink. Many kinds of salts are found in salt water. But most of the salt is the kind you use on food.

Where is salt water found?

Most salt water is found in oceans. An **ocean** is a large body of salt water. On the map, find the four main oceans. They are the Pacific, Atlantic, Indian, and Arctic oceans. Notice that the Pacific is the largest ocean. Half the water in the oceans is in the Pacific Ocean. Which ocean is the smallest?

Move your finger along the map from one ocean to another. As you can see, the oceans are connected. They are really parts of one large body of water.

Water on the Earth

The Four Main Oceans

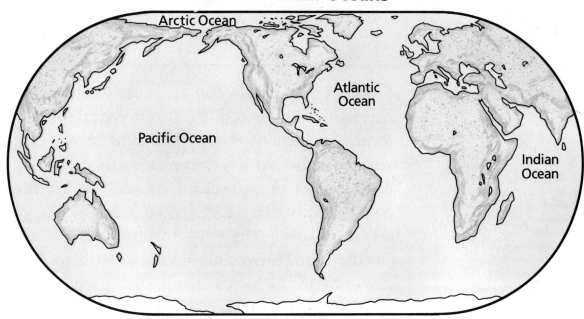

How does ocean water move?

Since oceans are connected, water can flow from one ocean to another. Water can be carried from one place to another by a current (KUR unt). A **current** is a large river of water that moves through a body of water. In the oceans, some currents flow near the surface. Other currents move through the deep ocean.

The Main Ocean Currents

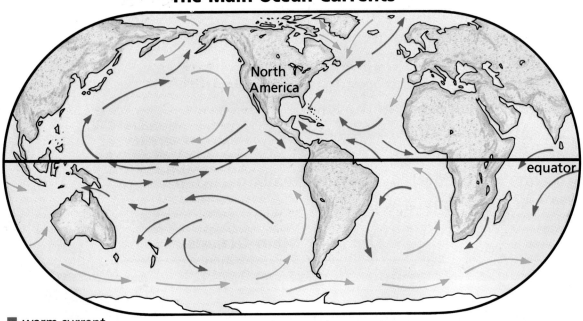

■ warm current
■ cold current

The map shows the main ocean surface currents of the world. These currents are formed mainly by winds that blow across the surface of the water. Some currents carry warm water away from the equator toward the North and South poles. Other currents carry cold water from the poles toward the equator. On the map, warm currents are red, and cold currents are blue. What types of currents affect the coasts of North America?

ACTIVITY

Explore Together

What happens when warm water meets cold water?

Materials

Organizer

aquarium · cold water · small jar with lid · hot water · blue food coloring

Procedure

Manager

A. Fill an aquarium with cold water.

Investigator

B. Fill a small jar with hot water. Then add several drops of blue food coloring to the water. Place the lid on the jar, but do not tighten it.

Investigator

C. Hold your thumb on the lid to keep it in place. Then lower the jar to the bottom of the aquarium.

Group, Recorder

1. Predict what will happen to the hot water if the lid is removed.

Investigator

D. While holding the jar on the bottom, use your thumb to push the lid from the jar.

Group

E. Observe what happens to the hot water.

Recorder

2. Make a drawing to show what happens when the hot water meets the cold water.

Writing and Sharing Results and Conclusions

Group, Recorder

1. What happens when warm water meets cold water?

2. The Gulf Stream is a warm current. Predict what happens when the Gulf Stream meets a cold current.

Reporter

3. How do your results and conclusions compare with those of your classmates?

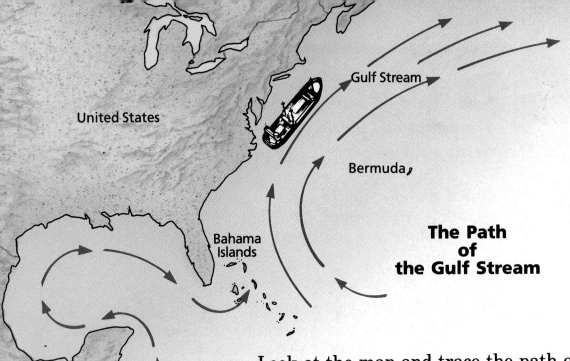

United States

Gulf Stream

Bermuda

Bahama
Islands

**The Path
of
the Gulf Stream**

Look at the map and trace the path of the current called the Gulf Stream. The Gulf Stream carries warm water north from the equator toward the east coast of the United States. There is 100 times more water in the Gulf Stream than in all the rivers on land.

The Gulf Stream is one of the strongest currents. Large ships like this tanker can be carried great distances by the Gulf Stream. Do you think the Gulf Stream would also carry plastic wastes from one part of the world to another? Explain your answer.

Lesson Review

1. How much of the earth is covered by water?
2. Where is most salt water found?
3. Name the four main oceans.
4. In which direction do warm currents move? In which direction do cold currents move?

Think! Suppose Christopher Columbus had sailed into the Gulf Stream near the Bahama Islands. Where might the Gulf Stream have carried his ships?

**Life Science
CONNECTION**

Use reference books to find out about the different life zones in the ocean. Write a report about the plants and animals in one life zone.

THINKING

Skills

Recording data on a graph

Sometimes you hear how high the temperature was on a certain day. You can compare that temperature to the high temperatures on other days. You can use a graph to compare the temperatures.

Practicing the skill

Gulf Coast Water Temperature	
Date	Temperature (°C)
February 1	17
April 1	19
June 1	20
August 1	23

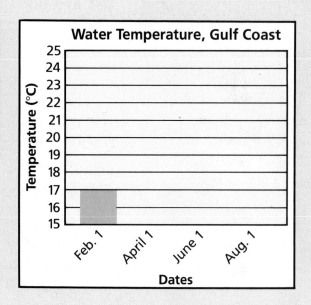

1. Study the table and graph. Both show that the temperature on February 1 was 17°C.

2. Copy the bar graph. Record the data for April 1, June 1, and August 1 on your graph.

Thinking about the skill

How did you know the height of the bar to draw for August 1?

Applying the skill

Average Temperature on a Tropical Island	
Month	Temperature (°C)
January	27
April	28
July	29
October	29

Construct a bar graph using the data from the table above.

2. Resources from the Ocean

Words to Know
resources
nodules
pollution

Getting Started Have you ever eaten seafood? Make a list of all the kinds of seafood you know. Which foods on your list are not fish?

▲ Living things in the ocean

▼ Fish and fish products

How are the oceans important to people?

The oceans provide people with many **resources** (ree SOR sez), or useful materials. Some ocean resources are food, minerals, water, and oil and natural gas.

Many kinds of fish are food for people, farm animals, and pets. Some fish and fish products are shown here. Besides fish, other ocean animals are used as food. People eat shellfish such as clams, oysters, shrimps, and crabs. People also eat octopuses and squids. Which of these foods do you eat?

Ocean plants are also used as food. Some people eat fresh or cooked seaweeds. Seaweeds are also used to make jellylike materials. These materials help make the products shown here thick and creamy. Which ones did you know had seaweeds in them?

People also farm the oceans for food. Sea farmers raise ocean plants and animals in shallow water near the shore. In Japan, seaweed is grown like a crop. In the United States, salmon and other fish are raised on sea farms like the one shown here. Shellfish such as clams, shrimps, and lobsters are also grown on sea farms in the United States. Someday large parts of the ocean may be fenced in and used to raise fish and shellfish.

▼ Products containing seaweed thickeners

▼ Chinook salmon farm

Where are minerals found in the oceans?

▲ Nodules on the ocean floor

Many minerals are found in the oceans. Minerals are natural solids found in the earth. Some minerals are found in small black lumps called **nodules** (NAHJ oolz) on the ocean floor. Nodules are about the size of small potatoes. The nodules shown here contain a metal called manganese (MAN gan ese). Manganese is used to make steel. What things in your school are made of steel?

Other minerals are salts dissolved, or mixed, in the water. Salts can be separated from ocean water by a process called de-salination (dee sal un NAY shun). This process is useful for two reasons. First, it removes salts from the water. Then the salts can be used to make table salt, medicines, and other products. Second, it makes fresh drinking water. Factories like the one shown here produce fresh water from ocean water.

▼ Desalination plant

Problem Solving
A Quicker Picker-Upper

Scientists are always trying to find better ways to clean up an oil spill. In the picture a scientist is using chicken feathers to soak up oil.

How do scientists try to solve the problem of removing oil from an ocean? First, they test new methods in a laboratory. Think about ways that you might try to solve this problem.

How can oil be removed from the surface of salt water?

Pour 60 mL cooking oil into a pan of salt water. Experiment to find ways to remove the oil from the salt water. Try to leave as much water in the pan as possible. Which method worked fastest? Do you think your methods would work on a large body of water like an ocean? Do you think your methods might harm ocean life? Explain your answers.

Where are oil and natural gas found?

Resources are also found under the oceans. Huge pools of oil and natural gas lie in rock sediments below the ocean floor. Most of this oil and gas is near the shore. It is reached by drilling wells through the rocks.

▲ Offshore oil well

This offshore well drills deep into the sediments and rock to reach the oil or gas. Then the oil or gas is brought to the surface in pipes. Ships carry the oil and gas to land. Underwater pipes also transport the oil and gas. What are some ways people use oil and gas?

What causes ocean pollution?

The oceans also have unwanted materials. Garbage is dumped into the oceans by barges like the one shown here. Sewage and chemical wastes from factories are also dumped into the oceans.

Dumping wastes into the oceans causes pollution (puh LOO shun). **Pollution** is the presence of harmful materials in water. Scientists know that even small amounts of pollution can harm ocean life. Plants do not grow well in polluted water. Animals become sick. People who eat seafood from polluted water can also become sick.

▼ Barge carrying garbage

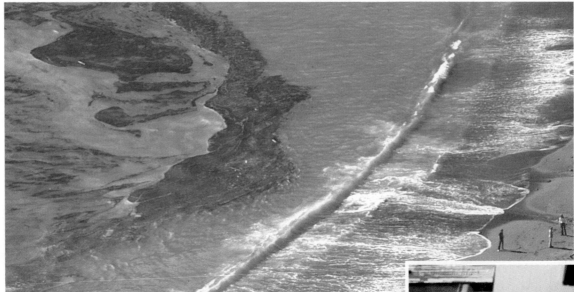

▲ Beach polluted by oil from a tanker accident

Oil spills are another cause of ocean pollution. Huge ships carry oil across the oceans. Sometimes the tanks in these ships leak oil into the ocean. Offshore wells also cause oil spills. As you can see in the picture, beaches are damaged by oil spills. Ocean plants and animals are also harmed. Oil-covered seabirds cannot fly or float. How are this bird's feathers being cleaned?

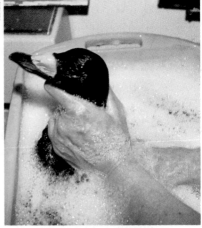

▲ Bird rescued from oil spill

Lesson Review

1. List two resources found in the oceans.
2. How are the oceans farmed?
3. What are nodules?
4. How can fresh water be obtained from the oceans?
5. Name two kinds of wastes that pollute the oceans.

Think! Do you think the nations of the world should agree to stop dumping wastes into the oceans? Give reasons for your answer.

Should ocean dumping be stopped?

Did you know that each year Americans throw out 220 million tons of garbage? Suppose this garbage was piled on huge barges, like the ones shown here. Then imagine the barges forming a line. The line of barges would stretch across the ocean from New York to England!

Now think of the millions of tons of garbage other countries throw out. Suppose this garbage was piled on barges. Think how long the line of barges would be then!

and Society

STS

Most garbage ends up in dumps called landfills. Food, plastic, metal, glass, and paper are buried in these huge pits. Factories leave chemicals there also. Landfills are filling up all over the world. Many countries have no space for new landfills. In our country, half of our states will run out of land-fill space by the year 2000.

Many countries with little space dump their wastes in the oceans. Most wastes sink. People do not see them pile up. But wastes are piling up in parts of the oceans. Ocean currents can carry them to other parts of the ocean. Some wastes are start-ing to wash up on beaches all over the world.

Scientists say we have reason to worry. Some wastes contain poisons or germs. These wastes can harm people who swim in the ocean. They also poi-son fish and shellfish that live in the oceans. People who eat sick or poisoned fish may get sick, too.

Critical thinking

1. What might happen if people keep dumping wastes in the oceans?
2. What are some ways to prevent harmful wastes from piling up in the oceans?

Using what you learned

1. Persuade a friend that ocean dumping is a dangerous way to get rid of garbage.
2. Classify the garbage you or your family throw out in one day. Then think of ways to cut down on the amounts of paper, plastics, and metal you throw out.

3. Lakes and Ponds

Words to Know
lake
pond
glacier

Getting Started Did you drink from a water fountain in your school today? Where do you think your drinking water comes from? Imagine if one day there was not enough water to drink.

What are lakes and ponds?

You learned that most of the fresh water on the earth is found on land. Some of this water is found in lakes and ponds. Where else is fresh water found on land?

A **lake** is a large body of water surrounded by land. Most lakes contain fresh water. But some, like the Great Salt Lake, have salty water. As you can see in the drawing, a pond is really a small lake. A **pond** is a small, shallow body of water surrounded by land.

▼ Plants and animals of a pond

How are lakes and ponds important?

Lakes and ponds are important to people. The water you drink may come from lakes. So may the water used to grow your food. What are some other ways people use lakes and ponds?

Lakes and ponds are also the home for many kinds of living things. Fish such as bass and perch live in the water. Ducks and geese build nests nearby. What other animals might live in or near a lake?

Many plants grow along the edges of lakes and ponds. Find the cattails in the drawing. Their flowers are long, brown, and furry. Why is *cattail* a good name?

Plants also grow on top of the water. Water lilies are floating plants. Perhaps you have seen their white or pink flowers and round flat leaves on a pond. Simple plants called algae (AL jee) also float on the water. One kind of algae is pond scum. Pond scum plants look like long green threads.

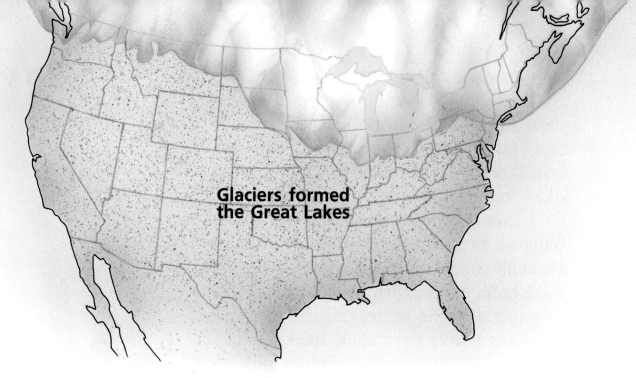

Glaciers formed
the Great Lakes

How are lakes and ponds formed?

Lakes and ponds are formed in several ways. Many lakes and ponds were formed by glaciers (GLAY shurz). A **glacier** is a huge body of slow-moving ice. Thousands of years ago, glaciers covered large parts of North America. The Great Lakes were formed when glaciers moved back and forth across the land. The glaciers left deep, hollow spaces in the land. When the glaciers melted, water filled the spaces and formed the lakes.

Lakes and ponds also are formed when a river or stream is blocked. Soil on hillsides can loosen and slide into a river. This soil can form a dam across a river. The dam blocks the flow of the river and forms a lake.

Other lakes are made when people build dams across rivers. The lake formed by this dam is called a reservoir (REZ ur vwahr). Reservoirs store water for farming and for drinking.

▼ Glen Canyon Dam
and Reservoir—
Lake Powell, Arizona

How are lakes and ponds harmed?

Lakes and ponds can be harmed by pollution. One kind of pollution is caused by certain wastes from cities and farms. The wastes from cities are laundry detergents (dee TUR junts) that wash down drains. The farm wastes are raw materials called fertilizers (FUR tuh lye zurz). When it rains, fertilizers wash from the soil into rivers and streams.

Fertilizers and detergents are carried into lakes by rivers and streams. These wastes contain nutrients (NOO tree unts). Nutrients are used by algae and other plants in the water.

In this polluted lake, nutrients cause algae to grow very fast. As the algae die, they start to decay. The decay of the dead algae takes oxygen from the water. Oxygen is needed by fish for breathing. As the oxygen is used up, fish start to die.

▼ Green algae growing in a lake

▲ Adirondack lake
 polluted by acid
 rain

A second kind of pollution is caused by acid rain. When coal and oil are burned, gases enter the air. These gases mix with rain to form acid rain. Acid rain has harmful chemicals that wash into lakes. These chemicals kill fish and other living things. The water in this lake looks clean and clear. But no fish live there. The water has been polluted by acid rain.

Lesson Review ━━━━━━

1. How are lakes and ponds important to people and other living things?
2. List two ways that lakes and ponds are formed.
3. How did glaciers form the Great Lakes?
4. List two ways that lakes become polluted.

Think! Why would it take a shorter time to pollute a pond than to pollute a lake?

Life Science
CONNECTION

What are some of the living parts of a pond ecosystem? What are some of the nonliving parts?

340

Chapter Connections

Say a key word from the graphic organizer to a partner. Have your partner list all the words and phrases from the chapter that go with your key word. Compare the list with the graphic organizer.

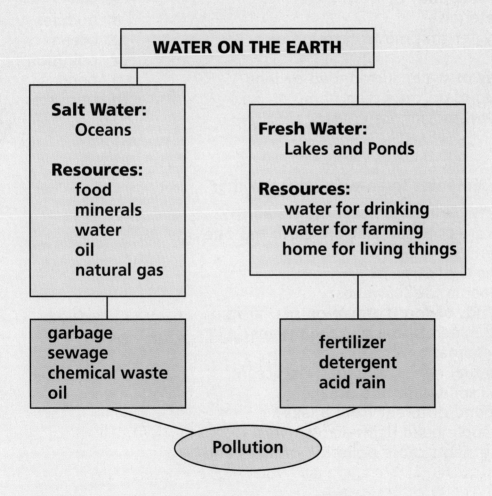

WATER ON THE EARTH

Salt Water:
   Oceans

Resources:
   food
   minerals
   water
   oil
   natural gas

garbage
sewage
chemical waste
oil

Fresh Water:
   Lakes and Ponds

Resources:
   water for drinking
   water for farming
   home for living things

fertilizer
detergent
acid rain

Pollution

Writing About Science • Describe

Write about a pond or lake in your area. What living things are found there? Is pollution a problem? Write a paragraph about the pond or lake.

Science Terms

Write the letter of the term that best matches the definition.

1. Presence of harmful materials in water
2. Large body of salt water
3. Small, shallow body of fresh water
4. Useful materials
5. River of water that moves through an ocean
6. Large body of water surrounded by land
7. Mineral lumps on the ocean floor
8. Body of slow-moving ice

a. current
b. glacier
c. lake
d. nodules
e. ocean
f. pollution
g. pond
h. resources

Science Ideas

Use complete sentences to answer the following.

1. Name the two kinds of water on the earth.
2. Why is it correct to say that the earth has one large ocean?
3. What is the Gulf Stream?
4. How do people use seaweeds?
5. List two kinds of foods grown on sea farms.
6. Where are minerals found in the oceans?
7. What is desalination?
8. Name two fuel resources under the oceans.
9. How do oil spills harm the oceans?
10. How is a pond different from a lake?
11. Why do people build dams across rivers?
12. How do nutrients cause pollution of lakes and ponds?

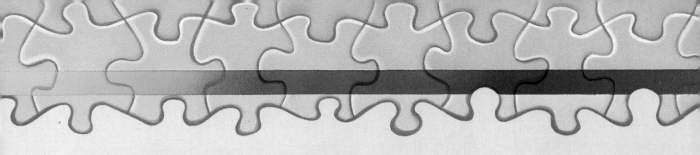

Applying Science Ideas

Use complete sentences to answer the following.

1. Why does polluting one ocean pollute them all?
2. Think of a plan for making sure people have enough fresh water to drink in the future.
3. Scientists try to predict whether an oil spill will wash up on any beaches before it can be cleaned up. Why do you think they study the path, speed, and strength of the currents near the spill?
4. Acid rain causes pollution of ocean water near the shores. How can acid rain pollution harm ocean resources?
5. Name one way that people can be harmed by ocean dumping.

Using Science Skills

The table shows how easily 35 lakes in California can be harmed by acid rain. Use the data from this table to construct a bar graph. Write the four groups of lakes along the bottom. Write the number of lakes up the left-hand side.

How Easily 35 Lakes Can Be Harmed By Acid Rain	
Group	Number of Lakes
Very easily harmed	14
Easily harmed	11
Less easily harmed	8
Least easily harmed	2

The Atmosphere

High-Rise Winds

"Good morning! The weather in the city today will be sunny. Winds will be calm and from the south. For those of you downtown, however, watch out for wind gusts near sky-scrapers. Be careful when turning corners and leaving buildings."

Can you imagine such a forecast? People who live in cities with skyscrapers can! In January 1982 a New York City worker was seriously hurt when a gust of wind blew her into a concrete planter. Over 6 years ago in Boston, Massachusetts, a blast of wind turned over a mail truck. Most people would blame the weather for these accidents. But engineers have found that, often, buildings are to blame.

Buildings block the wind. If buildings are all the same height, the wind blows over them. But if one building is much taller than others, it can direct gusts of wind toward the ground. These strong gusts of wind are called downwashes.

The shape of a building affects the downwash it causes. Some skyscrapers are built in steps, like a wedding cake. These buildings do not have strong downwashes. A downwash that starts at the top of such a building hits the roof of a wider part below. This weakens the downwash.

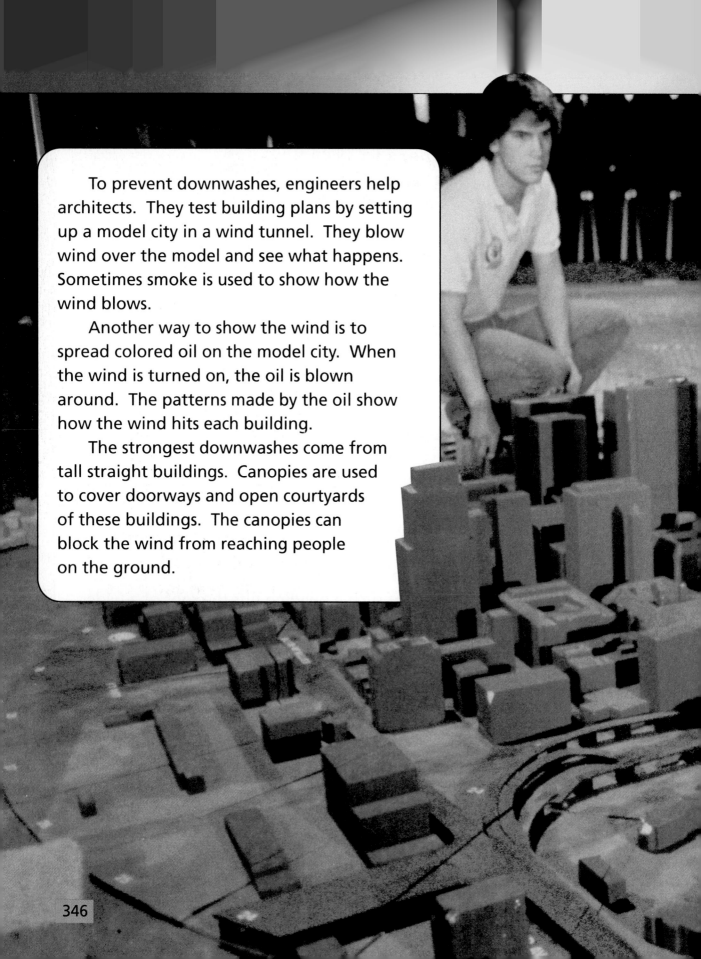

To prevent downwashes, engineers help architects. They test building plans by setting up a model city in a wind tunnel. They blow wind over the model and see what happens. Sometimes smoke is used to show how the wind blows.

Another way to show the wind is to spread colored oil on the model city. When the wind is turned on, the oil is blown around. The patterns made by the oil show how the wind hits each building.

The strongest downwashes come from tall straight buildings. Canopies are used to cover doorways and open courtyards of these buildings. The canopies can block the wind from reaching people on the ground.

Discover

What happens to buildings when the wind blows on them?

Materials   empty boxes of all sizes · table fan

Procedure

    Use large and small boxes as models of buildings. Then use a fan to test what happens when wind blows from different directions. Why is it important to keep the fan's distance from the models the same for each test? Which shapes of models were affected most by wind? How did the height of the models make a difference?

In this chapter you will discover what causes wind and other weather conditions. You will also learn about the atmosphere.

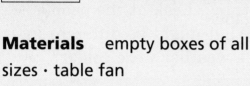

1. Heating the Atmosphere

Words to Know
atmosphere
radiation

Getting Started Each morning, many people find out how hot or cold it is outside. This information helps them to choose their clothing. Look at the people in the picture. What might be different in the picture if the weather were colder?

What heats the atmosphere?

The earth is surrounded by a thick blanket of air called the **atmosphere.** The atmosphere is made of gases, water, and small solid particles such as dust. The condition of the atmosphere at a certain place and time is called weather. One weather condition that affects your life every day is the temperature of the air. Make a list of the things you do differently on hot days and on cold days.

▼ Children outside on an autumn day

The atmosphere is heated by radiation from the sun. **Radiation** is energy that travels through space in the form of waves. Light energy is a kind of radiation that you can see. There are other kinds of radiation that you cannot see.

Radiation from the sun travels in waves through space to the earth. Look at the picture to see what happens to the radiation that reaches the earth. You can see that about half of the radiation is absorbed by the earth's surface. The absorbed radiation is changed to heat and warms the ground.

All warm objects give off heat. So the warmed ground gives off heat. Gases in the atmosphere absorb the heat from the ground. The absorbed heat warms the atmosphere.

▼ Radiation absorbed and reflected by the earth's surface

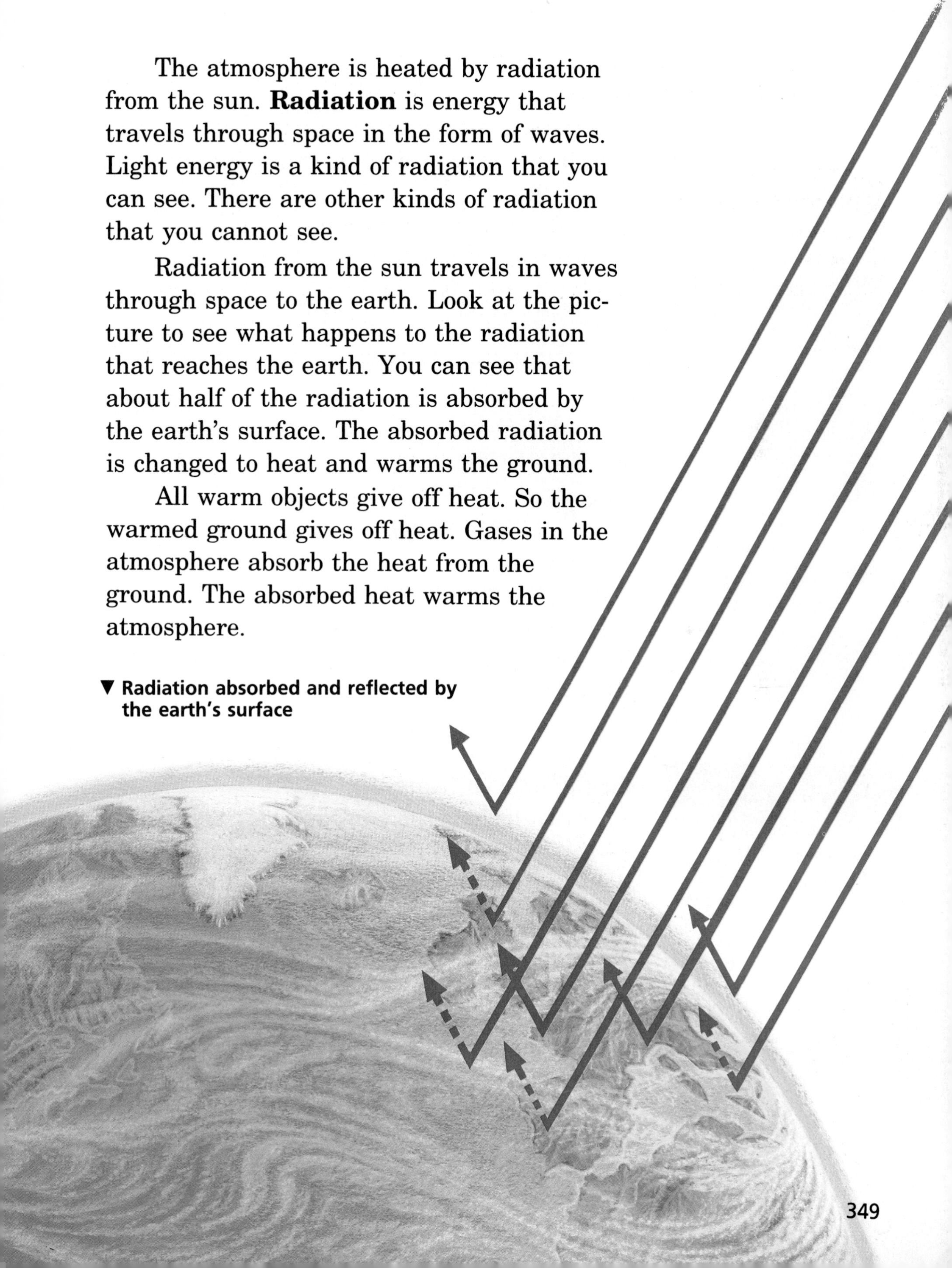

equator

▼ South America

▲ Sun's rays striking at almost no slant

What causes uneven heating of the atmosphere?

The earth's surface is not heated evenly. So the earth's atmosphere is not heated evenly. The angle at which the sun's rays strike the earth's surface is the main reason for the uneven heating.

Look at how the sun's rays strike the earth near the equator. The sun's rays strike the earth's surface at almost no angle. These rays heat the surface a great deal. So the air near the equator is usually very warm.

Now look at how the sun's rays strike the earth closer to the poles. Closer to the poles, the sun's rays strike the earth's surface at an angle. These slanted rays heat the earth's surface less than direct rays. How will this affect the air temperature?

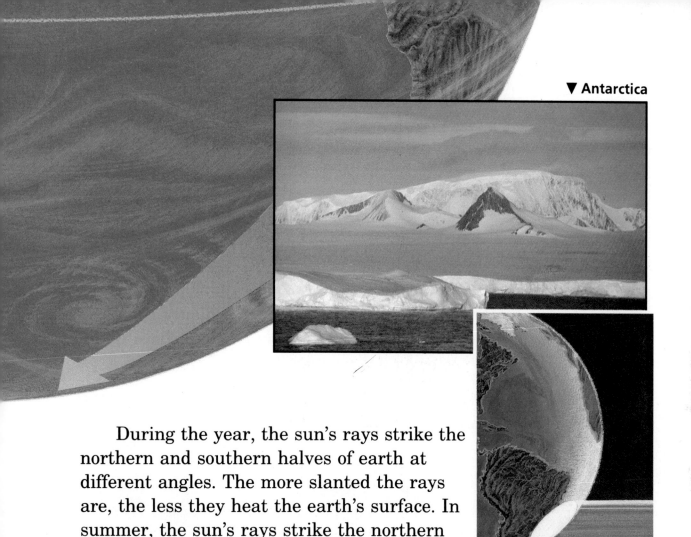

▲ Sun's rays striking at an angle

During the year, the sun's rays strike the northern and southern halves of earth at different angles. The more slanted the rays are, the less they heat the earth's surface. In summer, the sun's rays strike the northern half of the earth with very little angle. So the air is warmed the most. In winter, the sun's rays strike the northern half at the greatest angle. So the air is warmed the least.

There are other reasons for the uneven heating of the earth's surface. One reason is that some materials absorb radiation more quickly. These materials become warmer than do others. The air above these warmer materials is heated more. Concrete and most buildings absorb radiation quickly. Grassy areas, forests, and farmland absorb radiation more slowly. Dark-colored material absorbs radiation faster than light-colored material.

Land absorbs radiation faster than does water. So land will become warmer than water when they both absorb radiation. This is why the air near a body of water is often cooler than the air farther from the water.

This satellite photo shows that different surfaces on the earth give off different amounts of heat. The blue areas are the coolest. The red areas are warmer than the blue. The white areas are the warmest. What difference do you see in the color of the water and most of the farmland? What does this color difference mean?

▼ **Heat given off by different surfaces**

Lesson Review

1. How is the earth's atmosphere warmed?
2. What is the main reason for the uneven heating of the atmosphere?
3. How does the speed at which different materials absorb radiation affect air temperature?

Think! Why do you think it is better to exercise outdoors in light-colored clothes than in dark-colored clothes?

Life Science
CONNECTION

Find out about the greenhouse effect. Write a report about how living things are affected by the greenhouse effect.

THINKING

Skills

Setting up and conducting an experiment

Some questions can be answered by comparing how things happen. You can set up an experiment so that two sets of materials can be compared. The sets are the same except for one change that you make. You can compare the sets to see how the change affects what happens.

Practicing the skill

1. How does covering a beaker affect the air temperature in the beaker? You can do an experiment to find out.

2. Use two beakers. Put a thermometer into each beaker.

3. Put each beaker into a plastic bag. Change one set of materials by closing the bag. Leave the other bag open.

4. Place the beakers in sunlight. Record the temperature in each beaker every minute for 5 minutes. Compare the temperatures of the two beakers. Keep recording for several more minutes.

Thinking about the skill

Why is it important to put the bag over both beakers even though you closed only one of them?

Applying the skill

Does covering a beaker with dark plastic have the same effect on temperature as covering a beaker with clear plastic? Do an experiment to find out. What will your two sets of materials look like?

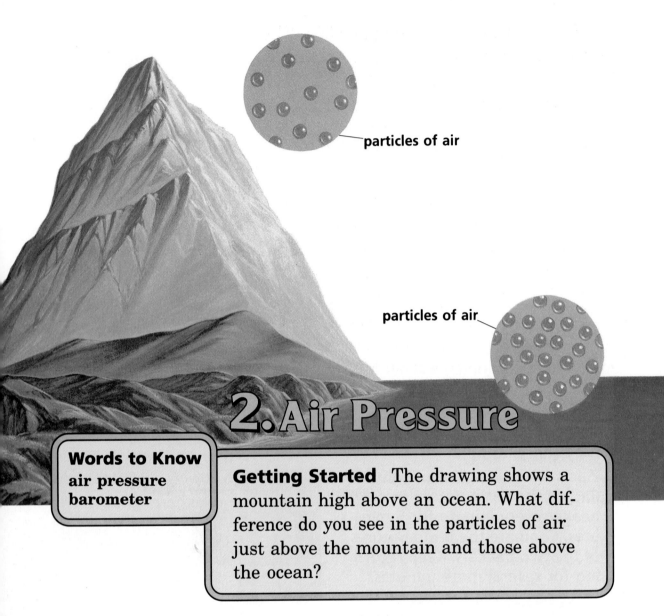

particles of air

particles of air

2. Air Pressure

Getting Started The drawing shows a mountain high above an ocean. What difference do you see in the particles of air just above the mountain and those above the ocean?

What is air pressure?

Gravity is a force that pulls matter toward the earth. Air is matter. So it is pulled toward the earth by gravity. This pulling makes the air press on the earth's surface. Air also presses on anything in the atmosphere. The pressing force of air is called **air pressure.** Air does not just press downward. It presses in all directions.

Look at the drawing on page 354. The higher you are in the atmosphere, the less air there is above you. Also, there are fewer particles of air higher in the atmosphere. So there is less air pressing on you and the air pressure is lower.

How is air pressure measured?

A **barometer** (buh RAHM ut ur) is an instrument used to measure air pressure. The picture shows one kind of barometer. It is made of a metal box with thin sides. When air pressure increases, the air pushes in the sides of the box. This causes a lever to move. The lever winds the chain, which moves a needle. The needle points to the air pressure. What do you think happens when air pressure falls?

Have you ever seen a rainbow? What about a double rainbow? Read about this beautiful sight in **Double Rainbows** in Horizons Plus.

▼ **Inside the barometer**

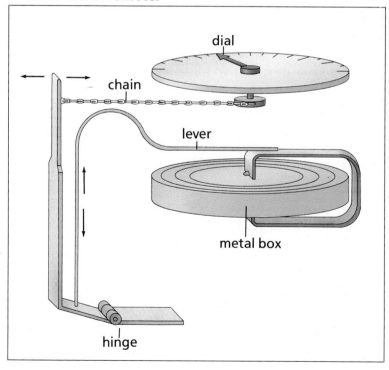

▼ **One kind of barometer**

Explore Together

How can you make a barometer?

Materials

Organizer

round balloon · scissors · jar · rubber band · sticky dot · plastic straw · tape · tongue depressor

Procedure

Investigator, Manager

A. Cut a balloon lengthwise. Stretch it over the mouth of the jar. Seal the balloon around the jar's mouth with a rubber band. Place the sticky dot in the center of the stretched balloon.

B. Cut off one end of the straw at an angle. Tape the uncut end to the dot on the balloon. The straw will be the pointer of your barometer.

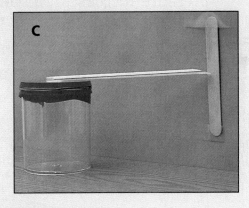

C. Tape the tongue depressor vertically on a wall. Place the jar as shown in the picture.

Recorder

D. Draw a line on the depressor even with the end of the pointer. Label that line *1*. This stands for reading number one on your barometer.

E. Look at the barometer each day for four days. Draw the line and reading number each day as in step **D**.

Writing and Sharing Results and Conclusions

Group, Recorder

1. Describe the movement of the pointer from day to day.

2. What makes the pointer move?

Reporter

3. How do your results compare with those of your classmates?

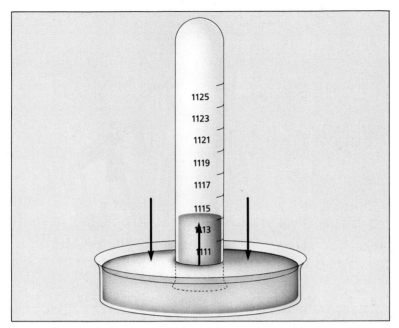

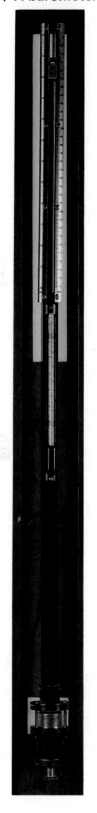

This picture shows another kind of barometer. As air presses on the surface of the liquid, it pushes the liquid up the tube. The higher the air pressure is, the farther the liquid is pushed up the tube. So the height of the liquid in the tube is used to measure air pressure. Air pressure is measured as the height of the liquid in millimeters. What is the air pressure shown?

Lesson Review

1. What is air pressure?
2. Why does air pressure decrease the higher you go in the atmosphere?
3. What instrument measures air pressure? Explain how one kind of these instruments work.

Think! Suppose you were using a barometer. As you ride an elevator from the ground floor to the fiftieth floor, you notice the liquid in the barometer go down. Explain what happened.

3. Winds

Getting Started Look at the picture of the flags in front of the United Nations building. You might use the word *brisk* to describe the wind blowing the flags. Name four other words you use to describe the wind.

Words to Know
sea breeze
land breeze

What causes the wind?

Moving air is called wind. You cannot see wind. But you can see objects such as the flags move when the wind blows. And you can feel wind as the air moves across your body.

Wind is caused by differences in air pressure. Air moves from places with higher pressure to places with lower pressure. The moving air is wind. The greater the difference in air pressure between two places, the faster the wind moves.

Particles of cool air are packed closer together than are particles of warm air. This makes cool air heavier than warm air. The heavier, cool air presses on the earth's surface more. So cool air has a higher air pressure than warm air.

Trace the movement of the air in the picture. The heavier cool air (blue arrow) sinks and pushes up the lighter warmer air (red arrow). So the wind moves from the place with high pressure to the place with low pressure. As the warmer air rises, it cools and sinks. The air keeps rising and sinking in a circular path. The wind is the air moving sideways near the ground.

▼ How air moves

Problem Solving
Blowing in the Wind

You may not realize it but there may be small winds in your classroom. You can find these winds with a wind detector made with tissue paper and pencil. Cut the paper into a 2 cm by 30 cm strip. Tape one end of the paper to a pencil. Hold this detector in a wind. It will move in the direction of the wind.

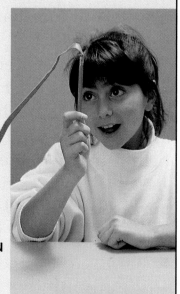

Can a wind detector be used to map the winds in your classroom?

Make a list of the places in your classroom where you expect to find winds. Decide how you would show the wind directions on a map. Then make a map of the winds in your classroom.

What are some kinds of winds?

A light wind is called a breeze. Breezes often occur where a warm surface is next to a cool surface. Breezes may form where land and water meet. During the day, land heats up faster than water. The air over the land becomes warmer than the air over the water. This means that the air pressure is lower over the land than over the water.

Look at the ocean shore in the drawing on the next page. The arrow shows that the cool air over the water sinks. It moves toward the land where the air pressure is lower. The wind blowing from the water toward land is called a **sea breeze.** What happens to the warmer air over the land?

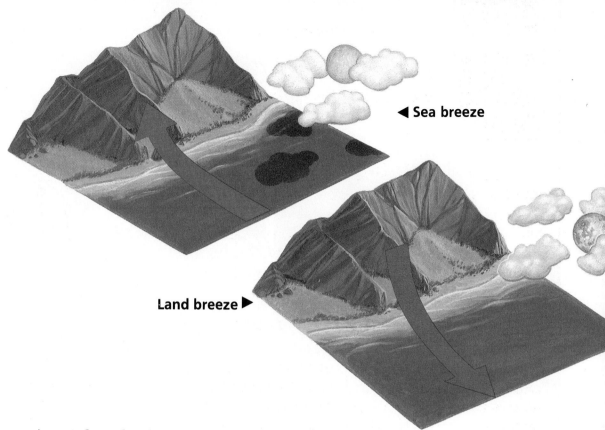

◄ Sea breeze

Land breeze ►

At night, the land cools more quickly than does the water. So the air over the land is cooler than the air over the water. This means that the air pressure is higher over the land. The cool air over the land sinks. It moves toward the lower pressure ocean air. The wind blowing from the land toward the water is called a **land breeze.**

Lesson Review

1. What causes wind?
2. How does wind move in a circular path?
3. Why does the wind blow from the water toward land during the day? Why does it blow from the land toward water at night?

Think! Imagine that you were designing a tall building for a windy city. Would you make a straight building or one shaped like steps? Explain your answer.

4. Water in the Atmosphere

Getting Started The pictures show some flowers in the morning and in the afternoon. What happened to the water that was on the flowers?

Words to Know
water vapor
humidity
relative humidity
dew point

What is humidity?

You know that air is a mixture of gases. One of the gases in the air is water vapor (VAY pur). **Water vapor** is water in the form of an invisible gas.

The water vapor in the air is called **humidity** (hyoo MIHD uh tee). All air does not have the same humidity. The amount of water vapor in the air changes from place to place and from time to time. Warm air can hold more water vapor than cold air. So as the temperature of air changes, the amount of water vapor the air can hold also changes.

The first jar in the picture is holding some marbles. But it could hold more. The second jar is holding all the marbles it can. So you can compare the number of marbles in the first jar with the total number of marbles it could hold if it were full.

◀ Comparing the number of marbles

The water vapor in air can be measured in the same way as you compared the marbles. **Relative humidity** is a measure of the amount of water vapor in a given amount of air compared with the total amount of water vapor the air could hold. Remember that warm air can hold more water vapor than cold air. Two samples of air with the same amount of water vapor in them do not always have the same relative humidity.

A high relative humidity means that the air is holding almost all the water vapor it could hold. A low relative humidity means that the air is holding little water vapor compared to the total amount that it could hold.

How do clouds form?

You have learned that warm air can hold more water vapor than cool air. If air cools, the air cannot hold as much water vapor as it could before. Sometimes more water vapor is in the air than it can hold. If there is "extra" water vapor in cooled air, the extra water condenses. Condense means to change from a gas to a liquid. How do you think the water got on the outside of the bottle of cold juice?

▼ **Water vapor condensing**

Look at the picture of the children outside on a cold day. The water vapor in the children's breath is condensing. The warm breath of the children came in contact with the cold outside air. This air cooled the children's breath to a temperature at which it could not hold as much water vapor.

The children's breath condensed, forming tiny water droplets. A collection of water droplets high in the atmosphere is called a cloud. Clouds form the same way as the water droplets from the children's breath.

For a cloud to form, air must first be cooled. Air must be cooled to a temperature at which it can hold no more water vapor. At this temperature, water condenses. The temperature at which water vapor in the air condenses is called the **dew point.**

Notice the level of the flat bottoms on the clouds in the picture. There is no condensed water vapor below that level. The temperature of the air below that level is higher than the dew point. The air above that level is at the dew point. So the water vapor there forms clouds.

▼ **Clouds form in air that is above its dew point**

Explore

How can you measure the dew point of air?

Did you ever notice that sometimes the grass is wet in the morning? That water on the grass is dew. Dew comes from water vapor that condenses in the air. The temperature at which water vapor in the air condenses is called the dew point.

Materials

graduate · 300 mL of room-temperature water · empty soup can · paper towel · thermometer · ice cube · stirrer

Procedure

A. Pour 250 mL of the water into the can. Dry the outside of the can if it gets wet. Measure and record the water's temperature.

B. Place the ice into the water.
  1. What will happen to the temperature of the water?
  2. Predict what will happen to the temperature of the air around the can.

C. Stir the water with the stirrer. Watch the outside of the can. When water forms on the outside, measure and record the temperature of the water in the can.

D. Remove the ice. Place it where your teacher tells you to.

E. Add the last 50 mL of water and stir it.

F. When the water on the outside is gone, measure and record the temperature of the water.

G. The dew point is between the temperatures measured in steps **C** and **F**. Add the two temperatures. Divide by 2.
  3. What is the dew point?

Writing and Sharing Results and Conclusions

1. Where did the water droplets on the outside of the can come from?
2. What might happen if you poured cold lemonade into a dry glass on a day with high relative humidity?
3. Would the air temperature and the dew point be closer on a day with high or low relative humidity?

Temperature alone does not cause clouds to form. One more thing is needed before water condenses—a solid surface. Water condenses only on solid surfaces. In the air, water condenses on tiny particles such as dust, salt, and ash which are part of the air. So for a cloud to form, air must be cooled to its dew point and tiny solid particles must be present in the air.

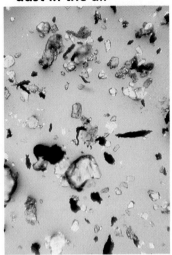

▼ **Microscope view of dust in the air**

What are the kinds of clouds?

Clouds have three main shapes. They can be grouped by these shapes. Stratus (STRAT us) clouds are thick, flat clouds low in the sky. They often cover the sky like a blanket. The word *stratus* means "layered" or "sheetlike." Stratus clouds usually look gray. They can be a sign of rainy weather. Rain from stratus clouds is often light but steady.

▼ **Stratus clouds**

▲ **Cumulus and cirrus clouds**

You have probably seen clouds that look like large fluffy balls of cotton. The fluffy, white clouds are cumulus (KYOO myoo lus) clouds. The word *cumulus* means "heaped." You can see these clouds during fair weather.

Feathery, wispy clouds high in the sky are cirrus (SIHR us) clouds. Some people think these look like curls of hair. In fact, *cirrus* means "curly."

Cirrus clouds are often made of tiny pieces of ice. It is very cold high in the atmosphere where these clouds form. So the water there freezes. Cirrus clouds are often a sign of warm weather. But there may be rain a day or two after you see these clouds.

Lesson Review

1. What is the difference between humidity and relative humidity?
2. How does a cloud form?
3. What is the dew point?
4. What are the three main kinds of clouds?

Think! If you saw thick, flat grayish clouds what kind of weather would you expect?

Physical Science
CONNECTION

Give an example of each of the three states of water found in the atmosphere.

368

Chapter Connections

Choose a partner. Explain the chapter's main ideas to your partner. Use the organizer as a guide.

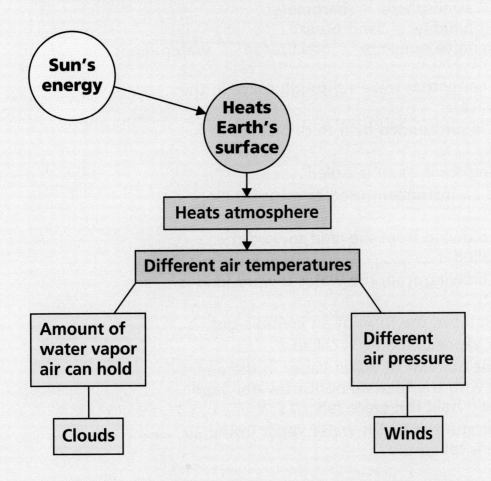

Writing About Science • Classify

Fold a piece of paper into four parts. At the top of each part write one of the following terms: *Heat*, *Air Pressure*, *Wind*, *Water*. Now watch and listen to a weather report on television. Record the information you see and hear in the right boxes. Compare your lists with a classmate.

Chapter 11 Review

Science Terms

Copy the sentences below. Use the terms listed to complete the sentences.

air pressure   atmosphere   barometer
dew point   humidity   land breeze
radiation   relative humidity   sea breeze   water vapor

1. _____ is energy that travels through space in the form of waves.
2. The earth is surrounded by a thick blanket of air called the _____.
3. The pressing force of air is called _____.
4. A _____ is an instrument used to measure air pressure.
5. The wind blowing from the land toward the water is called a _____.
6. The wind blowing from the water toward land is called a _____.
7. _____ is water in the form of an invisible gas.
8. The water vapor in the air is called _____.
9. _____ is the amount of water vapor in the air compared with the total amount of water vapor the air could hold if it were full.
10. The temperature at which water vapor in the air condenses is called the _____.

Science Ideas

Answer the following using complete sentences.

1. Explain how the atmosphere is heated.
2. Why might the air over the North Pole have a higher pressure than air near the equator?

3. The air over a large grassy field is cool. The air over the parking lot next to the field is warm. Do you think the wind would blow from the field toward the parking lot? Explain your answer.
4. How do humidity and relative humidity differ?
5. What are the two things needed for water in the air to form clouds?
6. "The slant at which the sun's rays strike the earth's surface is the main reason for the uneven heating of the earth's atmosphere." Explain this statement.

Applying Science Ideas

Answer the following using complete sentences.

1. When you inhale, air moves from the outside into your lungs. Is air pressure higher outside or inside your lungs while you inhale?
2. On the earth's surface, the pressure inside our bodies is about equal to the air pressure. What problem might there be for a person jumping out of an airplane high in the atmosphere.
3. Many years ago, before homes and offices were air-conditioned, many people would leave the cities in the summer. These people would spend the summer near a lake or ocean. Why, do you think, did they make this trip?

Using Science Skills

Suppose you have a lizard that needs much humidity in its cage. You can increase the humidity by putting a wet sponge in the cage and letting the water evaporate. Design an experiment. Find out if water will evaporate faster from a sponge that is cut into small pieces.

Careers in Earth Science

Geologist

When Shannon Goodwin was in the fifth grade, she received a geology kit as a present. That kit sparked Shannon's interest in rocks and minerals. Today, she is a **geologist** in the state of Washington. She studies the ground beneath us. But Shannon does more than just look at soil and rocks. She is helping to keep our drinking water safe.

The water people drink often comes from deep underground. Sometimes rainwater washes harmful materials through the soil to underground water. The harmful materials could poison people. So Shannon's job is to help find out if underground water is safe.

To find underground water, a drill is used. The drill digs up soil and rock. Shannon looks at the soil carefully and does tests on soil samples. If Shannon finds harmful materials, she tells a hydrologist. **Hydrologists** (hye DRAHL uh jihsts) are scientists who study water on or in the earth. They predict whether these materials will wash through the soil to reach underground water.

Will there be enough clean water for us in the future? This is what Shannon worries about. She says, "I like doing my part to help protect the earth's water."

If you think you might enjoy being a geologist, learn as much as you can about science. In college you can study soil, rocks, and minerals and become a geologist.

Connecting Science Ideas

1. You have read about sources of pollution. What sources might pollute the underground water that Shannon tests? **Chapter 10; Careers**

2. The atmosphere has been called "an ocean of air." Explain how the motions of the atmosphere and oceans are alike. **Chapter 10; Chapter 11**

3. Scientists were observing the atmosphere during a full moon. They noticed a bulge in the atmosphere on the side of the earth facing the moon. Use what you know about tides to explain the cause of this bulge. **Chapter 10; Chapter 11**

4. Rock salt is a sedimentary rock. How is rock salt formed? How might salt be obtained at desalination plants? **Chapter 9; Chapter 10**

5. You have learned that valuable minerals are on the ocean floor and in the earth's crust. Identify some problems of getting the minerals from each place. Decide which is harder. Explain why.
Chapter 9; Chapter 10

Computer Connections

Water on the earth can be found in oceans, seas, gulfs, lakes, ponds, and rivers. Choose the names of two bodies of water. Use reference books to find the location, size, and average depth of each one. Enter the information into a class database. Have your classmates enter information about other bodies of water.

Trace a world map from an atlas. Use the class database to help you locate and label different bodies of water on the map. Then use different colors to show the average depth of each body of water. Include a key to explain the colors you used.

from

IF YOU ARE
A HUNTER OF FOSSILS

Written by Byrd Baylor
Illustrated by Peter Parnall

Some rocks have secrets from the distant past to share with you. Join this hunter of fossils as she searches for treasures buried in rocks.

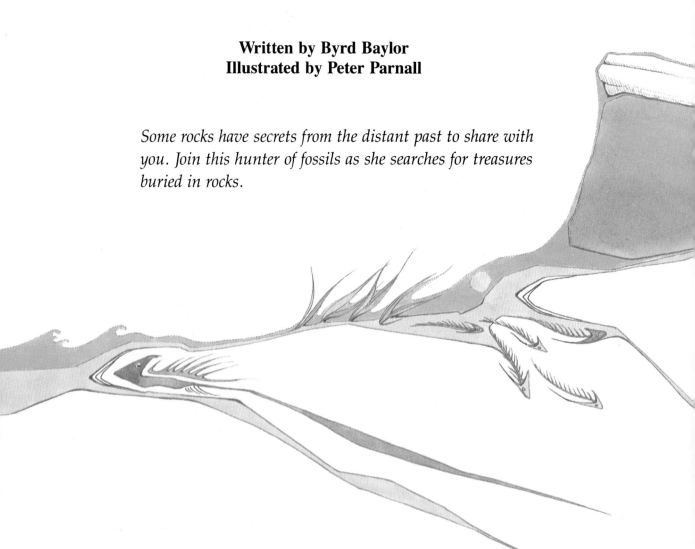

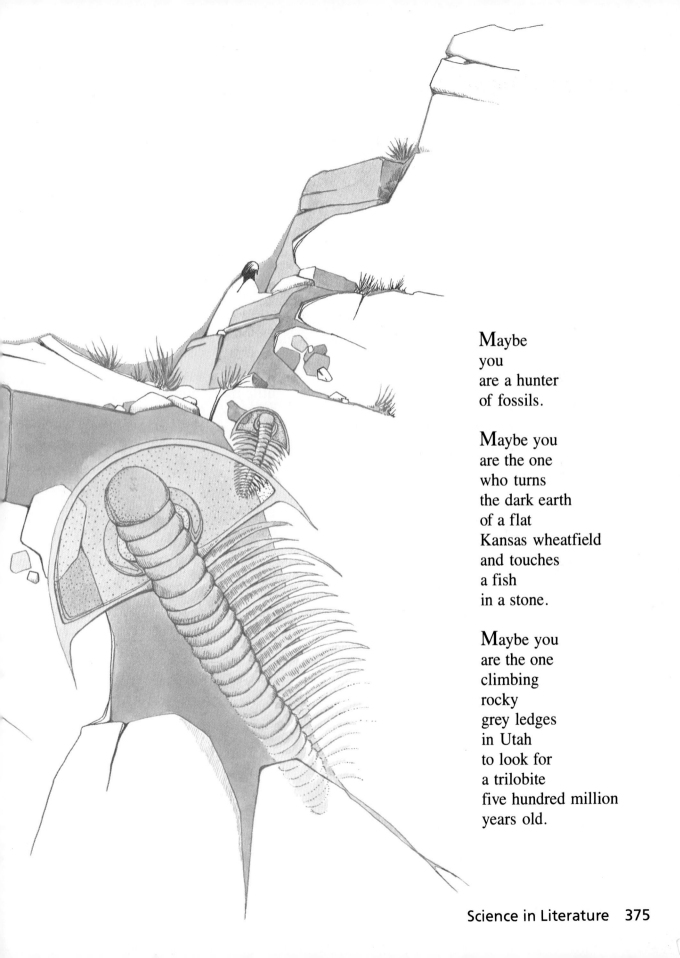

Maybe
you
are a hunter
of fossils.

Maybe you
are the one
who turns
the dark earth
of a flat
Kansas wheatfield
and touches
a fish
in a stone.

Maybe you
are the one
climbing
rocky
grey ledges
in Utah
to look for
a trilobite
five hundred million
years old.

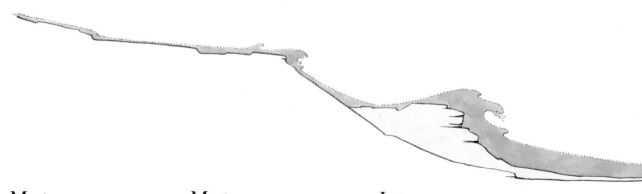

Maybe you
are the one
in Wyoming
with your feet
in a dinosaur track

or the one
who finds
a seed fern
in Pennsylvania shale,
so perfect
every
vein
still shows.

Maybe you
are the one
in the hills
of Nebraska
with a
rhinoceros bone
in your hand

or the one
who gathers
sponges
in the rocks
of an Iowa farm.

Maybe you
are a hunter of fossils—
like me.

I am the one
on the side of
a West Texas
mountain
reading
the rocks

looking
for signs
of the sea
that was
here.

Today
you'd find me
resting
on a chalky
limestone boulder
by a prickly pear.

There are
seashells
in this rock,
jumbled,
jammed together,
large and small.

I always stop
and touch
the ones that
curl
like
little ram's horns.
(*Exogyra*
is their name.)

Up here,
what's *real*
is the
shallow
warm
Cretaceous sea
that all these
seashells
knew.

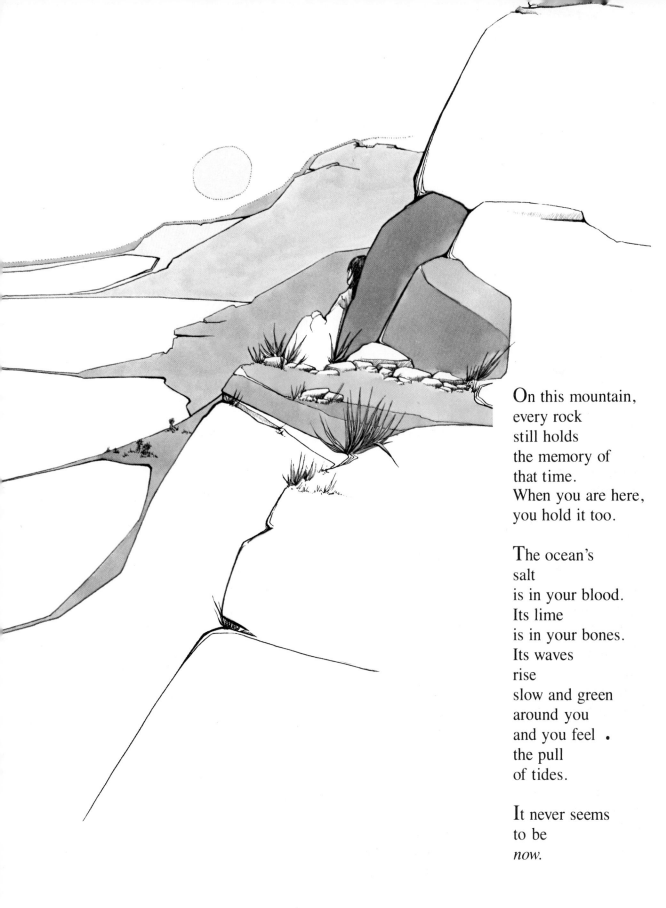

On this mountain,
every rock
still holds
the memory of
that time.
When you are here,
you hold it too.

The ocean's
salt
is in your blood.
Its lime
is in your bones.
Its waves
rise
slow and green
around you
and you feel .
the pull
of tides.

It never seems
to be
now.

Here,
time flows back
and forth
so easily
that
any day
can be
wrapped up
inside
some other day
that came
and went
a hundred million
years ago.

Here,
when I find
a brachiopod
or mollusk
or a round
sea urchin,
I don't just
see it
as it is . . .
on a mountain
locked
in rock.

I see it
in that
ancient
lapping
water.

I see
the tiny
clams
plowing
through mud.
I see
sea lillies
sway.

I see
all the creatures
with shells
and plates
and spines.
Slow moving,
glimmering,
they hide
in the crevices,

creep
into holes
in the rocks.

I see the
waving tentacles
and curving
spiral shells
of ammonites.
It is their day.
They are
the masters of
this sunken
sea-floor world.

Above them,
fish
swim lazily
by coral reefs.
Sharks
move
through
darkness.

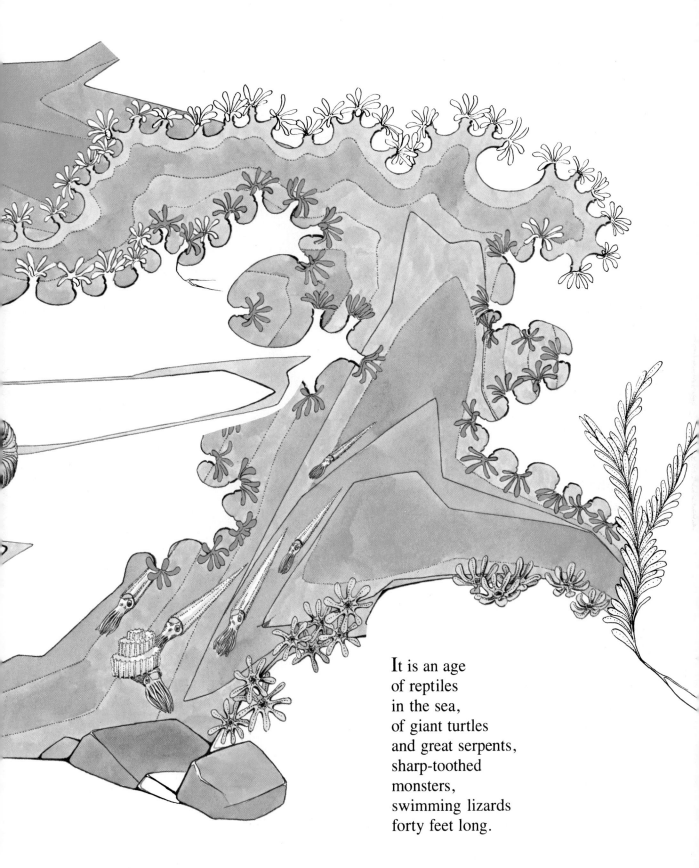

It is an age
of reptiles
in the sea,
of giant turtles
and great serpents,
sharp-toothed
monsters,
swimming lizards
forty feet long.

Sometimes
you even feel
the long
slow
terror
in that world
when water
turned
to mud.

It took
millions of years
for ocean slime
and sun
to fight it out

but
finally
sunshine
won.

Now
that sea is
a mountain of
rock
that I climb
with a shell
in my hand.

If you are
a hunter of fossils
you know
how the day
always
ends.

You know
how it is
to go home
feeling glad
that you walk
in the sun . . .
breathing
air.

You always
walk home
kind of proud.

You always
hold on
to that long
chain of life
as you
go.

Reader's Response

The author writes that fossil hunters feel proud at the end of the day. Why do you think they might feel that way?

Selection Follow-up

 Responding to Literature

1. The narrator tells us many facts about fossils. Discuss some of the things you learned with classmates who have read the selection.

2. If you could ask the narrator one question about fossils, what would it be?

3. You can learn a great deal from illustrations in a book. What do the pictures tell you about changes that have taken place in the land of West Texas since the time fossils were formed?

4. Perhaps a million years from now someone may find fossils of things that are alive today. Pretend you are that future hunter of fossils. Write a journal entry about what you might find.

 Books to Enjoy

If You Are a Hunter of Fossils by Byrd Baylor
What is the largest animal ever to fly? Read all of the book and discover its name.

Dinosaurs Walked Here and Other Stories Fossils Tell by Patricia Lauber
Fossils can tell us a great deal about life in the prehistoric world. In this book, the author explains how fossils yield information about that long-ago time.

Dinosaur Mysteries by Mary Elting and Ann Goodman
This book asks questions and describes mysteries about dinosaurs based on what scientists have learned from fossils.

SCIENCE HORIZONS

HUMAN BODY

Digestion

Strange Foods

"You're under arrest!" the police officer cried. "But what did I do?" asked the scared young man. "You ate a potato!" the police officer said sternly.

Do you believe that someone could be in trouble for eating a potato? Hundreds of years ago, people in France could not eat potatoes. Some people thought potatoes caused disease. So towns passed laws to keep people from eating potatoes and spreading the disease.

Today, people all over the world eat potatoes. They taste good, and they do not cause disease. We eat potatoes baked, boiled, mashed, and fried. In the United States alone, people eat over 1 million bushels of potatoes every day. That many potatoes would fill 80 rooms, each the size of your classroom!

People also used to fear tomatoes. Long ago, people grew tomato plants in their gardens. They grew the plants for their pretty flowers and leaves. But they never ate the tomatoes. They thought the tomatoes were poisonous. They would let the tomatoes drop to the ground and spoil.

A story that people tell is how one man changed people's minds about tomatoes. One day he stood on the courthouse steps in his town, in front of hundreds of people, and ate a whole basket of tomatoes. They did not even upset his stomach!

Actually, in the early 1800s tomatoes became very popular. They were even mixed with spices and used as medicine. The label on the medicine bottle said the medicine would cure any ache, pain, or illness. We still have this mixture around today, but not as a medicine. Today we call it tomato sauce!

Today, we eat tomatoes in many ways. They are in the sauce on pizzas. They are also used in spaghetti sauce. People eat sliced tomatoes on sandwiches and in salads. In what other ways do we eat tomatoes?

Discover

What do people know about the food they eat?

ACTIVITY

Materials   paper · pencil

Procedure

    People still believe many different things about food. Ask five adults to tell you one strange thing they have heard about food. Ask each of the five to explain the meaning of their strange belief. Write each answer. Which statements do you think are true? Which do you think are false? Show the statements to five of your classmates. Record which statements they think are true and false. How might you find out which statements are really false?

In this chapter you will learn about the different types of food you eat. You will also learn how to make correct choices about the food you eat.

1. From Cells to Systems

Getting Started Do you have a toy that runs on a battery? Suppose you turn on the toy and let it run for a while. Why does the toy keep moving? What will happen if you forget to turn it off?

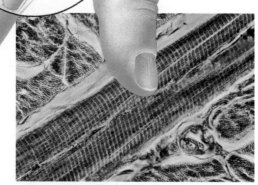

▲ Muscle cells

▲ Skin cells

What are the smallest parts of the body?

In what way are you like your toy? Your toy can move because it has energy. The energy comes from the battery. Without energy, you could not move. Your body needs energy to move, talk, think, sleep, and grow.

The parts of your body also need energy. Your hands need energy. Your fingers do, too. Even the smallest parts of the body need energy. The smallest part of the body is a **cell.** The body is made up of billions of cells. Most are so small that they can be seen only

388

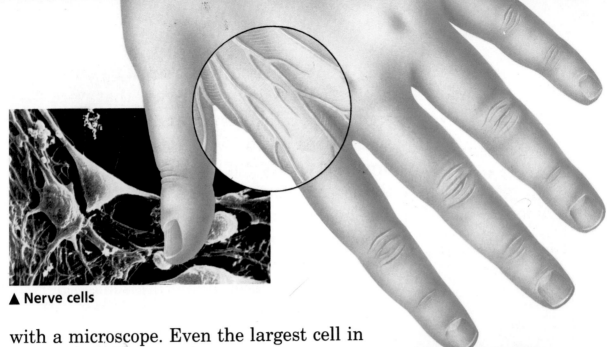

▲ Nerve cells

with a microscope. Even the largest cell in the body is only about the size of a pinpoint.

The body is made of many kinds of cells. Blood is made of blood cells, and bone is made of bone cells. As you can see, cells have different shapes and sizes. How would you describe the shape of these blood cells?

▲ Blood cells

How do body parts work together?

Have you ever tried to do a hard job, such as cleaning up the schoolyard? The job would be easier if you worked with a group of your classmates. In the body, cells of the same kind work together. This makes it easier to do certain jobs. A group of cells that work together is called a **tissue.**

Muscle tissue is made of muscle cells. Muscle cells work together and help move parts of the body. Bone tissue is made of bone cells. Bone cells work together and support parts of the body. What kind of cells make up skin tissue? In what ways do skin cells work together?

Groups of tissues also work together in the body. A group of tissues that work together is called an **organ.** Organs have special jobs in the body. Your heart is an organ. It is made of muscle tissue, nerve tissue, and other tissues that work together. The heart pumps blood throughout the body. Your brain is an organ that is made mainly of nerve tissue. The brain controls most of the body's activities. What are some other organs in your body?

▼ Bone tissue

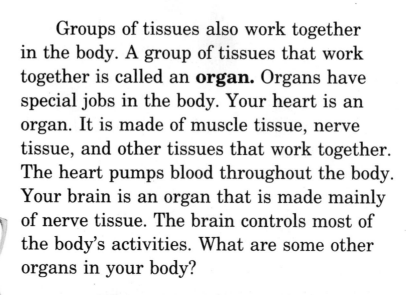

▲ Bone

Organs also work together in the body. A group of organs that work together is called an **organ system** (SIHS tum). The body has many important organ systems. The skeletal (SKEL uh tul) system is shown in the drawing. It supports and protects the body. The organs of the skeletal system are the bones. They are made of several kinds of tissues and cells. What would your body look like without bones?

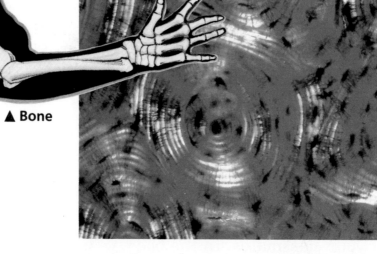

Another important organ system is the digestive (dih JES tiv) system. The organs of this system are listed in the table. As you can see, each organ does a special job. The organs work together and help your body use the food you eat.

Why is the digestive system important?

You have learned that the cells in your body need energy. Without energy, the parts of the body could not work. Your heart could not beat and your muscles could not move. The energy that cells need comes from the food you eat. Food also provides materials that cells need. Cells use these materials to grow, repair themselves, and produce new cells. By adding and repairing cells, your body grows and stays healthy.

The Digestive System

Mouth
- Teeth bite and chew food
- Saliva softens and moistens food, breaks down some food into nutrients

Esophagus
- Squeezes food into the stomach

Small Intestine
- Squeezes food to move it along
- Mixes food with digestive juices
- Absorbs nutrients from food and releases them into the blood

Stomach
- Mixes food with digestive juices

Large Intestine
- Removes water from food and releases it into the blood

▲ Different kinds of food

The food shown here is not in a form that can be used by your cells. Every piece of food you eat is too big to enter a cell. So food must be changed. Changing food into a form that cells can use is called **digestion** (dih-JES chun). During digestion, food is broken down into tiny particles called nutrients (NOO-tree unts). Nutrients are small enough to enter even the smallest cell in the body.

Lesson Review

1. What is the smallest part of the body?
2. How does a tissue differ from an organ?
3. Why do cells need food?
4. What happens to food during digestion?

Think! Imagine that your school is made up of cells. Think of a way that a group of "cells" might work together. For example, window "cells" might work together letting light into the classrooms.

Physical Science
CONNECTION

In what ways is the human body like a machine?

THINKING

Skills

Recognizing a definition

The word *hand* can have different meanings at different times. Sometimes to give someone a hand means to help him or her. You might also give someone a hand by clapping when he or she sings a song that you like. Knowing what is being done can help you to understand the meaning of a word.

Practicing the skill

Imagine watching an animal eat food. Which meaning of *food* could come from what you observe?

Meaning A: Something that is put into the mouth, moistened and chewed, and swallowed

Meaning B: A material that gives a living thing energy

Thinking about the skill

How can there be more than one meaning for a single word?

Applying the skill

Sometimes we talk about the energy food gives us. People need energy to move, talk, and think. There are other meanings for energy . Which meaning fits the kind of energy you use when you are on the playground?

Meaning A: What is needed to run, jump, and play

Meaning B: What a toy car gets from a battery

Meaning C: The ability to do work

2. The Digestive Process

Getting Started Think about your favorite food. Close your eyes and picture how it looks. Think about how it smells. As you do this, what happens inside your mouth?

12:00

Where does digestion begin?

When food is eaten, it goes through many parts of the digestive system. Each part does a special job in the digestion of food. Look at the pictures and drawings as you read about the path of food through the digestive system.

Food enters the **mouth,** the place where digestion begins. In the mouth two things happen. First, food is broken into smaller pieces as it is chewed by the teeth. Notice that you have different kinds of teeth.

Digestion in the Mouth

chewing food

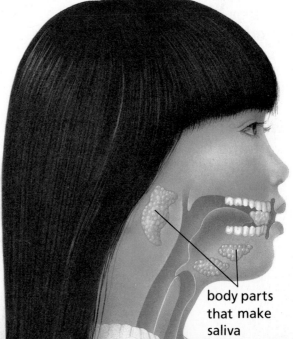

body parts that make saliva

394

Incisors have sharp edges that cut and bite food. Canines have sharp points that tear food. Molars have flat tops that crush and grind food.

As you chew, a second thing happens. A digestive juice called saliva (suh LYE vuh) mixes with the food. This liquid comes from body parts connected to the mouth. Saliva helps to make food soft and wet. Soft, wet food is easy to swallow. Saliva also breaks down some of the food into nutrients.

During this time the tongue is also at work. The tongue moves the food around in the mouth. This helps to mix the food with saliva. The tongue also pushes food to the back of the mouth, where it is swallowed.

By the time you swallow, one step in digestion is complete. Your teeth, tongue, and saliva have changed large pieces of food into a soft, wet ball.

Three Kinds of Teeth

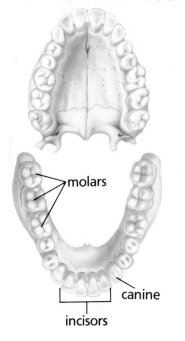

molars

canine

incisors

swallowing food

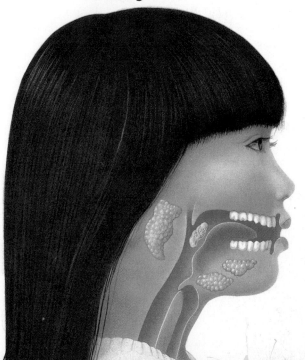

food moving down the esophagus

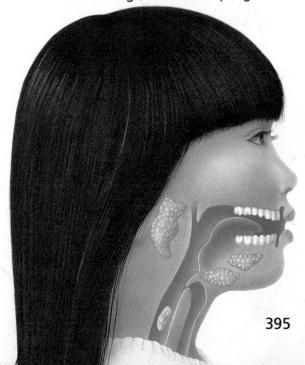

Explore Together

What happens to food in your mouth?

Materials

Organizer

safety goggles · 2 salt-free crackers · iodine solution in dropper bottle · timer

Procedure

Group

A. Put on your safety goggles. **Caution:** *Wear safety goggles for this activity.*

Manager

B. During digestion, foods that contain starch are broken down into sugar. You can test a piece of food to see if it contains starch by using iodine. If the iodine turns from brown to blue-black, the food contains starch. Place a drop of iodine on a small piece of cracker. **Caution:** *Iodine is a poison, do not let iodine come in contact with your skin or mouth.*

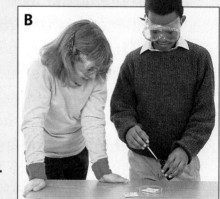

Group, Recorder

1. Does the cracker contain starch?

Manager

C. Time the Investigator as he or she performs step **D.**

Investigator

D. Take a few bites of another cracker. Chew the cracker for 1 minute.

Investigator, Recorder

2. What did the cracker taste like when you began chewing?

3. How did the cracker taste after 1 minute?

4. In what other ways did the cracker change as you chewed it?

Writing and Sharing Results and Conclusions

Group, Reporter

1. How can you tell that saliva broke down starch in the cracker?

2. What else happened to the cracker in the mouth?

396

What happens when food is swallowed?

When food is swallowed, it moves from the mouth into a tube called the **esophagus** (ih SAHF uh gus). The esophagus is made of strong muscles. Food moves down this tube in a few seconds. But it does not simply fall through. Instead, it is squeezed through by the muscles, as toothpaste is squeezed through a tube. The muscles are strong enough to push food downward to the stomach.

From the esophagus, food enters the stomach. The **stomach** is a baglike organ made of muscles. An empty stomach is about as big as your two fists. But as you eat, it stretches and becomes much larger.

Food stays in the stomach several hours. While food is there, the stomach muscles squeeze together. This mixes the food with more digestive juices. These juices come from the cells in the stomach wall. Like saliva, the juices help to break down food into nutrients.

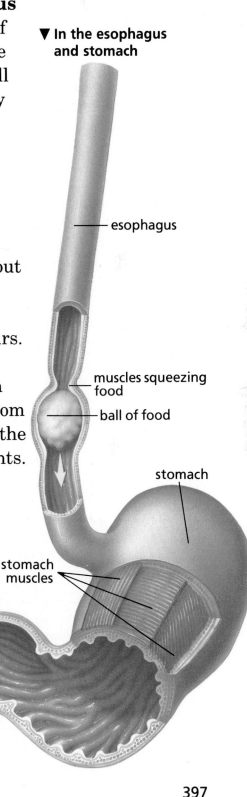

▼ In the esophagus and stomach

esophagus

muscles squeezing food

ball of food

stomach

stomach muscles

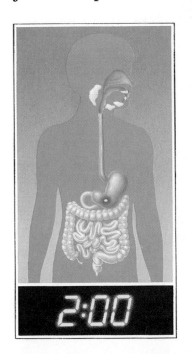

2:00

397

What happens when food leaves the stomach?

When food leaves the stomach, it is like thick soup. The liquid moves into the small intestine (ihn TES tun). The **small intestine** is an organ shaped like a long, narrow tube. Like the esophagus, the small intestine is made of muscles that push food along. But it may take 9 hours to squeeze food through this very long tube.

As the muscles squeeze together, the food is mixed with more digestive juices. These juices come from the small intestine and from organs connected to it.

Notice that the inside of the small intestine has many finger-shaped parts, called villi. The villi stick out into the liquid food. Nutrients from the liquid enter blood inside the villi. Then the blood carries the nutrients to all the cells of the body.

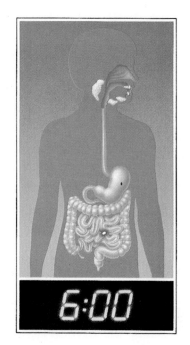

▼ The small intestine

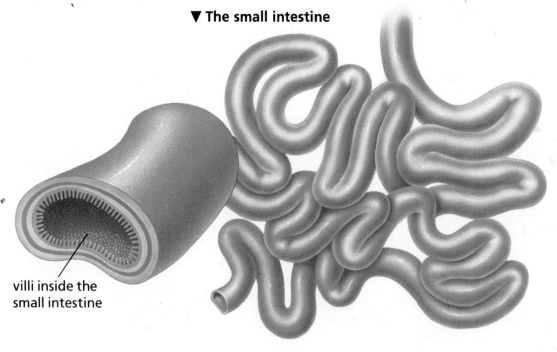

villi inside the
small intestine

398

Where does the digestive system end?

After the nutrients are absorbed in the small intestine, some liquid remains. It is made up of water and food that cannot be digested. This watery liquid moves into the large intestine. The **large intestine** is an organ shaped like a wide tube. It is much wider and shorter than the small intestine.

Water is removed from the liquid in this organ. There, water moves out of the large intestine and enters the blood. The unused food is pushed along by muscles in the large intestine. At the end of the large intestine, this material leaves the body as waste.

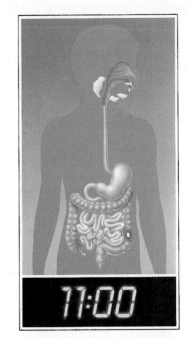

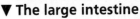

▼ The large intestine

inside the large intestine

Lesson Review

1. How do teeth and saliva help to digest food?
2. Where does digested food move into the blood?

Think! When astronauts are in space, they may float upside down while they eat. Why can food still move through the digestive system?

How does an artificial mouth test teeth?

You chew each mouthful of food you eat 26 times. That means your teeth cut, tear, chip, and grind 250,000 times a year. Chewing can wear your teeth down and change their shape and size.

The foods you chew can hurt them as well. Hard and crunchy foods, like peanuts or popcorn kernels, can break them. Strong liquids, like lemon juice and vinegar, can dissolve their outer covering. Sweet foods, like caramels and cherry pie, can leave a sticky film on them, causing cavities.

When teeth need to be repaired, dentists can use materials made of metal or plastic. But how can they test these materials to find out which ones will last the longest? They use a machine called ART, the artificial mouth.

ART has upper and lower plastic plates. Each plate holds one or more false or real teeth. ART moves like a real mouth. Its teeth chomp up and down. They also grind from side to side. Chomping and grinding wear down ART's teeth just like eating wears down your teeth. Scientists place teeth or fillings made of a certain material in ART's mouth. Then they see how long it takes for the material to wear out.

ART works quickly. It can show 5 years of wear on teeth in just a few weeks. ART is hooked up to a computer. The computer measures the size and shape of teeth before and after testing. It can measure wear on teeth even if the wear is only the width of a hair.

Scientists are working on a new and better ART. It will have an artificial tongue and cheeks. The new ART will be able to chew real food. Its tongue and cheeks will keep food in the right position. It will also have artificial saliva. The new ART will help scientists make better dental materials.

Critical thinking

Some people might say that the only way to test new dental materials is on real people with real teeth. Do you agree or disagree with this point of view? What are your reasons?

Using what you learned

How do some liquids wear teeth away? Get a piece of eggshell the size of a tooth. Eggshell is made of a material that is a lot like the material that makes up your teeth. Drop the piece into a bottle of soft drink. Check it every other day for two weeks. What happens?

3. Healthy Digestion

Getting Started Hold up one of your hands and make a fist. Now open and close your fist as fast as you can. How many times can you do this without stopping? Why, do you think, could you not do it all day?

How can you take care of your digestive system?

Where do you get the energy to make a fist? As you have learned, this energy comes from the food you eat. But before your body can get this energy, the food must be digested. So it is important to keep your digestive system healthy.

One way to take care of the digestive system is to eat the proper kinds of foods. Fruits and vegetables contain a material called fiber. Foods with fiber help to keep the digestive system healthy. What fruits and vegetables have you eaten today?

A second way to take care of the digestive system is to keep your teeth healthy. Dairy products should be part of your diet. They contain calcium, which helps to make teeth strong and healthy. You should also brush your teeth often and clean between your teeth with dental floss. This removes food and plaque (plak) from your teeth. Plaque is a sticky material that can cause tooth decay.

A third way to take care of the digestive system is to exercise every day. Then the food you eat will be digested more easily. What kinds of play are good exercise?

Active play, sports, and other kinds of exercise also make you feel better. Feelings affect the way the digestive system works. When you feel happy, for example, the muscles in your stomach and intestines work better. How are these children taking care of the digestive system?

▼ **Children playing softball**

Explore

ACTIVITY

How can you remove plaque from teeth?

Smile and show your pearly white teeth! You might think this is easy to do. But suppose you were George Washington. He had false teeth made of wood. In those days, people did not know how to prevent tooth decay. Many people lost their teeth and had to wear false teeth.

Materials
2 disclosing tablets · water in a paper cup · mirror · toothbrush · toothpaste · dental floss

Procedure

A. Do this activity at home. Ask an adult to help you.

B. Get 2 disclosing tablets from your teacher or your dentist.

C. Chew a tablet, but do not swallow it. Spit into a sink. Rinse your mouth with water.

D. Use a mirror to observe your teeth and gums carefully.

E

   1. Do you observe any dark spots on your teeth and gums? Dark spots show where plaque has formed.

   2. Make a drawing that shows where plaque has formed on your teeth.

E. Now brush and floss your teeth carefully.

F. Repeat steps **C** and **D**.

3. Compare the way your teeth look now with the way they looked in step **D**.

Writing and Sharing Results and Conclusions

1. Do brushing and flossing help remove plaque? How do you know?

2. Do you think you can do a better job of caring for your teeth? Explain your answer.

What are some problems of digestion?

This girl is doing the kind of exercise that helps to keep the digestive system healthy. But you should not do such active exercise right after you eat. Do you know why? The muscles in your digestive system use energy. The muscles you use to exercise also use energy. If you exercise, the digestive muscles may not get enough energy to keep on working. Food may stay in the stomach and intestines longer. Then you may get a stomachache. Stomachaches are a common problem of the digestive system.

Another problem is choking on food. Suppose you do not chew your food well enough before swallowing it. Then food may get stuck in the windpipe. The windpipe is a tube near the esophagus. The windpipe carries air to your lungs. When it is blocked, a person starts to choke. A choking person cannot breathe or speak.

The best way to help a choking person is shown in the pictures. Do not practice this procedure on a person. (1) First, get behind the person. Wrap your arms around the person's waist. (2) Then make a fist with one hand. (3) Put your other hand over your fist. Press hard into the person with quick upward pressing. This will force air up the windpipe and push the food out.

▼ Helping a choking person

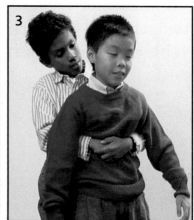

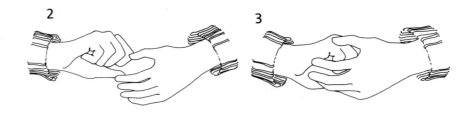

Lesson Review

1. List three things you can do to keep your digestive system healthy.
2. What can cause a stomachache?

Think! When you are worried or frightened, the muscles in the digestive system may work more slowly. What digestive problem might happen then?

Chapter 12 Putting It All Together

Chapter Connections

Copy the graphic organizer. Cut out the boxes and mix them up. Then rearrange them in the correct order.

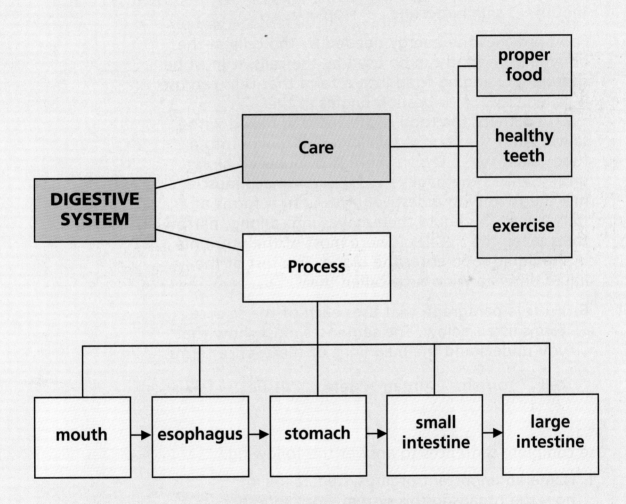

Writing About Science • Narrate

In this chapter you learned about the digestive system and its care. Tell a story about the things someone did to improve the health of this important organ system.

Science Terms

A. Number your paper from 1 to 6. Use the terms below to complete the sentences.

digestion   esophagus   large intestine
mouth   small intestine   stomach

Food provides the energy needed by the cells of the body. Before food can be used by the cells, it must be changed. Changing food into a form that cells can use is called ___(1)___. Digestion begins in the ___(2)___. There the food is chewed and mixed with saliva. After the food is swallowed, it moves into a tube called the ___(3)___. There it is squeezed along until it enters the baglike ___(4)___. Stomach muscles mix the food with digestive juices until it forms a thick soup. This liquid then moves into a long, narrow tube called the ___(5)___. There most of the nutrients in the liquid food enter the blood. The rest of the liquid enters a wide tube called the ___(6)___.

B. Write a paragraph that uses each of the science terms listed below. The sentences must show that you understand the meanings of the science terms.

cell   organ   organ system   tissue

Science Ideas

Use complete sentences to answer the following.

1. Name an important organ system. Explain how the organs in this system work together.
2. How is food changed during digestion?
3. Which foods contain fiber?
4. What is plaque?
5. Why isn't it a good idea to jump rope right after eating a big meal?

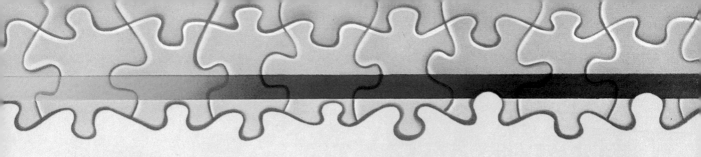

6. Identify each of these parts of the digestive system. Explain how each part helps in digestion.

A

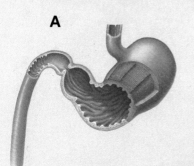

B

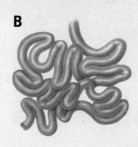

C

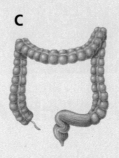

7. What should you do if someone is choking on food?

Applying Science Ideas
Use complete sentences to answer the following.

1. People who are sick or recovering from operations are given only liquids and soft foods to eat. Why, do you think, are they given these kinds of foods?

2. Suppose you have lunch today at twelve noon. When you go home at three o'clock, where in your digestive system will the food probably be then?

3. The small intestine is very long. The large intestine is very short. Why do these two organs have these names?

4. What is ART and what does ART do?

Using Science Skills
Which meaning fits the way the word *body* is used in this chapter?

Meaning A: A body is made of cells, tissues, organs, and organ systems.

Meaning B: A body is anything made of matter.

Chapter 13

Circulation and Respiration

Away With Asbestos

Suppose your teacher found a white material on the floor of your classroom. Now the classroom is closed off. You are having class in the gym. You see people wearing masks and special clothing in your school. They are searching for something.

What might these people be looking for? They are probably checking for asbestos. Asbestos is a strong material that does not burn. For many years it was used in building homes, schools, and offices. It helped to keep them from getting too hot or too cold inside.

Asbestos can take the form of very small fibers. These fibers look like tiny threads. Your teacher might have seen these threads.

Why is asbestos a problem? Ceiling tiles and other building materials that contain asbestos can crack or tear. This releases asbestos fibers into the air. Scientists have shown that the fibers get stuck in the lungs. The fibers can cause serious lung diseases.

So people do not want to touch materials or breathe air that contains asbestos. Suppose the people who are looking for asbestos find it in your school. What do they do with it?

Sometimes experts can repair damaged materials that contain asbestos. They can make sure that no more fibers are released. But if they find loose asbestos, they must re-move it. First they vacuum it up with a special vacuum cleaner. Then they wet it completely so no more fibers get into the air. Finally, they put it in heavy plastic bags which they bury in special areas.

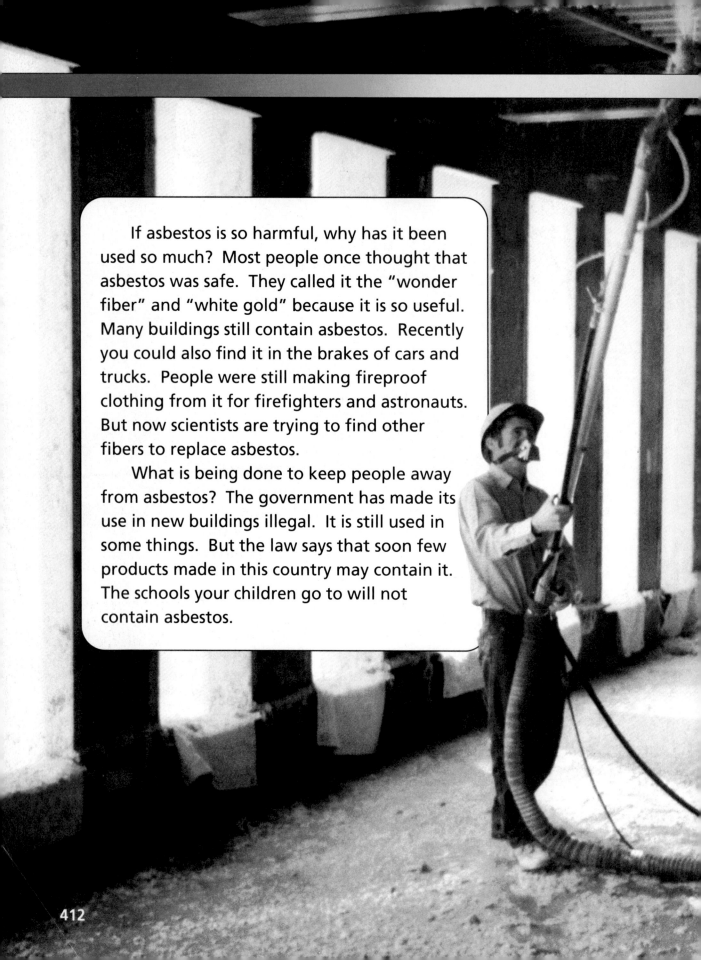

If asbestos is so harmful, why has it been used so much? Most people once thought that asbestos was safe. They called it the "wonder fiber" and "white gold" because it is so useful. Many buildings still contain asbestos. Recently you could also find it in the brakes of cars and trucks. People were still making fireproof clothing from it for firefighters and astronauts. But now scientists are trying to find other fibers to replace asbestos.

What is being done to keep people away from asbestos? The government has made its use in new buildings illegal. It is still used in some things. But the law says that soon few products made in this country may contain it. The schools your children go to will not contain asbestos.

Discover

How clean is the air you breathe?

Materials five squares of white cardboard covered with graph paper · string · petroleum jelly · masking tape · hand lens

Procedure

There may not be much asbestos around you. But you are breathing a lot of other things. How can you find out what is in the air?

Cover the squares of cardboard with a thin layer of petroleum jelly. Tie or tape a piece of string to each one. Hang them in various places around your school, both indoors and outdoors. Collect them after one day. Pick three of the squares from indoor and outdoor places. Using the hand lens, count the number of dirt particles on each. Then compare the numbers of dirt particles. Where is the air the dirtiest? Is the air dirtier indoors or outdoors? Give reasons.

In this chapter you will learn about other things in the air that can harm your lungs. You will also learn that the heart and lungs work together in the body.

1. The Circulatory System

Getting Started Hold a small mirror in front of your mouth. Now breathe out onto the mirror. What forms on the mirror? Where in your body does it come from?

How is oxygen used in the body?

Every time you breathe, you take air into your body. Air contains oxygen. Within cells, oxygen combines with digested food. In this way, energy is released. Cells need energy so that they can live and grow.

When oxygen combines with food, water and carbon dioxide gas form as wastes. These wastes must be removed from the body. When you breathe out, carbon dioxide and water leave the body. Which of these wastes did you see on the mirror?

▼ One kind of transport system

414

How do cells get oxygen and get rid of wastes?

The food you eat today was probably transported, or carried, to your town by trucks. Trucks and highways are part of a transport system that carries materials from one part of the country to another.

The body also has transport systems. These systems transport materials from one part of the body to another. Look at the bluish lines under the skin in your hands. They are part of a transport system called the circulatory (SUR kyoo luh tor ee) system. The **circulatory system** is a transport system that carries food and oxygen to cells. It also picks up wastes from cells. The circulatory system has three parts. They are the blood, the heart, and the blood vessels.

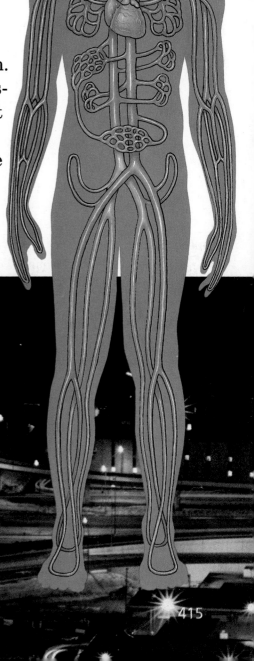

Circulatory System

What is blood?

Blood is a liquid with cells and other solid parts floating in it. Blood carries materials to and from all parts of the body. The movement of blood through the body is called circulation (sur kyoo LAY shun).

Look at the blood in the picture on the left. How many kinds of cells do you see? The small cells are red blood cells. They look like doughnuts without a hole. Red blood cells pick up oxygen in the lungs. Then they carry the oxygen to all the body's cells.

The large cells are white blood cells. Notice that there are fewer white cells than red cells. White blood cells can move on their own. As they move, their shape changes. There are different kinds of white blood cells. But all white cells help the body fight germs. Some white cells make chemicals that kill germs. Other white cells, like the one shown, wrap themselves around germs and eat them.

▼ **Drop of blood as seen under a microscope**   ▼ **White blood cell surrounding germs**

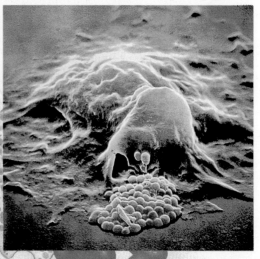

What are the parts of the heart?

The **heart** is a strong hollow muscle about the size of a fist. The heart pumps blood throughout the body. As long as you are alive, your heart muscle never stops working. How is this different from muscles in your arms and legs?

Notice that the heart has chambers, or spaces. The top chambers have thin walls. Each top chamber is an atrium (AY tree um). There is a right atrium and a left atrium.

 **Sure Hands, Strong Heart,** page 438, tells the true story of the courageous doctor who performed the first heart operation.

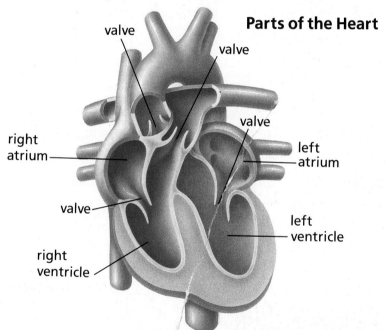

Parts of the Heart

valve

valve

valve

right atrium

left atrium

valve

left ventricle

right ventricle

The bottom chambers are larger and have thick muscular walls. They are the main pumping chambers of the heart. Each bottom chamber is a ventricle (VEN trih kul). There is a right ventricle and a left ventricle. Between each top and bottom chamber is a flap of tissue called a valve. The valves open and close to keep the blood flowing in one direction.

How does the heart pump blood?

Every time the heart beats, blood flows into and out of the heart. As you read, look at the drawing and trace the path of blood through the heart.

1. Blood from the body enters the right atrium. This blood has very little oxygen and a great deal of carbon dioxide.

2. The right atrium contracts, or gets smaller. As it contracts, blood is squeezed through a valve into the right ventricle.

3. Then the right ventricle contracts. This forces blood out of the heart to the lungs. In the lungs the blood gets rid of the carbon dioxide and picks up a fresh supply of oxygen. When oxygen is picked up, the blood becomes bright red.

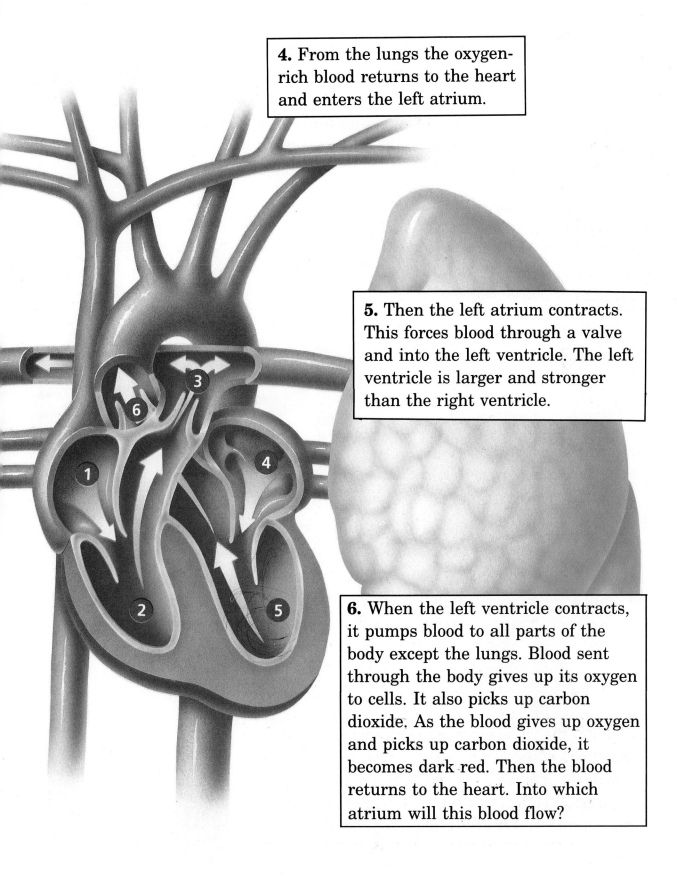

4. From the lungs the oxygen-rich blood returns to the heart and enters the left atrium.

5. Then the left atrium contracts. This forces blood through a valve and into the left ventricle. The left ventricle is larger and stronger than the right ventricle.

6. When the left ventricle contracts, it pumps blood to all parts of the body except the lungs. Blood sent through the body gives up its oxygen to cells. It also picks up carbon dioxide. As the blood gives up oxygen and picks up carbon dioxide, it becomes dark red. Then the blood returns to the heart. Into which atrium will this blood flow?

How do blood vessels differ?

Blood flows to and from the heart through blood vessels. **Blood vessels** are connecting tubes that carry blood. There are three types of blood vessels.

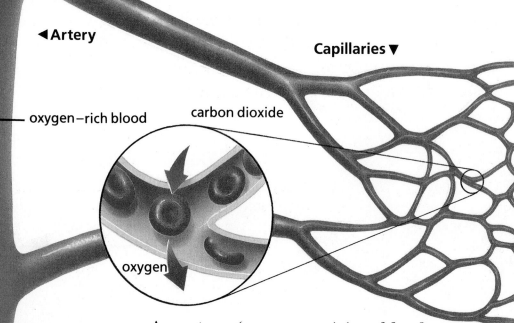

◄ **Artery**

Capillaries ▼

oxygen–rich blood

carbon dioxide

oxygen

An artery (AHRT ur ee) is a blood vessel that carries blood away from the heart. Each time the heart beats, blood is pushed into the arteries with great force. This stretches the arteries. The stretching of the arteries is called the pulse. The pulse can be felt in places where arteries lie just under the skin.

A vein (vayn) is a blood vessel that carries blood back to the heart. Like the heart, veins have valves that keep the blood flowing in one direction.

A capillary (KAP uh ler ee) is a tiny blood vessel that connects an artery and a vein. Capillaries are so small that red blood cells can only squeeze through them one at a time.

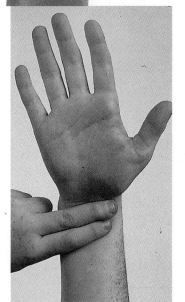

▲ **Feeling the pulse**

Now look at the drawing to see how blood vessels are connected. Blood flows from large arteries into smaller and smaller arteries. Then the blood flows into the capillaries. There, oxygen and food pass through the capillary walls and into the cells. Blood also picks up wastes at this time. From the capillaries, blood flows into the smallest veins. Then blood flows into larger and larger veins. Where will the veins carry the blood?

▼ **Valve in a vein**

open valve   closed valve

Vein ▶

oxygen-poor blood —————

Lesson Review

1. List three parts of the circulatory system.
2. Name two kinds of cells in blood.
3. What are the main pumping chambers of the heart?
4. List three kinds of blood vessels.

Think! Suppose a blood test shows that you have a high number of white blood cells. Why might this be a sign that you have an infection?

2. The Respiratory System

Getting Started Take a deep breath and blow up a balloon. Air has filled the balloon. Where was this air just before it entered the balloon? Place one hand on your chest and take another deep breath. What happens to your chest as you breathe in?

▼ Breathing out

What is the respiratory system?

As you read this book, you breathe about 15 to 20 times each minute. With each breath, oxygen from the air you breathe enters your body. The transport system that brings oxygen into the body is the **respiratory** (RES-pur uh tor ee) **system.**

The respiratory system and the circulatory system work together during respiration (res puh RAY shun). Respiration takes place in cells. During respiration, oxygen combines with food and energy is released. Carbon dioxide and water are given off as wastes.

The parts of the respiratory system are shown in the drawings on the next two pages. As you read, trace the path of air through these parts.

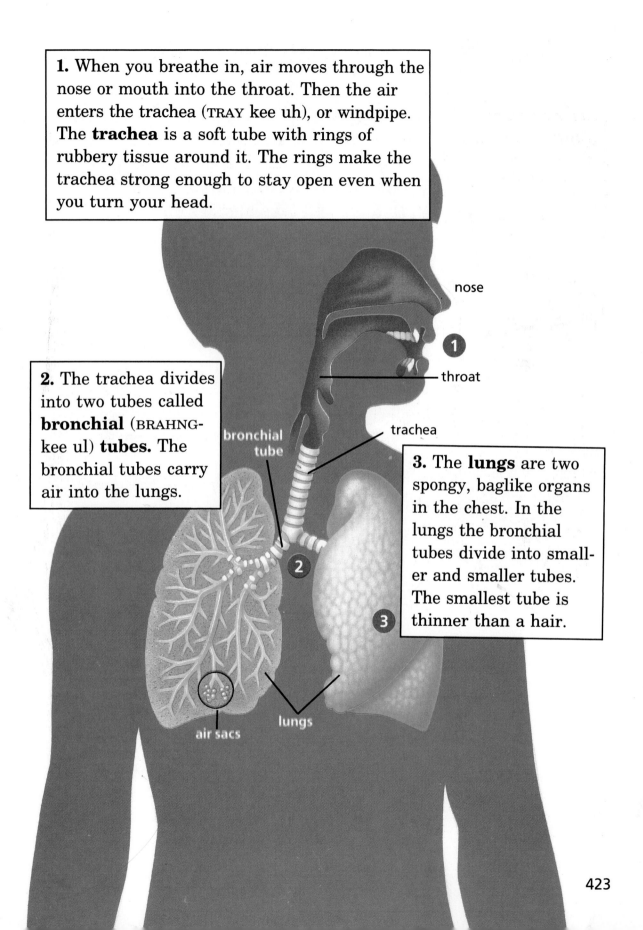

1. When you breathe in, air moves through the nose or mouth into the throat. Then the air enters the trachea (TRAY kee uh), or windpipe. The **trachea** is a soft tube with rings of rubbery tissue around it. The rings make the trachea strong enough to stay open even when you turn your head.

2. The trachea divides into two tubes called **bronchial** (BRAHNG-kee ul) **tubes.** The bronchial tubes carry air into the lungs.

3. The **lungs** are two spongy, baglike organs in the chest. In the lungs the bronchial tubes divide into smaller and smaller tubes. The smallest tube is thinner than a hair.

nose

throat

trachea

bronchial tube

lungs

air sacs

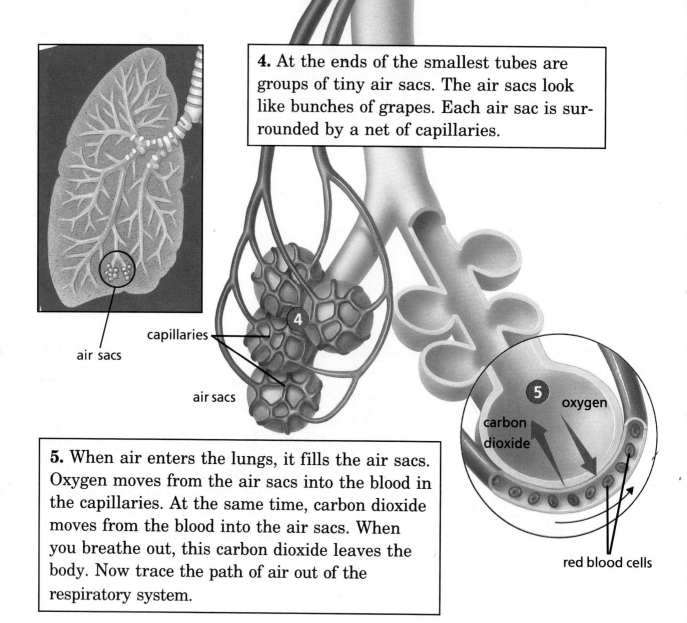

4. At the ends of the smallest tubes are groups of tiny air sacs. The air sacs look like bunches of grapes. Each air sac is surrounded by a net of capillaries.

air sacs

capillaries

air sacs

5. When air enters the lungs, it fills the air sacs. Oxygen moves from the air sacs into the blood in the capillaries. At the same time, carbon dioxide moves from the blood into the air sacs. When you breathe out, this carbon dioxide leaves the body. Now trace the path of air out of the respiratory system.

oxygen

carbon dioxide

red blood cells

What happens when you breathe?

When you breathe in, air fills the lungs. Breathing in is called inhaling. When you breathe out, air leaves the lungs. Breathing out is called exhaling.

The work of breathing is done mainly by a muscle called the diaphragm (DYE uh-fram). The **diaphragm** is a thick sheet of muscle just below the lungs.

It's the chance of a lifetime!
Play the Amazing Body Game when you read ***The Amazing Body Maze*** in Horizons Plus.

Explore Together

How does the diaphragm help fill the lungs with air?

Organizer

Materials
top half of a 1-L plastic bottle · medium balloon · small rubber band · scissors · large balloon · large rubber band

Procedure

Investigator

A. Place the medium balloon through the top of the bottle. Stretch the mouth of the balloon over the bottle opening. Hold the balloon in place with the small rubber band.

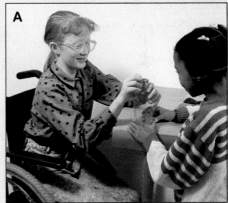

Investigator

B. Cut off the neck of the large balloon. Stretch this balloon across the bottom of the bottle.

Manager

C. While the Investigator holds the bottle, place the large rubber band around the bottom of the bottle to hold the balloon in place.

Group, Recorder

1. Compare this model with the diaphragm and lungs.
2. Predict what will happen when you pull down on the large balloon.

Investigator
Group, Recorder

D. Pull down on the large balloon.
3. Observe what happens to the balloon inside the bottle.

Writing and Sharing Results and Conclusions

Group, Recorder

1. Explain how the action of this model compares to how the lungs and diaphragm work.

Reporter

2. How do your results and conclusions compare with those of your classmates?

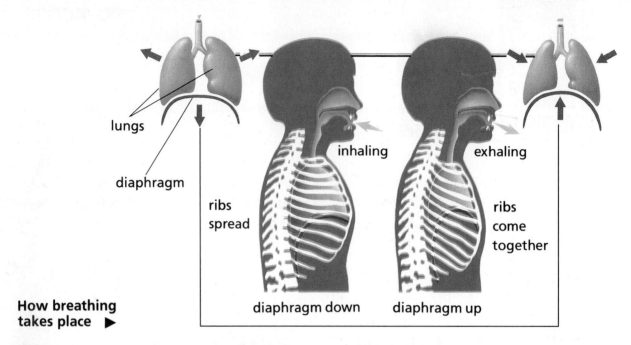

lungs

diaphragm

inhaling

exhaling

ribs
spread

ribs
come
together

diaphragm down   diaphragm up

**How breathing
takes place** ▶

What happens to the chest and ribs
when you inhale and exhale? The drawings
show how breathing takes place.

Inhaling begins when the diaphragm
moves down. At the same time, the ribs
spread apart. So the space inside the chest
gets larger. Then air can flow in and fill the
lungs.

Now look at what happens during exhaling. Notice that the diaphragm moves up and
the ribs come together. As the space inside
the chest gets smaller, air is forced out of the
lungs. But within seconds the diaphragm
moves down, and inhaling begins again.

**Earth Science
CONNECTION**

*From what you
have learned about
respiration, what parts
of the body can air
pollution affect?*

Lesson Review

1. How does air get from the nose to the lungs?
2. What happens to oxygen inside the air sacs?
3. How does the diaphragm move during
   exhaling?

Think! Why would a sleeping person breathe
less often than when awake?

THINKING

Skills

Using observations to make predictions

You may have observed that you often get hungry at the same times of day. What you have observed can help you to predict when you will be hungry again. After you have observed something many times, you can predict what will happen.

Practicing the skill

1. Fill a large plastic bottle with water. Put a cap on the bottle.

2. Have your partner hold the bottle upside down in a large tub that has water in it 4–5 cm deep. Remove the cap, keeping the opening of the bottle below the water in the tub.

3. Carefully put a tube into the bottle. Put a straw into the tube. Blow as much air into the straw as you can in one breath. Mark the new water level in the bottle. Then measure how much the water level dropped.

4. Compare your data with those of other teams. Predict how far the water level will go down when another person blows air into the bottle.

5. To check your prediction, repeat steps **1–3**.

Thinking about the skill

Why might you make different predictions for different classmates?

Applying the skill

Dip the end of a straw into soapy water. Point the straw down and blow soap bubbles. Have a classmate measure how big the bubbles are just before they fall off or pop. Predict how large the bubbles a classmate can blow will be.

427

3. Keeping Healthy

▲ Exercising for healthy heart and lungs

How can you take care of the circulatory system?

As you learned, transport systems carry materials to the body's cells. So it is important to keep these systems healthy. Doctors say that the time to start taking care of your heart and lungs is when you are young.

One way to take care of the circulatory system is to exercise. The children shown here are very active. Exercise makes muscles stronger. Remember that the heart is a muscle. So exercise helps to keep the heart strong. How have you exercised today?

A second way to take care of the circulatory system is to eat the right foods. Eating fatty foods may be harmful. Fats are found in snacks like ice cream and potato chips. The snacks shown here have very little fat. Which of these snacks do you eat?

Fatty foods can cause a buildup of materials inside the arteries. The inside of the arteries may then become blocked. As the drawing shows, blood cannot easily pass through a blocked artery.

▲ Snacks that have little fat

▼ Healthy artery and blocked artery

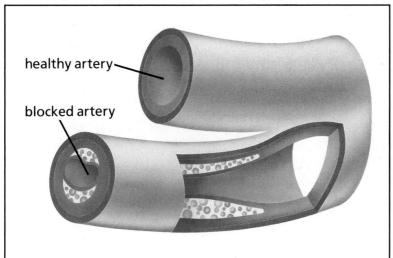

healthy artery

blocked artery

How can you take care of the respiratory system?

Many things that keep your heart healthy also keep your respiratory system healthy. One way to take care of the respiratory system is to exercise. Exercise makes the diaphragm stronger. A strong diaphragm helps a person take in more air. With more air in the lungs, more oxygen can be sent to cells.

▼ Dancing is good exercise.

ACTIVITY

Explore

How does exercise change your pulse rate?

"**H**old it, I'm out of breath!" Have you ever said these words after running a long distance? When you exercise, your muscles need more oxygen. By breathing faster, more oxygen enters your lungs. Your heart also beats faster. So blood is pumped more quickly, and more oxygen is carried to muscles.

Materials
timer · chair · calculator

Procedure

A. Work with a partner. While sitting quietly in a chair, find your pulse on the underside of your wrist.

B. Count the number of pulse beats in 1 minute. Have your partner use a timer to tell you when to start and stop counting. Record this number in a table.

C. Repeat step **B** two more times.

D. Use a calculator to find your average resting pulse rate by adding the three numbers and dividing by three.

   1. What is your average resting pulse rate?

   2. Predict what will happen to your pulse rate after you exercise.

E. Jog in place for 1 minute. Find your pulse rate again. Record this number in the table.

F. Repeat step **E** two times. Rest for 5 minutes between each trial. Use a calculator to find your average jogging pulse rate.

Writing and Sharing Results and Conclusions

1. Why do you calculate the average pulse rate?

2. How does your average resting pulse rate compare with your average jogging pulse rate?

3. Why is there a difference in the two average rates?

4. How do your results and conclusions compare with those of your classmates?

◀ Ragweed

▲ Ragweed pollen as seen through a microscope

A second way to keep the respiratory system healthy is to breathe clean air. Air that contains dirt, dust, and smoke can harm the lungs. Air may also carry pollen. Pollen is a powdery material made by plants. People can be allergic (uh LUR jihk) to pollen. If pollen enters their nose and throat, it causes sneezing, a runny nose, and a scratchy throat. Many people are allergic to the pollen of ragweed shown here. Are you allergic to pollen? If so, what kinds of pollen are you allergic to?

A third way to take care of the respiratory system is not to smoke cigarettes. Smoking can cause lung infections and diseases such as lung cancer. Smoking also causes heart disease. As the bar graph shows, it is very hard to stop smoking. So it is better never to start. Why do you think people start smoking?

1,000 People Who Try to Give Up Smoking

1000	
900	
800	
700	
600	
500	
400	
300	
200	
100	
0	

Likely to Succeed   Likely to Fail

431

▲ Rest at home when you have a cold

Sometimes, germs get into the respiratory system and cause diseases. One of the most common respiratory diseases is a cold. Cold germs get into the nose, throat, and lungs. No medicine will cure a cold. But rest helps the body get rid of the germs.

Resting at home may also help prevent the spread of cold germs. Every time you sneeze or cough, germs are sprayed into the air. People nearby may breathe in the germs. When you cough or blow your nose, germs also spread to your hands. What can you do to help prevent the spread of colds?

Lesson Review

1. How can eating fatty foods be harmful?

2. List two ways to keep the respiratory system healthy.

Think! Why do people wear masks when they remove asbestos from buildings?

Chapter Connections

Choose a partner. Write the words from the organizer on your paper, but mix them up as you write them. Exchange papers with another pair of partners. Rewrite the list to show which words belong together.

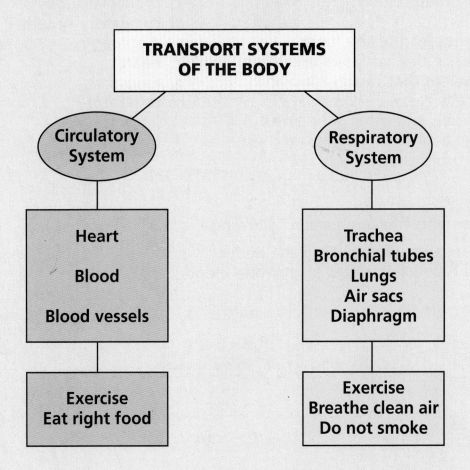

TRANSPORT SYSTEMS OF THE BODY

Circulatory System

Respiratory System

Heart

Blood

Blood vessels

Trachea
Bronchial tubes
Lungs
Air sacs
Diaphragm

Exercise
Eat right food

Exercise
Breathe clean air
Do not smoke

Writing About Science • Research

Many people do aerobic exercises to improve the strength of their heart. Find out what an aerobic exercise is and then create one of your own. Teach it to the class.

Science Terms

Write the letter of the term that best matches the definition.

1. Transport system that brings oxygen into the body
2. Muscle that pumps blood
3. Windpipe
4. Two tubes that lead to the lungs
5. Sheet of muscle that works in breathing
6. Transport system that carries food and oxygen to cells
7. Liquid with cells and other solid parts in it
8. Two spongy, baglike organs in the chest
9. Connecting tubes that carry blood

a. blood
b. blood vessels
c. bronchial tubes
d. circulatory system
e. diaphragm
f. heart
g. lungs
h. respiratory system
i. trachea

Science Ideas

Use complete sentences to answer the following.

1. What do transport systems do in the body?
2. How do red blood cells differ from white blood cells?
3. Write the correct term for each letter on the drawing.

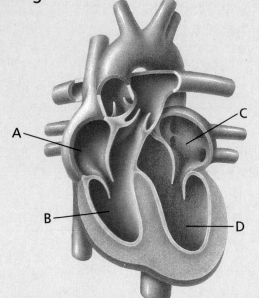

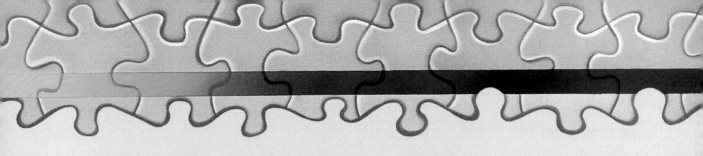

4. Which blood has very little oxygen—blood entering the right atrium or blood entering the left atrium?
5. Where does blood go when it leaves the left ventricle?
6. How does an artery differ from a vein?
7. What happens to oxygen inside the capillaries?
8. Write the correct term for each letter on the drawing.
9. How do the lungs fill with air?
10. In what ways do exercising and eating right help to keep the circulatory system healthy?

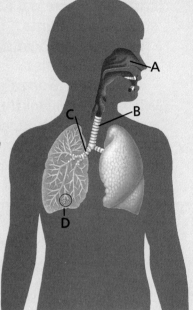

Applying Science Ideas

Use complete sentences to answer the following.

1. Why is the heart sometimes called a double pump?
2. A person running a race produces more carbon dioxide in muscle cells than when resting. How would faster breathing help a runner get rid of this carbon dioxide?
3. Arteries carry blood away from the heart. Most arteries carry oxygen-rich blood. But one group of arteries carries blood with very little oxgyen. Where are these arteries? (Hint: Look back at the drawing of the heart on pages 418–419.)

Using Science Skills

Count the number of breaths you take in 1 minute. Repeat this process for 2 more minutes. Compare your results with those of another classmate. Predict how many breaths another fourth grader might take.

Careers in Health Science

Children's Dentist

Dr. Edward Gonzalez is a **dentist,** and all of his patients are children. There is a reason for his choice of patients. "Being around children is the best part of my job," says Dr. Gonzalez.

Edward Gonzalez always liked working with children. When he was a teenager, he spent his summers as a camp counselor. During high school, Edward decided to be a dentist. In science class, he liked learning about the human body and how it works.

If you are thinking about becoming a dentist, take extra science classes in high school and college. After college you will have to go to dental school. Here you will learn much more about the human body, especially the teeth. You will learn how to take care of and repair teeth.

Dr. Gonzalez works with many people in his office. **Dental assistants** take X-rays. They also prepare the dentist's tools. A **dental hygienist** cleans teeth. But Dr. Gonzalez says that children and their parents are his best helpers. Together they follow his instructions on how to keep teeth healthy.

Years ago, children got a lot of cavities, or holes, in their teeth. Dentists would clean and fill in the holes with metal. Now dentists can help prevent children from getting cavities. Many children have their teeth treated with fluoride at the dentist's office. Fluoride is a material that prevents tooth decay. Sometimes a clear coating is painted on the teeth to protect them. Dr. Gonzalez hopes that someday all children will have healthy teeth.

Connecting Science Ideas

1. Imagine that you are a children's dentist. What would you say to children about the importance of their teeth? **Careers; Chapter 12**

2. You have read that your body is made up of cells, tissues, and organs. Name a cell, a tissue, and an organ in the circulatory system. **Chapter 12; Chapter 13**

3. You have learned about the digestive, circulatory, and respiratory systems. Explain how exercise is healthful for each of these systems. **Chapter 12; Chapter 13**

4. On pages 400–401 you read about an artificial mouth. What do scientists find out by using it? Imagine scientists making an artificial heart. What could they find out by using it? **Chapter 12; Chapter 13**

5. Compare the digestive system with the respiratory system. What does each system take into the body? How do the materials from each system get to other parts of the body? **Chapter 12; Chapter 13**

6. You have learned that some materials are harmful when taken into the respiratory system. Identify some materials that might be harmful to the digestive system. **Chapter 12; Chapter 13**

Calculator Connections

While sitting, measure your pulse for 15 seconds. Write down the number. Use a calculator to find the number of times your heart beats each minute. Then use the calculator to find the number of times your heart beats each hour. There are 24 hours in a day. How many times does your heart beat each day? How many times does your heart beat each year?

from

Sure Hands Strong Heart

THE LIFE OF DANIEL HALE WILLIAMS

Lillie Patterson

You are about to meet Dr. Daniel Hale Williams, a pioneer in the field of surgery. About 100 years ago, Dr. Dan made medical history when he performed life-and-death surgery on a man's heart.

July 9, 1893, was hot and humid in Chicago. The scorching heat wave wrapped the city like a sweltering blanket and blistered the sidewalks. Rising temperatures sent thermometers zooming toward one hundred degrees.

Doctors and hospitals were kept busy. The new Provident Hospital was no exception. Dr. Dan kept close watch on his patients. Making his rounds, he looked as immaculate as always, despite the heat. After his late-afternoon rounds were over, he retired to the closet-like room he used for his office.

Suddenly, a young student nurse burst into the room, her long starched skirt rustling as she ran.

"Dr. Dan!" she gasped. "An emergency! We need you."

Without a word Dr. Dan dropped the report he was reading and hurried to the room set aside for emergency cases. The lone hospital intern, Dr. Elmer Barr, came running to assist.

The emergency case was a young man. He had been brought in by his friend, who gave sketchy information. The patient's name: James Cornish. His age: twenty-four years. His occupation: laborer. The illness: he had been stabbed in the chest.

Dr. Dan discovered that the knife had made an inch-long wound in the chest, just to the left of the breastbone. There was very little external bleeding. Nevertheless, Cornish seemed extremely weak, and his rapid pulse gave cause for concern. The X ray had not yet been invented, so there was no way to determine what was happening inside the chest.

Dr. Dan knew from experience that such cases could develop serious complications. James Cornish must be kept in the hospital, he decided. And he must be watched closely.

That night Dr. Dan slept in the hospital. He did this often when there were serious cases. As he had feared, Cornish's condition worsened during the night. He groaned as severe chest pains stabbed the region above his heart. His breathing became labored. A high pitched cough wracked his sturdy frame. The dark face on the pillow was bathed in perspiration.

Dr. Dan watched the wounded man carefully all night. The next morning, as he took the patient's pulse, he voiced his concern to the intern. "One of the chief blood vessels seems to be damaged," he said to Dr. Barr. The knife must have gone in deep enough to cut the internal mammary artery, he explained. The heart itself might be damaged.

James Cornish showed symptoms of lapsing into shock.

Both doctors knew that something had to be done, and done quickly. Otherwise Cornish would surely die within a matter of hours.

But What?

The only way to know the damage done would be to open the chest and look inside. In 1893, doctors considered this highly impracticable. For surgery, the chest was still off limits.

He knew that medical experts repeatedly warned against opening the thorax, the segment of the body containing the heart and lung. Heart wounds were usually considered fatal.

The risks were there for him and for Cornish. If he did not attempt an operation, Dr. Dan reasoned, the patient would die. Nobody would blame the doctor. Such cases often died.

On the other hand, if he opened the chest and Cornish died anyway, there would be certain condemnation from medical groups. His reputation as a surgeon would be questioned, perhaps lost.

The odds were against both him and Cornish. But Daniel Hale Williams had never allowed the odds to intimidate him.

Dr. Dan lifted his chin, the way he did when he faced a challenge. The storm of doubts suddenly swept away, leaving his mind clear and calm as a rain-washed April morning.

The surgeon quietly told his decision to the intern. Two words he spoke. "I'll operate."

The word spread quickly through Provident Hospital. Like a small army alerted to do battle, student nurses rushed to get the operating room ready and prepare the patient. They knew Dr. Dan's strict rules regarding asepsis, or preventing infection. The instruments, the room, furniture; everything that came in contact with the patient must be free of microbes that might cause infection.

Meanwhile, Dr. Dan sent a hurried message to a few doctors who often came to watch him operate. The intern, a medical student, and four doctors appeared. Dr. George Hall of Provident's staff was there. So was Dr. Dan's friend, Dr. William Morgan. The circle of watchers gathered in the operating room; four white, two black.

Dr. Dan scrubbed his hands and arms thoroughly. Then, with a nod toward his colleagues, he walked over and looked down at Cornish, now under the effects

of anesthesia. Strong shafts of sunlight slanted through a window, giving the doctor's curly red hair a glossy luster. His thin, sensitive mouth drew taut with concentration.

The surgical nurse, proud of her training, stood at attention.

Scalpel!

A loud sigh escaped one of the doctors when the light, straight knife touched Cornish's bare skin. After that there was silence from the onlookers.

None of them knew what would happen next. How would the body react when air suddenly hit the chest cavity? Would vital chest organs shift too far out of place? Dr. Dan could not benefit from the experiences of other doctors. No paper had been written, no lectures given to guide him. Dr. Dan was pioneering in an unexplored territory. He was on his own.

The surgeon worked swiftly. He had to. The surgeon of 1893 did not have a variety of anesthetics or artificial airways to keep the patient's windpipe open. Blood transfusion techniques were unknown. Penicillin and other infection-fighting drugs had not been discovered.

Quickly, Dr. Dan made the incision, lengthening the stab wound to the right. Expertly, he cut through the skin and the layers of fat beneath it. Now he could see the breastbone and the ribs. He made another cut to separate the rib cartilage from the sternum.

Long years of studying and teaching human anatomy gave his every movement confidence. Working with precision, he made his way through the network of cartilages, nerves, blood vessels. A few inches from the breastbone he cut through the cartilage to make a little opening, like a trapdoor.

Bending his head close to the patient's chest, he peered through the opening he had made. Now he could examine the internal blood vessels.

Now he could see the heart!

The tough bundle of muscles throbbed and jerked and pulsated, sending food and oxygen through the body. Dr. Dan examined the pericardium, the fibrous sac that protected the pear-shaped heart and allowed it to beat without rubbing against other parts of the body.

At each step, Dr. Dan reported his findings to the group of observers. The vital pericardium was cut—a tear of about an inch and a quarter in length. He probed further. Yes, there was another puncture wound, he reported, about one-half an inch to the right of the coronary artery. Had the knife moved a fraction of an inch, Cornish would have bled to death before he reached the hospital. Also—Dr. Dan paused—the left mammary artery was damaged.

Dr. Dan kept on talking and working. The small wound in the heart itself should be left undisturbed, he advised. It was slight. The tear in the pericardium was a different matter. That had to be repaired.

Now the surgeon's hands moved with a rhythm born of knowledge, practice, and instinct. Strong hands; flexible enough to pluck tunes from guitars and violins. Sure hands; steady enough to string high telephone wires. Quick hands; made nimble from years of cutting hair and trimming beards and mustaches.

These hands now raced against time to save a life. Dr. Dan tied off the injured mammary artery to prevent bleeding.

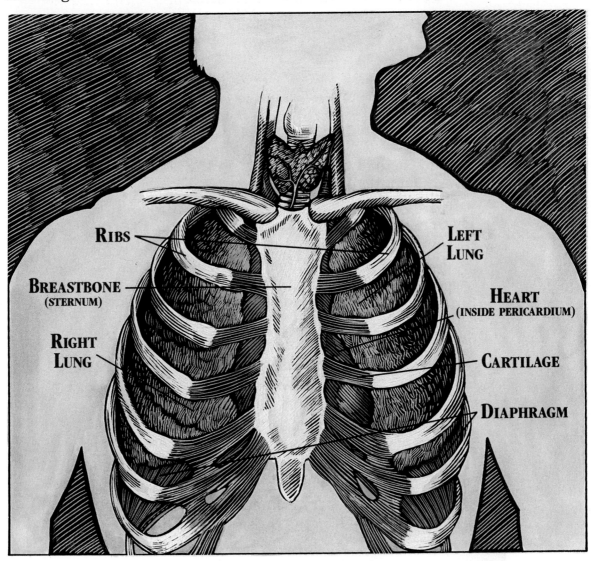

Forceps!

Now he had to try and sew up the heart's protective covering. Meticulously, he irrigated the pericardial wound with a salt solution of one hundred degrees Fahrenheit. There must be no chance of infection after the chest was closed.

Using the smooth forceps, he held together the ragged edges of the wound. Against his fingers the fist-sized heart fluttered and thumped like a frightened bird fighting to fly free.

Sutures!

Despite the rapid heartbeats, the master surgeon managed to sew up the torn edges of the pericardium. For this he used a thin catgut. After that he closed the opening he had made, again using fine catgut.

Another kind of suture would be used for the skin and cartilages, he informed the circle of watchers. He changed to silkworm gut, using long continuous sutures. This allowed for quick entry if infection or hemorrhage developed later. Over the outer sutures he applied a dry dressing.

The operation was over. James Cornish was still alive.

Dr. Dan straightened his aching back. Only then did he stop to wipe the perspiration from his face.

Like figures in a fairy tale suddenly brought to life by magic, the circle of doctors began to move and talk. They rushed to congratulate the surgeon. "Never," said one, "have I seen a surgeon work so swiftly, or with so much confidence."

Each of them dashed from Provident to spread the news. Daniel Hale Williams had opened a man's chest, repaired the pericardium, closed the chest; and the patient's heart was still beating.

Fifty-one days after James Cornish entered Provident with little chance of living, he was dismissed—a well man.

A news reporter from Chicago's *Inter Ocean* newspaper came to Provident to interview the surgeon and get the story first-hand. He found Dr. Dan more anxious to talk about his interracial hospital and the program for training nurses than to talk about the historic operation. The reporter had to coax details from him.

Nevertheless, the reporter's story came out with an eye-catching headline: "SEWED UP HIS HEART!" Another heading read: "DR. WILLIAMS PERFORMS AN ASTONISHING FEAT...."

The *Medical Record* of New York later carried Dr. Dan's own scientific account of the techniques and procedures he had used during the operation. His case created world-wide attention, for it was the first recorded attempt to suture the pericardium of the human heart.

The phrase "Sewed Up His Heart" became closely associated with the name of Daniel Hale Williams. The historic operation on James Cornish helped to advance the progress toward modern heart surgery.

Reader's Response

If you had been at the hospital with Dr. Dan, would you have advised him to operate? Why or why not?

Sure Hands Strong Heart

 Responding to Literature

1. Dr. Dan thought James Cornish would die if he did not have the operation. Do you think James Cornish would have survived without the surgery? Discuss your answer with classmates who have read the story.

2. Why do you think medical experts warned against opening the part of the body containing the heart and lungs?

3. What does the title of the story tell you about Dr. Dan?

4. Imagine that you were the reporter who interviewed Dr. Dan. Write a headline for an article about your interview.

 Books to Enjoy

Sure Hands, Strong Heart: The Life of Daniel Hale Williams by Lillie Patterson
If you want to find out about other milestones in Dr. Dan's life, read his complete biography.

Cuts, Breaks, Bruises, and Burns by Joanna Cole
Would you like to find out how the cells in your body work to heal wounds? If so, this is the book for you.

Why Does My Nose Run? And Other Questions Kids Ask About Their Bodies by Joanne Settel and Nancy Baggett
What makes you burp? What causes you to swallow? This book answers these questions and many other questions about how your body works.

Glossary ———————————————

Some words in this book may be new to you or difficult to pronounce. Those words have been spelled phonetically in parentheses. The syllable that receives stress in a word is shown in small capital letters.

For example: **Chicago** (shuh KAH goh)

Most phonetic spellings are easy to read. In the following Pronunciation Key, you can see how letters are used to show different sounds.

PRONUNCIATION KEY

a	after	(AF tur)
ah	father	(FAH thur)
ai	care	(kair)
aw	dog	(dawg)
ay	paper	(PAY pur)
e	letter	(LET ur)
ee	eat	(eet)
ih	trip	(trihp)
eye	idea	(eye DEE uh)
y	hide	(hyd)
ye	lie	(lye)
oh	flow	(floh)
oi	boy	(boi)
oo	rule	(rool)
or	horse	(hors)
ou	cow	(kou)
yoo	few	(fyoo)
u	taken	(TAY kun)
	matter	(MAT ur)
uh	ago	(uh GOH)

ch	chicken	(CHIHK un)
g	game	(gaym)
ing	coming	(KUM ing)
j	job	(jahb)
k	came	(kaym)
ng	long	(lawng)
s	city	(SIH tee)
sh	ship	(shihp)
th	thin	(thihn)
thh	feather	(FETHH ur)
y	yard	(yahrd)
z	size	(syz)
zh	division	(duh VIHZH un)

A

adaptation (ad up TAY shun)   A body part, a body covering, or an action that helps an animal survive. p. 101

air (air)   A mixture of gases, including oxygen and carbon dioxide. p. 137

air pressure (air PRESH ur) The force of air pressing on the earth. p. 354

amphibian (am FIHB ee un)   A cold-blooded vertebrate that lives part of its life in water and part on land. p. 76

appliance (uh PLYE uns)   A device used to change energy from one form to another. p. 209

atmosphere (AT mus feer)   A thick layer of gases, water, and small solid particles that surrounds the earth. p. 348

axis (AK sihs)   An imaginary line through the center of an object, around which that object turns. p. 262

axis

B

barometer (buh RAHM ut ur)   An instrument used to measure air pressure. p. 355

behavior (bee HAYV yur)   The actions of an animal. p. 110

bird (burd)   A warm-blooded vertebrate that has a body covering of feathers. p. 84

blood (blud)   A liquid with cells and other solid parts floating in it. p. 416

blood vessels (blud VES ulz) Tubes that carry blood throughout the circulatory system. p. 420

boiling point (BOIL ihng point) The temperature at which a liquid boils, or changes from a liquid to a gas. p. 180

bronchial tubes (BRAHNG kee ul toobz)   Tubes that carry air into the lungs. p. 423

C

camouflage (KAM uh flahzh)   A color or shape that helps an animal blend in with its environment. p. 106

cell (sel)   The smallest part of the body. p. 388

Celsius scale (SEL see us skayl) The temperature scale in which temperature is measured in degrees Celsius. p. 229

chemical change (KEM ih kul chaynj) A change that forms different kinds of matter. p. 182

chlorophyll (KLOR uh fihl) The green matter in plants that traps light in the food-making process. p. 51

circulatory system (SUR kyoo-luh tor ee SIHS tum) The transport system that carries food and oxygen to cells and picks up wastes from cells. p. 415

cold-blooded animal (KOHLD-blud ihd AN ih mul) An animal whose body temperature changes as the outside temperature changes. p. 69

community (kuh MYOO nuh tee) All the living things in an ecosystem. p. 138

compound machine (KAHM-pound muh SHEEN) A device made up of two or more simple machines. p. 201

condensation (kahn dun SAY-shun) The change of state from a gas to a liquid. p. 180

conduction (kun DUK shun) The movement of heat through matter as particles bump into each other. p. 235

conifer (KAHN uh fur) A plant that produces seeds within cones. p. 34

consumer (kun SOOM ur) A living thing that eats other living things. p. 131

convection (kun VEK shun) The movement of heat through liquids and gases by currents. p. 237

core (kor) The layer of the earth beneath the mantle and at the center of the earth. p. 295

crust (krust) The outer layer of the earth. p. 294

current (KUR unt) A large river of water that moves through the ocean. p. 324

D
decomposer (dee kum POHZ ur) A living thing that gets energy by breaking down dead plant or animal parts. p. 133

density (DEN suh tee)   The property of matter that describes the amount of matter packed into a given space. p. 169

dew point (doo point)   The temperature at which water vapor in the air condenses. p. 365

diaphragm (DYE uh fram)   A thick sheet of muscle just below the lungs that does the work of breathing. p. 424

digestion (dih JES chun)   Changing food into a form that cells can use. p. 392

direct rays (duh REKT rayz)   Rays from the sun that strike the earth's surface straight on. p. 268

E

ecosystem (EK oh sihs tum)   A place where living and nonliving things affect each other. p. 127

effort (EF urt)   A force applied to a machine. p. 197

environment (en VYE run munt)   Everything that surrounds and affects a living thing. p. 100

esophagus (ih SAHF uh gus)   The tube in the digestive system that carries food from the mouth to the stomach. p. 397

evaporation (ee vap uh RAY shun)   The change in state from a liquid to a gas. p. 179

F
Fahrenheit scale (FER un hyt skayl)   The temperature scale in which temperature is measured in degrees Fahrenheit. p. 229

feather (FETHH ur)   A light body part that is found on a bird's skin. p. 84

fibrous root system (FYE brus root SIHS tum)   A kind of root system that has several main roots with many smaller branching roots. p. 38

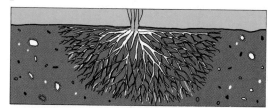

fin (fihn)   A fanlike part of an animal's body that helps the animal move, steer, and balance in the water. p. 70

fish (fihsh)   A cold-blooded vertebrate that lives in water. p. 70

flowering plant (FLOU er ihng plant)   A plant that produces seeds in flowers. p. 33

force (fors)   A push or pull on an object, caused by another object. p. 192

fossil (FAHS ul)   The remains or traces of a living thing preserved in rock. p. 308

freezing point (FREEZ ing   point) The temperature at which a liquid freezes, or changes from a liquid to a solid. p. 180

G

gas (gas)   The state of matter that has no definite volume or shape. p. 176

gills (gihlz)   Thin, feathery parts of an animal's body filled with blood and used for breathing. p. 71

glacier (GLAY shur)   A huge body of slow-moving ice. p. 338

H

hardness (HAHRD nihs)   How easy it is to scratch a mineral. p. 292

heart (hahrt)   The strong hollow muscle that pumps blood throughout the body. p. 417

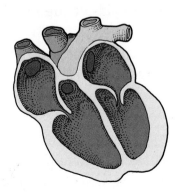

heat (heet)   Energy that moves from warmer matter to cooler matter. p. 220

high tide (hye   tyd)   The time at which the water level of the ocean reaches its highest point on land. p. 276

host (hohst)   A living thing that a parasite feeds on and harms. p. 140

humidity (hyoo MIHD uh tee) Water vapor in the air. p. 362

I

igneous rock (IHG nee us   rahk) Rock formed from melted rock that has cooled and hardened. p. 298

inborn behavior (IHN born bee HAYV yur)   A behavior an animal is born with and does not have to learn. p. 110

indirect rays (ihn duh REKT rayz)   Rays from the sun that strike the earth's surface at a slant. p. 268

insulator (IHN suh layt ur) Matter through which heat does not move easily. p. 239

invertebrate (ihn VER tuh briht) An animal without a backbone. p. 69

K

kinetic energy (kih NET ihk EN ur jee)　The energy of a moving object. p. 202

L

lake (layk)　A large body of water surrounded by land. p. 336

land breeze (land breez)　Wind that blows from the land toward the water. p. 361

large intestine (lahrj ihn TES-tun)　A digestive organ shaped like a wide tube. p. 399

lava (LAH vuh)　Melted rock that reaches the earth's surface. p. 298

leaf (leef)　The part of a plant where most of the plant's food is made. p. 46

learned behavior (lurnd bee-HAYV yur)　A behavior an animal learns and is not born with. p. 116

life cycle (lyf SYE kul)　All the stages in the life of a living thing. p. 72

liquid (LIHK wihd)　The state of matter that has a definite volume but no definite shape. p. 175

low tide (loh tyd)　The time at which the water level of the ocean reaches its lowest point on land. p. 276

lunar eclipse (LOO nur ih KLIHPS)　What occurs when Earth blocks the sun's light from the moon. p. 273

lungs (lungz)　**1.** Organs through which animals get oxygen from air. p. 77. **2.** Spongy, baglike organs in the chest. p. 423

luster (LUS tur)　The way light reflects from a mineral's surface. p. 289

M

magma (MAG muh)　Melted rock inside the earth. p. 298

mammal (MAM ul)　A warm-blooded vertebrate that has hair and feeds milk to its young. p. 88

mantle (MAN tul)　The layer of the earth just beneath the crust. p. 295

mass (mas)　A measure of the amount of matter in something. p. 164

matter (MAT ur)   Anything that takes up space and has mass. p. 164

melting point (MELT ihng   point) The temperature at which a solid changes to a liquid. p. 179

metamorphic rock (met uh MOR-fihk   rahk)   Rock that forms from rock that is changed by heat and pressure inside the earth. p. 312

metamorphosis (met uh MOR fuh-sihs)   The changes in form that occur from egg to adult in some animals. p. 78

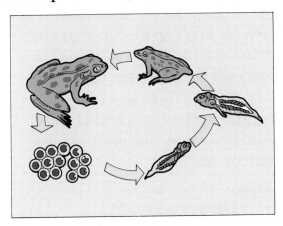

mimicry (MIHM ihk ree)   An adaptation in which an animal looks like a harmful animal. p. 109

mineral (MIHN ur ul)   A natural solid substance found in the earth's crust. p. 288

mouth (mouth)   The place in the digestive system where digestion begins. p. 394

N
nodule (NAHJ ool)   A small black lump of minerals found on the ocean floor. p. 330

O
ocean (OH shun)   A large body of salt water. p. 323

orbit (OR biht)   The path that one body in space follows around another body in space. p. 263

organ (OR gun)   A group of tissues that work together. p. 390

organ system (OR gun SIHS tum) A group of organs that work together. p.390

ovary (OH vuh ree)   The bottom part of the pistil. p. 55

P
parasite (PAR uh syt)   A living thing that feeds on and harms another living thing. p. 140

particles of matter (PAHRT ih-kulz uv MAT ur)   Small bits that make up matter. p. 167

petals (PET ulz)   The parts of a flower that surround and protect other parts of the flower. p. 55

photosynthesis (foht oh SIHN-thuh sihs)   The process by which plants produce food. p. 50

physical change (FIHZ ih kul chaynj)   A change that does not form new kinds of matter. p. 178

physical property (FIHZ ih kul PRAHP ur tee)   A property of matter that can be observed or measured. p. 168

pistil (PIHS tihl)   The female part of a flower. p. 55

planet (PLAN iht)   A body in space that moves in a regular path around the sun. p. 260

pollen grain (PAHL un   grayn) A small part that holds the male cells of a plant. p. 55

pollination (pahl uh NAY shun) The process by which pollen grains move from a stamen to a pistil. p. 56

pollution (puh LOO shun)   The presence of harmful materials in water, in air, or on land. p. 332

pond (pahnd)   A shallow body of water surrounded by land. p. 336

potential energy (poh TEN shul EN ur jee)   Stored energy. p. 202

predator (PRED uh tur)   An animal that hunts and eats other animals. p. 139

prey (pray)   An animal that is hunted and eaten by another animal. p. 139

producer (proh DOOS ur)   A living thing that makes food by using the sun's energy. p. 130

R

radiation (ray dee AY shun) **1.** The movement of energy in the form of waves. p. 237. **2.** Energy that travels through space in the form of waves. p. 349

relative humidity (REL uh tihv hyoo MIHD uh tee)   The amount of water vapor in the air compared with the amount of water vapor the air could hold if it were full. p. 363

reptile (REP tul)   A cold-blooded vertebrate that has lungs and dry skin. p. 80

resistance (rih ZIHS tuns)   A force applied by a machine. p. 197

resource (ree SORS)   A useful material. p. 328

respiratory system (RES pur uh-tor ee   SIHS tum)   The transport system that brings oxygen into the body. p. 422

revolution (rev uh LOO shun)   The movement of one body in space on a path around another body. p. 263

rock (rahk)   A solid that is made of one or more minerals. p. 294

root (root)   The part of a plant that anchors the plant in the ground. p. 36

root hair (root   hair)   Tiny threadlike structure that grows from a root into the soil. p. 37

rotation (roh TAY shun)   The turning of an object on its axis. p. 262

S

scale (skayl)   A hard, flat plate that protects an animal's body. p. 71

sea breeze (see   breez)   Wind that blows from the water toward the land. p. 360

season (SEE zun)   One of the four periods of the year — spring, summer, autumn, and winter. p. 266

sedimentary rock (sed uh MEN-tur ee   rahk)   Rock that forms from hardened sediments. p. 304

simple machine (SIHM pul   muh-SHEEN)   A device that changes the size or direction of a force. p. 196

small intestine (smawl   ihn TES-tun)   A digestive organ shaped like a long narrow tube. p. 398

soil (soil)   The part of the ground where plants grow. p. 134

solar eclipse (SOH lur   ih KLIHPS)   What occurs when the moon blocks some or all of the sun's light from a place on Earth. p. 274

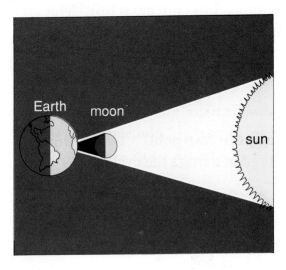

solid (SAHL ihd)   The state of matter that has a definite volume and shape. p. 175

stamen (STAY mun)   The male part of a flower. p. 55

states of matter (stayts   uv   MAT-ur)   The three forms of matter — solid, liquid, and gas. p. 174

stem (stem)   The part of a plant that supports the leaves, flowers, or cones. p. 42

stomach (STUM uk)   The baglike digestive organ made of muscles. p. 397

stomate (STOH mayt)   A tiny opening on the underside of a leaf. p. 47

streak (streek)   The color of a powdered mineral. p. 292

succession (suk SESH un)   The changes in the communities of an ecosystem over many years. p. 142

T

tadpole (TAD pohl)   The fishlike stage in a frog's life cycle. p. 78

taproot system (TAP root   SIHS-tum)   A kind of root system that has a main root that grows straight down. p. 39

temperature (TEM pur uh chur)   A measure of how fast the particles in matter are moving. p. 224

tides (tydz)   The regular rise and fall of the earth's water. p. 276

tissue (TIHSH oo)   A group of cells that work together. p. 389

trachea (TRAY kee uh)   A soft tube in the respiratory system with rubbery rings around it. p. 423

V

vein (vayn)   The part of a leaf that holds tubes that transport food, water, and minerals. p. 46

vertebrate (VER tuh briht)   An animal with a backbone. p. 69

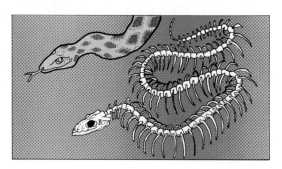

vibrate (VYE brayt)   To move back and forth. p. 221

volume (VAHL yoom)   The amount of space that matter takes up. p. 165

W

warm-blooded animal (WORM-blud ihd   AN ih mul)   An animal whose body temperature stays the same, even when the outside temperature changes. p. 69

water (WAWT ur)   A nutrient needed by all living things in an ecosystem. p. 135

water vapor (WAWT ur   VAY-pur)   Water in the form of an invisible gas. p. 362

work (wurk)   What is done when a force moves an object. p. 194

Index

Credits

Chapter 13 410–411: © Jerry Burgess/Photo Researchers, Inc. 411: David Walberg/*Time Magazine*. 412–413: D. Bruster/Bruce Coleman. 413: Dan DeWilde for SB&G. 414–415: Steve Elmore Photography. 416: *r.* Lennart Nilsson, *Behold Man*, Little Brown & Co. 425: IMAGERY for SB&G. 427: Frank Siteman for SB&G. 428: *r.* C. Allan Morgan/Peter Arnold, Inc.; *b.r.* © Joseph Nettis/Photo Researchers, Inc. 431: *l.* IMAGERY; *r.* Biological Photo Service. 432: Dan DeWilde for SB&G. 436: Courtesy of Dr. Edward Gonzales. 436–442: Ken Barton.

ACKNOWLEDGMENTS

Grateful acknowledgment is made to the following publishers, authors, and agents for their permission to reprint copyrighted material. Any adaptations are noted in the individual acknowledgments and are made with the full knowledge and approval of the authors or their representatives. Every effort has been made to locate all copyright proprietors; any errors or omissions in copyright notices are inadvertent and will be corrected in future printings as they are discovered.

p. 15:   From "To Save the Whales" by James S. Kunen and Maria Wilhelm, in *People Weekly,* November 7, 1988. Used with permission.

p. 20:   Based on the article "Humpbacks: Their Mysterious Songs" by Roger Payne, Ph.D., in *National Geographic* magazine, January 1979. Courtesy of National Geographic Society.

p. 22:   From "Humpbacks: Their Mysterious Songs" by Roger Payne, Ph.D., in *National Geographic* magazine, January 1979. Courtesy of National Geographic Society.

p. 22:   From "Chuck Nicklin's World" in *Whales and Man: Adventures with the Giants of the Deep* by Tim Dietz. (Dublin, NH: Yankee Publishing, Inc., 1987). Courtesy of Yankee Publishing, Inc.

p. 26:   From "At Home with Right Whales" by Roger Payne, Ph.D., in *National Geographic* magazine, March 1976. Courtesy of National Geographic Society.

pp. 150–158:   From *McBroom Tells the Truth* by Sid Fleischman, illustrated by Walter Lorraine. Text Copyright © 1966 by Sid Fleischman. Illustrations Copyright © 1981 by Walter Lorraine. Reprinted by permission of the author and the illustrator.

pp. 246–254:   From *Sugaring Time* by Kathryn Lasky, photographs by Christopher G. Knight. Copyright © 1983 by Kathryn Lasky. Copyright © 1983 by Christopher G. Knight. Reprinted with permission of Macmillan Publishing Company and of Sheldon Fogelman.

pp. 374–382:   From *If You Are a Hunter of Fossils* by Byrd Baylor, illustrated by Peter Parnall. Text Copyright © 1980 by Byrd Baylor. Illustrations Copyright © 1980 by Peter Parnall. Reprinted by arrangement with Charles Scribner's Sons, an imprint of Macmillan Publishing Company.

pp. 438–446:   From *Sure Hands, Strong Heart* by Lillie Patterson. Copyright © 1981 by Abingdon Press. Adapted and reprinted by permission.